Rapid Relief
from Emotional Distress

Other Books by Gary Emery

Rapid Relief
from
Emotional
Distress

Gary Emery, Ph.D.,
and
James Campbell, M.D.

Fawcett Columbine · New York

The names and circumstances of clients and other identifying characteristics in case histories have been changed to protect their privacy.

A Fawcett Columbine Book
Published by Ballantine Books
Copyright © 1986 by Gary Emery, Ph.D., and James Campbell, M.D.

All rights reserved under International and
Pan-American Copyright Conventions. Published in
the United States by Ballantine Books, a division of
Random House, Inc., New York, and simultaneously
in Canada by Random House of Canada Limited,
Toronto.

Library of Congress Catalog Card Number: 86-92113

ISBN: 0-449-90249-8

This edition published by arrangement with Rawson Associates.
Cover design by James Harris
Manufactured in the United States of America
BVG 01

To Pat

—G.E.

To my parents, Mildred and Ernest Campbell,
and to my farming roots, which
have helped me see life's basics more clearly;
and to my sons, Paul and Justin

—J.C.

Contents

Acknowledgments

Many people have helped to bring about this book. The most important has been my wife, Pat Day. She provided crucial input from the beginning to the end. Anne Knowles helped make the book more readable and accessible. Eleanor Rawson and Grace Shaw gave us many helpful editorial suggestions.

Gary Baffa, Monty Dunn, Ralph Lampson, Richard Schenkman, Al Shore, David Stark, and Nathan Tracy added ideas to the book.

I am particularly grateful to Dan Dunne. Not only did he add many valuable ideas, but he also introduced me to other writers doing similar work. They include David Reynolds, whose approach to life (accept your feelings, know your purpose, and do what is necessary) makes perfect sense; Patricia Carrington, who has developed many strategies for accepting reality, no matter how terrible it appears; and Robert Fritz, who has pointed out that to become the creative force in your own life, you have to focus simultaneously on both your vision and "current reality," a phrase he coined.

As you read on, you will be encouraged to acknowledge yourself. In this spirit, I would like to acknowledge myself for holding the vision of this book.

—G.E.

I thank my clients first, because they have been my true teachers. Secondly, I thank Gary Emery, my mentor and friend, and Pat Day, who have been the real force in making this book become a reality. I would also like to thank Jack Dorman and Dr. Stanford Perlman, who took time to read and comment on earlier versions of the manuscript.

—J.C.

Before You Begin This Book—
Be Sure to Read This

For the past twenty years I have wanted to find a simple, effective system people can use to relieve emotional distress. Some of the systems with which I experimented worked only partially; others failed altogether. A few were so complicated and took so long that they hardly seemed worth the time and effort people put into them. I was looking for a method that worked and worked quickly to move people away from their emotional suffering and toward what they want instead.

Then I met Jim Campbell, a Fellow in the Psychiatry Department at UCLA. In the intervening years, I've gotten to know Jim well. When faced with an obstacle he immediately asks, "Okay, what can I do to move around it?" At heart he is an efficiency expert. His foremost question is, "How can I do this job more quickly and easily?"

When Jim first told me about a new rapid therapy, I thought he might be testing to see how gullible I was. I could hardly believe what he told me: He had developed new techniques that could help patients overcome clinical depression and anxiety in *five or six sessions.*

Perhaps you can understand my reaction when you consider that traditional psychotherapy advocates treatment for *five or six years.* In the last few years therapists have developed what is called "brief psychotherapy"—one or two years of treatment. Outcome studies in the more recent cognitive (or "thinking") therapy found that people could overcome their depression or other emotional distress in fifteen or twenty sessions, although many professionals said this was impossible and doubted the findings. And Jim was talking about five or six sessions!

Furthermore, he told me that 80 percent of the clients he saw could use the new method successfully. It was a method we later came to call "choice versus change rapid therapy."

The basic premise is this: *Needing to change yourself, others, or the world before you can be happy is the cause of your emotional distress.* You get relief from this distress by seeing that you create your own experiences through choice and by putting this principle into practice.

Rapid relief from emotional distress comes when you move from the change system ("I need to change people and events so that I can be happy") to the choice system ("I choose to accept the current situation and to create what I want").

Jim elaborated on the choice versus change approach over the next several months. Despite my early skepticism, I came to believe that the ideas made sense. I began to test them with clients . . . and in my own life. I was excited and pleased to see that most of my clients could readily grasp the ideas and almost immediately move out of their emotional distress. The method worked.

We face a big problem in psychology in that the professionals who make up the therapies often fall in love with their creations. They believe they have the whole truth instead of the working truth. As a result, they fail to look honestly at whether their therapy works. We are presenting our working truth—what works best right now. Our aim is to get better results; we are always willing to let go of some technique or approach if we can find a better way.

It is easy to get hung up on the means to a goal. The means (therapy) can become so interesting, comforting, or self-satisfying that both the therapist and client forget that the idea was to get better.

I learned the importance of focusing on results instead of process when I was six years old. My aunt, an eccentric woman, was living with us at the time. The general consensus was that she had a screw loose. In most everything she did, she got hung up on the process and forgot the goal. One day she literally had a screw loose—on the vacuum cleaner. She wanted my two brothers and me to tighten it so that it would hold the top of the vacuum cleaner securely, but the screw obviously was stripped. Turn as we might, the screw never tightened. My aunt, however, made us keep turning it around in the hole, hung up on the process (turning the screw) and forgetting the desired result (fixing the vacuum cleaner).

Many of the current psychotherapies are much like the endlessly turning screw in my aunt's vacuum cleaner. I was looking for a therapy that got the screw tightened.

After a year of testing the new choice-versus-change rapid therapy, I decided to compare it with cognitive therapy. I had helped to develop cognitive therapy and have written five books on it. More than a dozen studies have found cognitive therapy to be an effective treatment for depression. I compared twenty depressed clients who were treated with traditional cognitive therapy to twenty depressed clients who were treated with this new rapid therapy. In the cognitive therapy group, fifteen of the twenty moved from moderate or severe depression to being undepressed. In the rapid therapy group, seventeen of the twenty eliminated their depression.

The striking difference was in the number of sessions required to eliminate the depression. The cognitive therapy group had an average of twelve sessions, while the rapid therapy group had an average of five sessions— *less than half the number of sessions the traditional group required to get better.* Although my study was an unscientific and informal one, it added further support to the idea that people can eliminate emotional distress more rapidly than usually thought and, at the same time, learn ways to prevent further distress.

Some of the people I treat with choice-versus-change rapid therapy continue to come for therapy long after they are over their initial emotional distress. They come for more lessons in the business of living, just as professional tennis players continue to take lessons. Because of this new kind of treatment, I consider myself a life skills coach rather than a therapist.

Most therapists try to guide their patients in a delicate search for the right keys to psychological health and the right ways to use them. This can take years.

We offer an alternative approach that works quickly. You already have the key within yourself.

GARY EMERY
Los Angeles, California

In 1971 I entered private practice in Phoenix after two years at a Strategic Air Command base in Puerto Rico. I had been the base's first and only psychiatrist. I had graduated in 1969 from Michael Reese Hospital in Chicago, one of the leading psychoanalytically oriented residency programs in the country. When I left there, I felt qualified to evaluate and treat just about anyone with a psychiatric problem.

Shortly after I began my practice, I began to look for aids to help clients make more rapid progress. Although I had been trained in psychodynamic psychotherapy, I found that most patients lacked the time and the money for this type of therapy, even when kept "brief." I kept my eyes open for material that might be helpful and screened numerous books, audio tapes, and seminar materials.

I eventually came across some interesting and possibly useful material from the Barksdale Foundation in Idyllwild, California. L. S. Barksdale had started the foundation to study self-esteem; he had produced several books and audio tapes on building self-esteem. I began providing his books and tapes to clients, and I started looking at depression as a self-esteem issue rather than as a psychodynamic issue. As a result, I found that clients began to get better much faster and that the number of prescriptions I wrote for medication was cut in half.

This approach led to such rapid improvement in some clients' symptoms that I was afraid I was doing something wrong. I was concerned that perhaps I was creating transference cures (people were getting better to please me) or that the patients were having a flight into health (only pretending to be better) or were experiencing some other undesirable psychiatric effects. When I followed up on the clients, however, I found that their improvement was more real and more lasting that what I achieved with other clients through traditional psychoanalysis.

I continued to practice the new concepts and began to understand them better. Over time I reduced the concepts from the self-esteem books into as few concepts as I could and still maintain impact. When I used these principles more quickly and directly in therapy, I found that clients improved even more rapidly. Eventually I developed the choice-versus-change system model.

Most of the clients I saw did well using this model. I was seeing approximately 85 percent of referred adult outpatients fewer than eight times, and probably more than 50 percent of my adult clients were being seen fewer than five times. However, 15 to 20 percent did not seem to have the ability to use the concepts, although they appeared to understand them. I suspected that their apparent inability was associated with the way they had developed as children.

In 1980, I decided to go to UCLA to take a Child Psychiatry Fellowship. I chose UCLA because the program stressed how children develop psychological problems. During my second year at UCLA, I had Gary Emery as a supervisor. Some of the other supervisors seemed uninterested and on occasion even somewhat hostile to my views on emotional disorders. Gary was supportive and willing to test the models. He was then able to give me feedback on his results. We believe that we now have sufficient evidence to indicate that this approach can be helpful to many. We have seen scores of people relieve their emotional distress with it. Now we want to share it with you.

JIM CAMPBELL
Phoenix, Arizona

Rapid Relief
from Emotional Distress

I. STRATEGIES FOR RAPID RELIEF

1. How to Get Rapid Relief

I f you suffer from anger, guilt, shame, anxiety, or depression and are distressed over work, love, money, health, or a host of other problems, you are one of the walking wounded. You may be able to get up each day, eat breakfast, go to work, come home, eat dinner, and go to bed, but you're in pain.

You may believe that you need something outside of you to change in order to get relief ("I need to have my job back"; "I need her to love me"; "I need to get myself to stop drinking") but actually it's your need to change reality that causes your pain. Remove this "need to change" and you eliminate the pain.

How well you love, work, and play depends on whether you operate from a system focused on the need to change reality or from a system in which you create what you want by means of choice. Let go of the belief that you must change yourself, others, or the world and you will eliminate your stress and distress. Once you decide to design your life by choice, you make a quantum leap into a richer, more satisfying life.

Rapid Relief is Possible!

Most of our clients have major life problems: divorces, bankruptcies, deaths of loved ones, failed hopes and dreams. How quickly they switch out of their distress isn't related to the magnitude of their life problems, but rather to how quickly they can see that *they* have the ability to create the experiences they want in life.

Some clients with major losses (e.g., the death of a spouse) can eliminate their distress relatively quickly; other clients with minor problems (a job they dislike) may take much longer, and vice versa. But no matter what the emotional distress, once our clients begin to create their own lives by becoming aware of and making choices, they get relief.

When Jim served for two years as a psychiatrist for the Air Force in Puerto Rico, he had his first glimpse of the possibility of rapid relief. In his residency at Michael Reese Hospital in Chicago he had treated clients for

3

one or two years. In the Air Force, however, he had to make rapid decisions about a person's qualifications to stay in the service, and he had to provide quick treatment for any problems that existed so that the person could get back to work.

During this assignment Jim had his first rapid recovery of a client. An airman had been treated for panic attacks in the emergency room of the base hospital for three consecutive nights. On the fourth morning Jim received a call from the chief of the medical unit. Jim was to work this airman into his schedule because the airman's nightly panic attacks disrupted his work and were affecting his health. Jim was booked solid that day, so could give the airman only a few minutes between appointments.

He skipped the formal psychiatric interview when the airman came in and simply asked what was bothering him. The airman said he felt extremely uncomfortable working indoors. Jim pulled out a prescription pad and wrote that the patient was to be given an outdoor job for the time being and then made an appointment to see him at the next available time.

When Jim did see him again, he was doing fine. After seeing Jim's prescription, the airman's commanding officer had given him a job outside for a few days. Later the officer asked the airman to work inside again, where he was greatly needed. However, he gave him the option of returning outside if he felt panicked again. The airman agreed and returned to his regular job, where he was able to work without difficulty. Becoming aware of his *choices* (to work indoors *or* outdoors) enabled him to *accept* the situation and make a choice (to work indoors). He stopped trying to control his anxiety, which actually escalated it, and made a different choice instead. His panic attacks stopped. Several months later the commanding officer looked up Jim and thanked him for the "terrific job" he had done for the airman. The effective simplicity of the approach and the recollection of the gratitude Jim received opened him to the possibility of a therapeutic approach for rapid relief from emotional distress.

Rapid relief from emotional distress is possible because both the distress and the relief come from you. Events and people don't cause anything in your psychological world of experiences and feelings—unless you allow them to do so. If you let events or other people dictate your psychological world, you will always be shoved around by outside forces. To feel good you will either have to struggle to change people and external and internal events or wait for them to change. You could be miserable for the rest of your life, because many events in your life can never be changed. Once you make the choice to create your own life, you'll begin to feel relief. The only energy you need is the energy to stay alert to the choices you have and to compare them to the choices you are making. No matter how bad you feel right now, you have the key to relief in your hand.

Five Steps to Immediate Relief

1. Know that you create your psychological pain.
2. Know the difference between change and choice.
3. Use the ACT Formula.
4. Be precise in your language.
5. Use critical opportunities to increase your skill at making choices.

STEP ONE: Know That You Create Your Psychological Pain

The first step toward rapid relief is to realize what you are doing to create your pain. Your emotional pain is an allergic reaction to one basic toxic belief: *"Others (or events) need to change because they are responsible for my thoughts, feelings, and actions, and I need to change because I am responsible for others' thoughts, feelings, and actions."*

The Ten Change Symptoms   When you must change something you can't change, you get caught in an emotional bind. By the very nature of the unresolvable conflict, you have to experience emotional distress. When you focus on your need to change your current reality, you will experience one, or many, of the following inevitable unpleasant emotional reactions, or change symptoms:

1. Waiting—"They have to change before I can feel better."
2. Hurt—"Why did they have to say that to me?"
3. Frustration—"Why don't they change?"
4. Helplessness—"I can't change my feelings."
5. Resentment—"I hate them for making me feel this way."
6. Sense of Failure—"I try, but I can't make it different."
7. Depression—"I should be able to make them change; I can't change them so I'm a loser."
8. Surface Communication—"I can't say what I mean because if I do, I'll hurt their feelings."
9. Loneliness—"I can't be myself with them. I feel cut off, vulnerable, and lack intimacy."
10. Failure to develop a sense of self—"Because I let outside events and people determine my life, I don't know who or what I am. I feel invisible."

We've listed the ten distress reactions in progression from the least to the most troublesome. You usually follow them in the order listed. You can start with simple waiting and hurt ("My huband shouldn't have done that") and fall all the way into a clinical depression ("Nobody loves me; my life is one failure after another"). But you can quickly eliminate these emotional reactions once you stop your efforts to change something and instead *start to make choices to get what you want.*

To make the choice system work for you, you will find it helpful to keep a notebook, and we suggest you begin using your notebook by listing these ten byproducts of needing to change something. When you experience a negative emotion, you have this list and can refer to it. Soon you will learn to recognize when you are leaning on the change system instead of moving out and making choices.

STEP TWO: Know the Difference Between Change and Choice

In the choice system you believe: *"I'm responsible for choosing my thoughts, feelings, and actions, and others are responsible for choosing their thoughts, feelings, and actions."*

By responsibility we mean our ability to respond, or the range of responses you can directly make. In the choice system, you hold yourself accountable for *all* of your experiences because you recognize that *you* cause them, either directly or indirectly. When you are accountable for your life, you become the primary creative force in your life. Because *your choices create your experiences,* you can create the experiences you want by making new choices.

Choice is *not* another name for change. Change, which is best applied to the physical world, is a global concept ("I have to completely change my life") and difficult to accomplish. It requires tools ("I don't know how to change"), takes time and energy ("I can't change overnight"), and once accomplished, is something totally different that will remain permanent and stable ("Once I change, everything will be great"). Because change is so difficult, the natural tendency is to resist it ("It's hopeless, I'll never change").

Choice, on the other hand, is easy. The only energy you need is to be aware of what current options you have to select from. Choice is a basic psychological process and simple to do. You don't need any tools, only awareness. Selecting among options requires little or no time. Choice, unlike change, doesn't result in a stable result: Making choices that lead to happiness doesn't mean your happiness is insured. Choice usually leaves you with the same options you started with—nothing has changed.

The Ten Gifts of the Choice System   When you focus on creating something rather than on trying to change something, there is no inherent conflict. Creating what you want generates positive feelings:

1. Acceptance—"I can accept current reality because my happiness and creativity aren't dependent on needing events or others to change."
2. Energy—"I can do something right now to create the experience I want."

3. Knowledge—"I can learn something from any situation."
4. Resourcefulness—"I can look at current reality and create the choices I need."
5. Cooperation—"I can collaborate with others so that we all get what we want."
6. Success—"I choose visions that are within my ability to create."
7. Self-esteem—"I choose to accept and like myself as I am."
8. Laser communication—"I can tell the truth to myself and others."
9. Intimacy—"Because you are unable to hurt me, I can be myself, and because I'm not trying to change you, you can be yourself."
10. A good sense of self—"I know what I am and what I want out of life."

Copy down these ten gifts in your notebook, and include the sentence quoted after each one. When you find yourself in the midst of emotional distress, look at your choice list and ask yourself which positive experiences you want. *Then choose to create the experience and take action to make it happen.*

As you sharpen your ability to make choices, you will find that you automatically have more positive experiences in your life. You won't have to check your list and then consciously create these positive experiences because they will be yours already.

Are You in Change or Choice? At this moment you are either trying to change yourself or making choices to get what you want. One of Gary's clients, Anna, recognized that she was in the change system "but only halfway." During her first session with Gary, she said, "I do feel responsible for my husband's happiness, I'll admit that. I like to make him happy. But I would never try to make him responsible for me. I'm not the kind of person who tries to change others to make me happy."

Anna had come for therapy because she was depressed and having marital problems. She and her husband, Bill, were barely talking and hadn't had sex for several months.

A free-lance consultant, Anna worked out of her home. She took it upon herself to fix large gourmet meals for Bill. He was often late, however, because of the demands of his career and because he felt Anna was trying to control him. Every time he was late, Anna became angry, and she finally stopped cooking for him altogether.

As Anna began to learn the differences between change and choice, she came to see that anger was her way of manipulating Bill so that he would do what she wanted. She believed that her anger would show Bill where he should change, but she ultimately recognized that her manipulative tactics didn't get the results she wanted. She rarely felt a sense of intimacy with Bill; he was subtly aggressive with her by purposefully coming home late, and she suffered from chronic depression. Anna eliminated many of her problems when she accepted the fact that she couldn't change Bill and chose to have a good, honest relationship with him instead.

For example, when he was late, she chose to accept his lateness, to enjoy the evening anyway by savoring the meal herself (without letting it sit for an hour or two) and by watching a movie on cable TV or reading a good book until Bill came home. Or, if she felt like it, she chose to go out on her own. She told Bill that she wasn't going to use anger to manipulate him but wanted him to call when he knew he would be late so that she could plan her evening without him. Anna stopped trying to make Bill do what he wasn't willing to do; this eliminated her anger and the depression that followed.

Anna was able to switch out of her depression quickly. A month later, Bill came for several therapy sessions, initially because he was curious about what had worked so well for Anna. He saw that he had been reacting to Anna by becoming passive-aggressive. Once he accepted the fact that Anna was not responsible for his feelings, he saw that he could create the happy, cooperative relationship that they both wanted. Bill discovered that by being more accountable and keeping his agreements (calling Anna when he was late) he could get what he really wanted.

Gary was delighted when Anna called recently and said she and Bill were expecting their first child. Their marriage was better than ever, she reported, and they were still using the choice principles that they had learned.

Anna and Bill are not an isolated case. They are two of more than a thousand clients we have treated with this approach—at an 80 percent success rate. Many clients find that once they learn to use choice in their lives it can take a year or two of practice for the methods to become second nature. From time to time they find themselves back in the change system and distressed; but they learn to catch themselves more rapidly and are able to move back into *creating what they want rather than reacting to what they don't want* and thereby reinforcing it.

Are You an Agile Learner? Successful clients have similar characteristics that enable them to learn the differences between change and choice and to implement our methods almost immediately. We have come to call this group the "agile learners."

Agile learners characterize themselves with these self-assessments:

• *"I can admit to being wrong."* If you can say, "I made a mistake," you will be able to learn to use choice. The best way to learn is to invest in the truth, even if it means admitting your mistakes.
• *"I can easily say, 'I don't know.'"* Admitting ignorance is necessary to learning. You have to agree to be taught if you want to learn quickly. Honesty about what you don't know is the first step.

• *"I am willing to run experiments."* Learning is the exploration of un-charted territory. When you learn, you always move into the unknown. Be willing to run experiments to see if our approach works ("I'll do the exercises in this book and see what happens"), and you will be able to learn it with ease. When you know about something, *you own it and don't fear it.*

• *"I am an objective person."* If you are objective about situtations and unswayed by what feels true at the moment, you will learn the choice approach more rapidly.

• *"I am a resourceful person."* The more you believe that you create your own life, the more quickly you will learn. Learning is more than just putting information into your head. You have to assimilate the material and use it resourcefully. Reading the material is planting the seed; putting it into practice is harvesting it.

• *"I can trust others."* To learn, you need to have some basic trust. You need not blindly trust what others say, but you do have to suspend judgment and act *as if* you believe something in order to give it a fair test.

• *"I want to get better."* If you can move beyond an investment in being "sick" or "helpless," you will more quickly learn our new method. You transcend your problems *by letting go of the need for attention and sympathy.*

• *"I am good at accepting current reality."* The better you accept current reality, the faster you will see how unproductive your efforts are to change others and how productive making different choices can be.

• *"I own my own life."* The more accountability you take for your life instead of blaming others, the faster you will learn.

• *"I am successful in some areas."* If you have some success in your life, you will learn with more agility than if you have trouble in many areas of life.

Copy this profile of an agile learner in your notebook. Check off the characteristics that accurately describe you. Circle those in which you'd like to improve. As you read this book, you will find yourself becoming more agile at learning to let go of your need to change current reality and better at creating what you want. Refer back to this profile to see your improvement and to remind yourself of your goals.

Resistant Learners You may be wondering why the other 20 percent of our clients did not get better. Most people over twelve years old have developed to the point where they can use the choice principles presented in this book. Some people, however, do not have sufficient brain matura-tion (psychophysical development) and may not have the ability to use this approach. Among our resistant clients we find two characteristics: (1) They feel so righteous in believing that others should change that their anger and resentment block their ability to learn; (2) They believe so completely that the world and others should change that they are unable to believe they can make choices that would lead to rapid relief.

Each of us has spent many therapy sessions with clients to explain how investment in the belief that others need to change holds them in distress. We want them to "get it"; we always pull for our clients to be agile learners. We usually end a session by asking, "How do you think you can best put these principles into practice?" Inevitably some clients will say something like, "It depends on how my kids act this weekend." How well resistant learners can use choice depends on how strongly they demand that the world change to suit them. If their demand for change is too strong, they simply cannot learn the choice system.

If the principles we're giving you seem unclear, don't assume you are among those who will have trouble using this new way of thinking. Because distinguishing change from choice is new to you, you may have to digest the method before you can use it in your life. If you continue to have trouble, you may want to get some professional help putting the principles into practice. The odds are, however, that you will have little difficulty understanding or implementing this approach on your own.

STEP THREE: Use the ACT Formula

The ACT Formula helps you focus on choice:

1. *Accept* your current reality.
2. *Choose* to create your vision (what you want in life).
3. *Take action* to create it.

If you are experiencing painful, overwhelming emotions, say out loud:

> "*I accept* that right now I feel emotional pain in my life."
> "*I choose* to create the experiences I envision."
> "*I will take action* to create what I want in life."

If necessary, continue to say the three steps out loud until you begin to feel calmer:

"*I accept that right now I feel emotional pain in my life.*" Experience and feel your situation for forty-five seconds. Your current reality remains the same, but you accept it. You stop fighting to change it, so it stops trying to hold on to you. You're just there accepting your current reality.

"*I choose to create my visions.*" See yourself creating what you want. Hold the picture and focus on it. Let light and warmth surround it and fill it until all that light and warmth spills into your current reality.

"*I will take action to create what I want.*" Action will get you to your vision and keep you in the choice system. Each action step will be something you *can* do; your own current reality will supply it for you. You don't have to worry about how to get to your vision. The "how" will present itself to you.

In your notebook, write down the ACT Formula. Put it in your own terms. What do you need to accept and choose to happen? Be as general ("I choose to envision myself being at peace") or as specific ("I choose to envision myself filling out the job application") as you like.

One of Gary's clients, Lynne, used the ACT Formula to get relief from anxiety, resentment, and obsessive guilt. One example of her guilty obsessions was about letting her mother down. Lynne had decided early in college to forgo having children and to pursue a medical career vigorously instead. Although she was highly successful, in her late thirties Lynne felt more and more guilty about not having children.

"After my dad died, I felt like Mom had nothing left," said Lynne in her first therapy session. "I know Mom's proud of me, but I'm an only child, and because I work long, hard hours, it seems like a grandchild would be something special in her life. When I look at Mom she seems to be getting so old. And she's no help. She fuels the guilt by always bugging me about getting married and having kids. I really resent the situation. Why can't I do what I want with my life without all this guilt?"

Lynne had decided to come for therapy when she found that anxiety and her guilty ruminations interfered with her job and that her resentment of others kept her lonely and isolated. After learning the basic ACT Formula, Lynne decided to apply it to her mother. She told herself:

"I accept the idea that my mother won't have grandchildren and that she will be disappointed with me. I am willing to pay this price to be true to myself."

"I choose to create the vision of feeling good about my life-style and having a good relationship with my mother."

"I will take action by being honest with my mother about my intentions not to have children, by enjoying our visits, and by including her more often in my career successes."

At our next session Lynne was noticeably less anxious and had renewed energy to concentrate on her work. She spent the weekend with her mother and discussed the situation. When her mother expressed disappointment at growing old without grandchildren, Lynne repeated the ACT Formula to herself.

"I was astounded at how it worked," she said. "When Mom expressed her disappointment, I just accepted it. It seemed like I could love her more because I wasn't fighting her *or* the guilt. She didn't seem quite so frail. When I visualized the relationship I did want to have with her, I realized I wanted to do more with her. . . . I might take her on a trip to Europe." Once Lynne stopped resisting her mother, her mother gradually quit talking about grandchildren.

After five sessions, Lynne was free of her clinical anxiety and had learned how to eliminate guilt. She learned to use the ACT Formula to stop her normal fears from escalating into clinical anxiety. She accepted her fears and the possibility they could come true ("I could be fired"), chose to create the best case ("I envision getting good evaluations"), and took action to bring this about ("I'll do the best job I can"). She eliminated guilt by looking at the possible consequences of her choices; if she found she was unwilling to pay the price, she didn't make that particular choice. She continued coming to therapy for six months because, as she said, "I want to give myself the gifts the choice system offers."

STEP FOUR: Be Precise in Your Language

To understand how to use the idea of choice, break the word *responsibility* into two words: *response* and *ability*. You have response ability for the way you choose to act and think, which is related to how you feel. Others are not you, so they are unable to respond for you.

Language is critical to the way you think. *Many unspoken beliefs are buried in the words you use,* and unless you understand the concepts behind your words you end up making significant thinking errors. You lump different meanings together. As you learn more about choice and change, you'll discover that each system has its own distinct psychological language. The change system's language is derived from the physical world; it is based on blame and trying to change events. The choice system's language is derived from the psychological world and is based on awareness, choice, and creating desired experiences.

The system you are in determines the meanings you give to a word. One meaning may make sense in the physical world but mean the opposite in the psychological world. When you give away something physical (for example, money), you have less of it; when you give away something psychological (say, love) you have more of it. *Giving* when you're trying to change someone represents manipulation ("I'll give, but you owe me"), whereas *giving* out of choice is altruistic ("I give for the joy of it, with no strings attached"). *Helping* in the change system is motivated by change and blame ("I'll help because I want to change you"; "You'll blame me if I don't help"), whereas *helping* out of choice means something entirely different ("I'm helping simply because I want to").

Love, when used to change others, represents a restrictively narrow, conditional feeling that you ascribe to others ("I'll change so you'll love me"; "I'll love you if you change"). Then it is an indirect way to boost your self-esteem ("I need your love to feel good about myself"). *Choosing* to love is an expansive, unconditional feeling that you allow to come from within you ("I love you as you are").

As you become aware of the differences between trying to change something versus creating a new experience for yourself, be aware of the language you use. When you say, "I'll help you," do you really mean "I'll help you so you'll like me more"? When you love others, what does that mean to you? Do you need them to make you happy? Or does it mean you appreciate and accept them exactly as they are?

Be precise in your language so that you don't fool yourself with appearances. If you say, "I make him dinner every night because I love him" when you really mean "I make him dinner every night because I want something from him," you only fool yourself. The lyrics you use (lines with *love* or *help* in them) don't go with the music you use (the meaning of the word), so that even when you say, "I love you," or, "I'll help you," the song as a whole doesn't work. As you raise your awareness of the nature of the two systems, raise your awareness of the language you use.

STEP FIVE: Use Critical Opportunities to Increase Your Skill

You already know something about the benefits of choice and about the drawbacks of trying to change current reality. Begin to identify unhappy experiences in your life in terms of your need to change something. Pinpoint exactly who or what you are trying to change.

EXERCISE

Close your eyes and think about the last time you felt unhappy. Take a few minutes to recapture the experience and feelings. Don't hurry. It is important to recapture your feelings, so take your time. What caused you to feel unhappy? In your notebook, complete this sentence: "I felt unhappy because _____."

What did you write? Very likely you wrote that *someone* or *something* made you unhappy. Did you suffer from one of the ten painful symptoms?

Take a few minutes and think of three disappointments you've had in your life. A disappointment is a situation in which you wanted to get or have something (a job, a trip, a degree, a relationship) and you failed to get it. Choose experiences that had a beginning, middle, and end and that are now finished. List them in your notebook. Use a specific incident (for example, "The time I wanted to write an article" or "The time I wanted to get into law school").

Notice how the change system played a role in each event. Who or what did you blame for your bad feelings? Did you blame others? Yourself? What were you trying to change? Which of the ten symptoms did you experience in each experience? Keep these three experiences handy. You will be using them in later exercises.

Use moments of pain as training opportunities. Whenever you feel emotional pain, ask yourself who or what it is you are trying to change. Pain is a sign you've gone into the change system. Use these critical moments of pain not as times to berate yourself, but as golden opportunities to train yourself to *let go* of the need to change events, other people, or yourself. At every opportunity, practice switching to the choice world view. See pain as your chance to say, "Hey, I can choose to create my own life. What do I want to see happen?"

If you feel that someone or something is causing your distress (your wife left with another man; you were fired), be aware that how you react to a situation is *your* responsibility. You always have current reality to deal with (your wife is gone; you're unemployed), but you don't have to be at the emotional mercy of your situation.

When you see that you create your own response to your current reality ("I sank into depression when my wife left"; "I was furious when I got fired"), *you are free to use your thoughts and actions to help you create the experiences you want.* Recognize that you may have a delay in creating a new feeling because your feelings are made up of a psychological part (how you choose to look at a situation) and a physiological part. The physiological part consists of automatic body reactions and complex electrochemical impulses. Because you can only indirectly effect the physiological part, it may take a while to create new feelings.

The following are examples of how new experiences can be created:

"I accept the reality that my wife left me and that I feel depressed about it."

"I choose to create my vision of a happy, meaningful relationship with a woman who loves me."

"I will take action by joining a singles group, pursuing my interests in clubs rather than alone; I will keep myself fit and healthy so that I feel good about myself; I will widen the friendships I already have with single women."

Or:

"I accept the fact that I was unfairly fired from my job and that I am furious about it."

"I choose to create my vision of feeling good and having a job I love."

"I will take action by applying for similar positions in other companies; looking into other types of jobs I might like to do; seriously examining if I have other interests I might be able to turn into a career by more schooling; and finding out about financial aid at schools that could help me broaden my skills."

The crux of the choice system, then, is this: Despite the influences around you, the responsibility for how you choose to think, feel, *and act* is yours, and the accountability for what happens to you is yours—*as is the ability to create the life you want.*

Let go of the need to change yourself, other people, or events and you will be free to choose the life you want. Nothing "out there" can dictate how you think, feel, and act. Each of those is entirely your choice.

2. Letting Go of Pain

The common denominator in all emotional pain is a need to change current reality—which is unchangeable at the moment. The need can be specific ("I need my retarded child to be normal"; "I need a job"; "I need my daughter to be off drugs"; "I need my husband to come back") or general ("I need to change my whole life"). You try to change what is generally impossible to change, but you keep on trying and you thus keep on hurting. You may learn to live with the pain ("It's my cross to bear") or you may try to numb it with drugs, alcohol, or workaholism, but because you continue to need to change current reality, you continue to hurt.

Need equals pain. You can eliminate the pain by letting go of the need to change current reality. When you use the choice system to accept current reality, you dissolve your need and your pain disappears.

Jerry, one of Gary's clients, had a nineteen-year-old daughter, Katie, who was halfway through her sophomore year at college when she called and told her father she was pregnant and quitting school. She was unsure who had fathered the baby.

Jerry immediately plummeted into despair ("Why did this have to happen? How could she do this to me?"). He tossed and turned all night and by morning had a migraine. Over and over he mourned the loss of the happiness Katie had given him by getting into an Ivy League school. He had wanted her to amount to something, perhaps even to be an accountant like himself. He saw his dreams evaporating, and he began to have images of supporting Katie and her child for the next twenty years. He agonized about telling others in the family that Katie had let them down.

Jerry knew Katie would regret what she was doing. He phoned her and said, "You have to get an abortion." She said, "No," and hung up.

The more Jerry thought about Katie's pregnancy, the worse he felt. His central nervous system responded to his need signals ("I need things to be the way they were before") with hurt, a mixture of anger and sadness. He had trouble sleeping and eating, and he felt a heavy sense of fatigue throughout his body.

Jerry continued to ruminate about Katie's situation even though he was sick of thinking about it. He felt compelled to talk about the subject, even though he knew others were tired of hearing about it. He dreamed about it at night and throughout the day had intruding images of his and Katie's telephone conversation. He couldn't process the image of Katie's pregnancy through his "acceptor" (a metaphor we have developed for that part of the brain that allows you to take in new information).

Jerry was depressed about his daughter for several weeks. He was restless, irritable, and had trouble concentrating and remembering names and dates. He was emotionally unstable and became angry with his office staff. When his ex-wife told him that Katie would be all right, Jerry replied, "It'll take a miracle."

In his first therapy session, Gary told Jerry that as an alternative to the pain of trying to change Katie's situation, he could decide to accept it. Jerry eventually made that decision and started to process the information ("I really can't do anything about Katie's pregnancy. Who can say what is right for someone else? I believe she made a mistake and should have had an abortion. But it's her life"). Once he accepted current reality he was able to see that *what he really wanted was to feel good about his daughter and continue to love her and communicate with her.* He then took action to create this by calling Katie to see what her plans were. The more supportive he acted toward Katie, the better he felt about her.

We have seen hundreds of clients switch out of their pain once they accept current reality. One woman who suffered for years over her alcoholic son put it succinctly: "Acceptance is miraculous!" *You can get rapid relief from your emotional distress by accepting current reality* and focusing on the experience you want to have.

• You accept current reality by honestly acknowledging what exists. You tell yourself the truth. You don't ignore what you dislike, exaggerate it negatively, or exaggerate it positively.
• You look at it in a clear and objective way. After you have a clear picture of what you are rejecting, you consciously have to allow it to exist. Rather than fighting it or forbidding it to be, you permit it to be.
• You decide to let go and let be.
• You include what you are resisting in your picture of current reality rather than try to exclude it. Acceptance is a perception ("This is how it is"), a decision ("I'll let it be"), and a feeling ("I'll experience it as it is").

Feelings: How They Work

Your lack of acceptance creates negative emotions (feelings). Emotions (feelings) have played a crucial role in human development. Your four basic emotions—mad, sad, glad, and scared—can inspire you to action, nudge you to protect yourself, and urge you to cut your losses. Feelings motivate you to take action. *You do what makes you feel good, and you avoid what makes you feel bad.* After you take the action your feelings leave, as does your motivation.

Pleasure motivates you to move toward something. Your pleasure feelings, for example, motivate you to move toward a certain crowd of people ("They think my jokes are funny"); you continue to interact with these people until it no longer feels good ("They made fun of me because I don't drink").

Anxiety motivates you to run or escape from a possible loss ("I had to run for my life").

Anger motivates you to fight against a perceived loss ("I had to fight for my life"). You yell or you attack someone to get rid of your angry feelings, even though you know your outburst will make matters worse.

Sadness motivates you to shut down and withdraw after a loss. If you lose money in the stock market, your sad feelings motivate you to stop playing the market and protect the money you have left.

Emotional Overflow

Normally your emotions keep themselves in balance. Your emotional thermostat turns on the furnace when you get too cold and off when you get too warm. If you're scared long enough, you eventually will get mad and fight for your rights. And if you're angry long enough, you eventually will fear the consequences of your anger and back off.

Your need to change current reality, however, creates an excess of negative emotions. Too much sadness becomes depression, too much gladness becomes mania, too much fear becomes panic, and too much anger becomes rage. Your emotional thermostat malfunctions and you become emotionally distressed.

Your strong emotions (rage, panic, despair) are part of a primitive survival system. They might help in times of real physical danger (a physical attack or a fire), but in modern life this primitive motivational backup system (in which you automatically cement your psychological experiences to the physical world) is rarely needed. Using this system is an unnecessary, ineffective way to run your life.

Choice allows you to balance your emotions, unlike the old, unsatisfactory change system, which tries to balance the world. When you use psychological principles (acceptance, vision, and choice) to separate the physical world from your psychological world ("I accept the fact I didn't get this job, and I choose to create a job I want") you eliminate negative feelings. Your brain stops firing off distress signals because you no longer need the world to be different. You create the experiences you want by using psychological principles in order to free yourself from physiological responses.

Feelings: Using Them to Pressure Yourself

When you need to change the world, you use your unpleasant feelings as self-manipulation. You nudge or goad yourself to solve your problem.

You make yourself anxious so that you won't forget all the work that needs to be done.

You get angry so that you'll stand up for yourself and set limits.

You become depressed so that you can withdraw, regain your strength, and feel good again.

Emotional Crisis Management

Jason, a law student, said, "When I feel too good I can't study because I want to do something that's fun. To make myself study, I have to make myself feel bad. Once after I ate ten packages of Twinkies, I thought, I feel so bad I might as well study. Studying eventually makes me feel good again, and then I feel like doing something else. But then I have to make myself feel bad to study again. If nothing else works, I imagine flunking out of law school."

You have two parallel mechanisms—your emotional and your goal-reaching mechanisms. The two often interact and influence each other. Your anxiety about a car accident can motivate you to use your seat belt. Using emotions to motivate your actions is often an automatic, unaware process.

You can, however, use your goal-reaching mechanism without any emotional impact. For example, you could decide to use your seat belt simply because you decide to.

Jason did this. He learned how to use acceptance, vision, and choice to replace his emotional motivation. He accepted his feelings ("I accept I'm feeling good and don't feel like studying"), visualized what he wanted to happen ("I want to get a good grade on the test"), and made the choice to study even if he didn't feel like it ("I'll choose to study because I want to be a lawyer").

You *can* use your feelings to pressure yourself, but you're nearly always better off using vision and choice to create what you want. You don't have to put yourself through an emotional wringer when you use vision and choice.

For example, when you can use choice, fear is no excuse for being untrue to your vision: You just act. You accept the reality of your fear ("I'm afraid of being rejected"); choose and envision what you want (to go on a date); and take action to get it (make a phone call).

Feelings: How They Use You

You are at the mercy of what you refuse to accept. What you resist captures your attention and enslaves you. Your focus becomes fixed on what you don't want. If you refuse to accept your feelings, you will be pushed around by them.

When you need to change current reality, your feelings begin to run your life ("I can't give speeches because I'm too anxious"; "I can't do my work because I'm too depressed"; "I can't talk to them because I'm too angry"). What you want takes a back seat to your automatic reactions. Your feelings become excuses or self-created handicaps ("I can't do anything until I feel better").

Big Choices, Little Choices

You can't always feel the way you would like to feel at each moment. However, *you do have the option to step over your feelings*—your primitive motivational system—*and move toward your vision.*

Gary stayed up late one night and didn't feel like writing the next morning. Before he sat down to start writing, his wife, Pat, asked if he'd like to take the morning off to look at computerized refrigerators. He did feel like doing that. He loves gadgets and it sounded like fun. However, his *big* choice was to finish this book, so he made the *little* choice to write this section. Gary said, "I chose to do it and imagine enjoying it. Initially, I didn't enjoy writing it. However, now that I'm into it, I'm having a good time and I like what I'm writing."

Moving Off the Fence

Your feelings always take you back to the *status quo*. Shirley, one of Jim's clients, is a good example. She shifted back and forth between withdrawing from others and being lonely and moving toward others and getting scared when she got close. Her feelings of loneliness pushed her to seek out others, and her feelings of being hurt and vulnerable caused her to back away if she got too close. She ended up on the fence, where she felt the least amount of pain.

Shirley got off the fence by learning to be responsible for her choices and not responsible for others' choices. Her loneliness came from feeling unconnected to others. Paradoxically, she first had to separate from others psychologically before she could connect with them. (This socialization process works the same for children. They have to separate from their parents before they can bond with others.)

Shirley had to get in touch with her own psychological reality. First, she learned to stop making others responsible for her experiences. She learned that even if others didn't cooperate, she didn't have to feel bad ("They can choose what they want, and I can choose to accept this without being critical of them or of myself").

Once she stopped blaming others for her feelings ("Men make me so angry"), she could see what she was doing to create the situation ("I don't tell men what I want and then I get mad if they don't do what I want"). She was then able to start to create what she wanted ("I'll tell men what I want even if they think I'm pushy"). As a result of being self-accountable, Shirley developed a sense of her own individuality. Once she saw she could create her own separate psychological reality, she started to experience a greater reality about people. At her last session, she smiled and said, "It's funny, but I used to feel lonely even when I was with people. Now I can remember somebody and feel close even though the person may be thousands of miles away."

Jim told her that while this was great she should not believe she had changed. She could always go back and get stuck in her core conflict between wanting to be close and her fear of being close. However, she now knew how to resolve the conflict and move beyond it.

Once Shirley stopped feeling lonely, she didn't have to become dependent on others to feel better. She made friends and went on dates because she *wanted to,* not because she *needed to.* Once she did start a serious relationship with a man, she didn't have to run away to feel better.

Your feelings are like the English weather—constantly in flux, constantly changing. That's why you can't trust them. To avoid being blown off course, keep your eye on where you want to go. Move toward your vision even if you don't feel like taking action at the moment.

When you're in distress you erroneously believe your feelings will never change ("I'll feel terrible forever"). This is one of the reasons you believe you have to change or control them. Struggling to change or control them, however, prolongs unpleasant feelings. *Your feelings will change on their own and toward the direction you want if you focus on choice instead of change.*

Feelings: How to Deal with Them the Way You Want

Does being responsible for your feelings mean you can direct them at will and feel any way you want to? Your feelings are made up of a complex biological and psychological interplay. You often have little say over the onset of your spontaneous moods and feelings, which are physical phenomena.

Still, you have the response ability for your feelings, because you are the one who can do the most about them. You have the response ability or choice in *how you want to see your feelings* (their causes, meanings, and purposes). You have choice in *how you express them* (state, act out, override). You have the choice about *how you experience your feelings* (repress, feel, ignore). You have the choice of how *indirectly to effect your feelings* (change or choice system). And, most importantly, you have the choice as to *how you take in your feelings* (accept or reject).

Here are some useful guidelines for dealing with your feelings:

Hold yourself accountable for your feelings ("I'm directly and indirectly responsible for my anger") rather than assign the accountability (or blame) to others ("You made me mad").

Hold your vision despite what you're feeling at the moment ("I want this marriage to work even though right now I feel its hopeless") rather than let yourself be blown about by your feelings ("I feel so awful I don't even care what I want").

Express your feelings if it will help you reach your vision ("When you do that, I feel . . .") rather than use your feelings to manipulate others ("Why do you do this to me?").

Express your feelings in a constructive way ("I feel bad when you're sarcastic, and I'd like to resolve this somehow") rather than destructively ("You're sadistic!").

Experience your feeling ("I'll feel my feeling for forty-five seconds and then focus on what needs to be done") rather than repress or try to change your feelings ("I can't stand feeling like this").

Honestly acknowledge what you are feeling ("I'm feeling down at the moment") rather than deny or lie to yourself ("I don't feel bad").

Use choice to create the feelings you want ("I'll choose to have a good time") instead of trying to change others or events in order to feel good ("Why are they like this?").

Don't use your feelings to evaluate or judge yourself Just because you feel guilty doesn't mean you're a criminal; if you don't feel guilty it doesn't mean you're not a criminal. Avoid evaluations of yourself or others when you are having strong feelings.

Use the word *FEEL* as shorthand to remember these guidelines:

*F*ocus on your feelings.
*E*xpress them constructively.
*E*xperience them.
*L*et them go.

Acceptance: Taking Information In and Letting Pain Go

In the physical world, when you take in or accept something you're stuck with it. In the psychological world, taking in (accepting information) is the way you let go of pain. This process may seem counterintuitive, but that's how the psychological world works.

EXERCISE

Refer back to your list of three disappointments. Identify in each case what you needed to have changed—in yourself, in another person, or in the event. Was there something you needed to be different in your schooling? Did you need your parents to be different? Did you need your physical appearance to change?

Acceptance is taking in unwanted information about current reality ("I lost my job"). Once you have this information, you are better able to create what you want. How you *take* (accept) *it* (the information) *in* is crucial to leading a happy and satisfied life. Do you take it in easily? Do you take it in poorly? Do you tell yourself, "I can't take it!"

When Jerry first heard that Katie was pregnant, he tried to act as if the situation did not exist. When he got out of the blame mode, he was able to accept Katie's situation. He stopped blaming her for his bad feelings ("I felt let down because I expected her to hold me up") and stopped blaming himself for her predicament ("She's an adult and accountable for her own life"). He removed the blame and was able to accept current reality as it was. Once he accepted current reality, Jerry realized he wanted to help his daughter in any way he could. He offered to pay for her maternity expenses and told her that if she ever did want to continue her schooling, he would help her pay for child care.

The Acceptor

The acceptor is a metaphor we have developed for that part of your brain that takes in new information about the world. Although it is not an actual, physical part of the brain, our clients have found it useful to use the word *acceptor* to visualize the process of acceptance. Before your acceptor processes the information, it goes through two other stages. First, you filter the information through the memory system in your right hemisphere (your unconscious), where your past emotional memories color the event. Next, the image goes from your right hemisphere to your left hemisphere, which is the conscious or aware part of your brain. This is the interpretation department. The image is checked against your belief system to see if it is acceptable. Both stages occur in a split second.

When the Consciousness Flow Is Blocked If current reality is acceptable, you process it from your consciousness (left brain hemisphere) back to your long-term memory (right brain hemisphere) through your acceptor. Your acceptor is like a channel between the two sides of your brain.

You process a stream of consciousness about current reality through your acceptor. What is useful you keep and what isn't you forget.

When you get a match between what you intend to have happen and what you see happening, you have motion toward your goal. However, when you have a mismatch, a clash between what you expect and what you see occurring, you experience e-motion, or lack of motion toward your goal. When the acceptance process breaks down, you experience emotional distress. This breakdown is caused when:

1. You construct an image of current reality. This is often a distorted image ("Bill thinks I'm a fool");

2. You have a mismatch between what you need to have happen and the image ("I need to have others' approval");

3. Your reaction to the image blocks the flow of consciousness ("I feel bad").

FIGURE 1

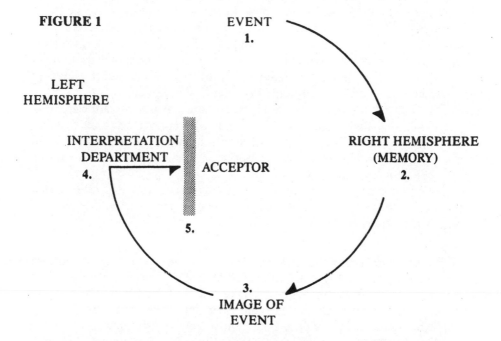

HOW THE ACCEPTOR GETS BLOCKED:

1. Event ("Mary didn't call").
2. Perception of event moves to right hemisphere and is colored by past memories ("I've been rejected before").
3. New image is produced ("Mary's rejecting me"); moves to left hemisphere.
4. Image is filtered through interpretation department and matched against beliefs ("I need to be loved").
5. Mismatch between image and belief blocks acceptor and creates negative feelings ("I'm hurt and sad").

Your beliefs ("To be happy I need others to change") conflict with your images, your pictures of the physical world. (The beliefs were usually formed early in life, often around some trauma you didn't fully process.) The clash of images and beliefs creates body vibrations or feelings. The limbic frontal circuits, the part of your brain from which emotions come, are circular structures. The clash causes them to reverberate like a tuning fork. The reverberation is a self-signal (a feeling) for you to take some action to change the physical world.

How to Feel in the Flow Dr. Eli Robins and associates at Washington University School of Medicine at St. Louis have recently made a major discovery in the brain physiology of emotions. They found that people prone to anxiety attacks have a marked imbalance in blood flow between the right and left sides at the parahippcampalgyrus, the part of the brain that controls emotions. The blood backs up on the right side of the brain and doesn't flow smoothly to the left side. Any changes in the blood flow affect the nerve cell activity of the two sides of the brain. The excess blood in the right hemisphere could be triggering the frightening images anxious people have. The researchers believe that this type of imbalance may play a role in other forms of emotional disorders, such as depression.

This research supports the idea of acceptance. When you are accepting the world, you feel more in the flow and more connected to everything. When you refuse or are unable to accept something, you feel blocked and out of the flow. When you suffer emotional distress, you feel a barrier between yourself and the rest of the world.

Once you take in what you have been rejecting, you will often feel a physical release and your senses will become more acute—colors are brighter, sounds are clearer.

Smooth Flow versus Sluggishness Some people have open acceptors; they easily process the daily demands of living, if necessary absorbing major losses, such as the death of a mate, with little difficulty. The ups and downs of life flow smoothly through their acceptors. Their theme song might be, "Row, row, row your boat gently down the stream. . . ."

Other people have sluggish acceptors. They often feel blocked ("I can't stand what's going on"), and even when their acceptors work, they accept only a trickle of current reality ("I can hardly put up with this"). The gap or mismatch between what they need and how they see current reality is large. They have more distorted images of reality ("Others will humiliate me") than people with open acceptors, and they react more strongly ("I need others' love"; "I need to be perfect"; "I need to be in control"; "I can't trust others"; "I don't belong"; "I can't do it").

Overly reactive people have trouble accepting that it's Monday or Tuesday or February or August. They jerk through life rather than flow through it. When events differ from their expectations, their acceptors jam up and they have trouble processing their life experiences.

Do You Have Mental Blocks? How well does your acceptor work? Use the following scale to see how smoothly you accept current reality. Rate each item from 0 to 5, with 0 meaning the statement doesn't apply and 5 meaning it completely applies to you.

1. I had many losses or traumas as a child ("One of my parents died"; "I was physically abused").

0   1   2   3   4   5

2. I was overprotected as a child ("I didn't stay over at friends' houses"; "My parents didn't allow me to fail").

0   1   2   3   4   5

3. I often act immaturely ("I throw tantrums"; "I pout"; "I quit if I don't get my way").

0   1   2   3   4   5

4. I'm often rigid ("I hate to change plans"; "I like to do everything in a certain way").

0   1   2   3   4   5

5. I take disappointments poorly ("I'm a sore loser"; "I see disappointments as personal affronts").

0   1   2   3   4   5

6. I often feel frustrated ("It's always something"; "Why me?" "Not again!").

0   1   2   3   4   5

7. I'm very judgmental and opinionated ("I don't like that"; "That's awful").

0   1   2   3   4   5

8. I'm a perfectionist ("Picky, picky, picky").

0   1   2   3   4   5

9. I'm often intolerant of others ("Why can't people be more like me?").

0   1   2   3   4   5

10. My parents had major trouble accepting changes (jobs, moves, separations).

0   1   2   3   4   5

11. I set goals that are way beyond my reach ("This time next year I'll have a mansion in Malibu next to Bob Dylan's house").

0   1   2   3   4   5

12. I can't tolerate not knowing ("I've got to know how I did on the test"; "I need to do more research").

0   1   2   3   4   5

13. I believe there has to be one right way ("I'll just have to find the right system").

0   1   2   3   4   5

14. I'm often indecisive ("The red sweater or the blue sweater?").

0   1   2   3   4   5

15. I often mistrust myself or others ("I'm suspicious of what they really want").

0   1   2   3   4   5

16. I often feel like an outsider ("What are they thinking about me?").

    0   1   2   3   4   5

17. I often feel inferior ("Others know more than I do").

    0   1   2   3   4   5

18. I need to feel in control ("Don't tell me that, I can't handle it").

    0   1   2   3   4   5

19. I often feel powerless ("They have all the power").

    0   1   2   3   4   5

20. I often feel rejected ("They don't like me").

    0   1   2   3   4   5

This quiz touches on the major issues in your ability to accept reality. Add up all your scores:

0–20	= You generally have a few problems with acceptance.
21–50	= You have recurring problems with acceptance and can benefit greatly by learning to accept current reality better.
51–70	= You have major problems with acceptance and need to focus on learning to accept current reality better.
71 and above	= You have a life-style based on resisting reality. You need daily practice in accepting current reality.

Each item relates to how you take in and process current reality. For example, your ability to accept adversity is often related to early learning experiences. If as a child you had severe trauma (a psychotic mother, for example), you may have trouble accepting later losses. You may have developed a belief that you can't stand losses or setbacks. It is *as if* your acceptor, after having to expand too much as a child, has since collapsed and narrowed. Similarly, if you were overprotected as a child, you'll also probably have trouble with acceptance. You may expect everything to go well. Because of underuse, your acceptor fails to develop fully and you have difficulty processing unpleasant experiences.

Too Much Too Soon Even if you're good at accepting adversity, you may have trouble if too much happens all at once. An accumulation of big and small setbacks can block your acceptor. Once you start resisting reality, you have trouble accepting anything—the weather, the way you look, the way your wife talks, and how your kids act.

Generally acceptance goes unnoticed. You process experiences in an even flow until there is a conflict. Then you experience pain. It is as if you put in some debris that blocks your acceptor. As with your digestive system, you only notice your acceptor when something is wrong, such as ruminating (obsessively repeating an idea to yourself) or having difficulty sleeping.

Signs of Blockage If your acceptor is blocked, you're not interested in anything but the problem. Because you spend your energy fighting current reality, you are chronically fatigued and "stressed out." You may cry all the time or you may be unable to cry. You may feel compelled to talk about the problem or be unable to talk about it at all. Excesses in sleeping, drinking, and working are attempts to deal with your resistance to current reality.

The Worm's Eye View

When you resist current reality, you constrict your awareness of available choices. You fail to divide the psychological world (your attention) from the physical world (what you're trying to change). The conscious portion of your brain (left hemisphere) fills up with racing, obsessive thoughts and you become fixated on what you want to change. You go into a trancelike state and react to the image as if it were true.

In his book *The War Against Sleep,* Colin Wilson, an influential writer about split-brain research, calls the left hemisphere pessimistic because it looks too closely at life—like trying to decide on the worth of the *Mona Lisa* by examining the canvas with a magnifying glass or microscope.

In short, the "worm's-eye view" of the left brain is negative by nature. The "bird's-eye view" of the right brain is positive by nature, revealing vistas of meaning and interconnectedness that are invisible to the worm.

You have many thinking distortions when you're upset because you lack perspective; you're looking too closely at the problem and missing the big picture.

The worm's-eye view has an evolutionary purpose. When you resist something, your attention narrows. You focus exclusively on what you need to change. To survive, early humans had to focus on what was unacceptable. If our ancestors had ignored or overlooked what was unacceptable—a tiger, for example, or possible starvation—we would not be here.

EXERCISE

Place your hand in front of your face and look around for a few moments. Now put your hand down and look around.

When you resist something, it's similar to walking around with your hand in front of your face. Start to notice the difference in your range of awareness when you resist current reality and when you accept it. To get rapid relief, you need to use psychological principles (awareness, choice, vision); therefore, the physical principle of *resist change* is nearly always counterproductive because it reduces awareness.

We treated a client who resisted current reality so strongly that she often overlooked the many other options open to her. She once made plans to go to Palm Springs for the weekend with friends and was looking forward to it, but they canceled out. At first she resisted ("How could they do this to me?").

When she decided to accept current reality instead of fight it, other options started to open. She took action and called some old friends she hadn't seen in several years and ended up creating a great weekend for herself.

What you see is what you get. Mother Nature seems to send us what we dislike the most. If you can't stand dirt, you *see* dirt everywhere. What you fear is sure to come visiting at your doorstep. If you try to block out what you don't want to hear, you can't help but hear it. Have you ever known people who hate being fat or hate being sick or hate being angry? Their problems seem to cling to them because they concentrate on them so fully that they shut out other, good things.

When a client says, "I can stand anything but this one problem" (rejection, disloyalty, failure), Jim says he knows *that* is what the therapy is going to be about. The more an individual needs to change something, the more it tends to stay the same.

In the choice system, you can use the psychological principle "what you see is what you get" to your advantage: *You hold the vision of what you want until you get it.* The trick is to focus on what you want until it happens. By holding the vision you increase your awareness of what specific actions to take to create it.

Needing to Change Your Need to Change

When you realize that you have been trying to change reality, be on the lookout even for your attempts to change that orientation. You may try to use your willpower to do this ("I've got to change my thinking"), or you can force yourself to think about something else ("I'm not going to think about trying to change my husband"). However, these methods seldom work; they're the same methods that created your distress. Even if you can repress or bury an experience, it always returns. Someone mentions your old boyfriend or girlfriend and you feel like crying. The unaccepted memory or repressed behavior rises up like a hand from the grave to grab you.

Facing the Beast   You have to start by accepting your resistance. What you resist most are your feelings—they often seem like monsters. Acting out your lack of acceptance by avoiding what makes you feel bad ("I can't tell him the truth"; "I can't talk in public") feeds the beast (your anxiety). When you avoid something (public speaking), you reinforce the illusion that the event (the speech) or others (the audience) have the ability to make you feel bad. Moving toward what is frightening ("I'll ask her out") or uncomfortable ("I'll try even though I'm unsure") causes the beast to disappear.

Avoidance has a cumulative effect ("I'll avoid all men because they can hurt me") and causes life to become increasingly difficult and barren ("Is this all there is?"). Approaching what you fear is effective because you accept and acknowledge current reality and you thus free creative energy.

Acceptance keeps you current. Everything you refuse to accept in your past robs you of living fully in the present. If there is something that happened to you last week that you can't accept, then you're not taking in and enjoying what is happening right now. If you have a large backlog of unprocessed experiences, you will have a strong sense of missing out on life—and you will have a greater fear of dying.

Once you tell yourself the truth about current reality ("I'm fifty-five years old, have a stressful job, and eat and smoke too much; this makes me a candidate for a heart attack"), you can create what you want ("I'll check myself out with the doctor and get myself healthy"). You develop the clarity and energy to move beyond your current obstacle and create what you want.

Becoming Wiser When you are in the flow, you take what is useful (the nutrients) from current reality and eliminate the rest. If your acceptor leaks like a sieve, you fail to learn from your experiences. You keep making the same mistakes.

The closer in time you are to an event, the greater your ability to learn from it. The more quickly you accept current reality, the better. For example, if you just got fired, take an honest look at what happened. Map out the stages and write down in your notebook what happened; see whether you helped create the problem ("I developed an attitude problem and devalued the job"). The longer you wait, the fuzzier your memory about an event becomes; *you start to imagine what happened* instead of seeing what really happened. Always write down immediately what you want to happen in the future so that you can put that knowledge into practice.

Influences on Your Acceptor

Biological Influences When your biological system is "off center," accept this as current reality. At times you may have to put off processing or accepting a troublesome situation until you are feeling physically stronger. You need a certain amount of psychological energy to run your psychological world effectively. Anything that depletes this energy—anger, envy, greed, fear, a physical ailment, alcohol, drugs—makes acceptance more difficult. Instead of expending more energy to fight your biological state, you can release energy by accepting what you are resisting ("I'll accept the fact that I'm feeling under the weather").

When your energy is down, your acceptor works less effectively. You're less able to accept current reality when you're sick, tired, hungry, excited, or stressed.

Social Influences   When you start creating your own life, you stop being bullied by cultural imperatives. For example, if you are the only one of a large family to remain single and your family pressures you to get married, you can accept the situation by taking responsibility for your own choices ("*I'm* the only one who can put psychological pressure on me").

Until you hold only yourself accountable for your choices, you'll have trouble accepting something if you're the only one with the "problem," if what you have to accept goes against group norms, if the group puts up psychological barriers to your accepting it, or if you may lose social status for doing so.

Psychological Influences   When you are "for" acceptance, your acceptor flows. A psychological bias against acceptance undermines acceptance. If you're against something, you set up barriers to acceptance. For example, if you're a negative person ("No, no, no!"), you will have problems accepting current reality.

Your bias may be due to misconceptions about acceptance. The most common misconception confuses physical meanings of acceptance (resignation, giving up, settling for, losing control, being weak) with the psychological meaning of acceptance: *an honest look at current reality for the expressed purpose of creating what you want.* Acceptance is the first step you take, not the last.

Taking the First Step

Some experiences are more difficult to accept than others. You may have to begin by accepting only a small part of an experience or by accepting it for a few moments at a time.

Assess Your Resistance   Use the questions that follow as an acceptance scale to measure how much trouble you have accepting an experience. Think of something you're resisting or trying to change. Go through the scale and rate your resistance on each item.

1. What I'm resisting is important.
$$0 \quad 1 \quad 2 \quad 3 \quad 4 \quad 5$$
2. What I'm resisting is unexpected.
$$0 \quad 1 \quad 2 \quad 3 \quad 4 \quad 5$$

3. What I'm resisting is unfair.

    0   1   2   3   4   5

4. What I'm resisting is symbolic.

    0   1   2   3   4   5

5. What I'm resisting is my fault.

    0   1   2   3   4   5

6. What I'm resisting is someone else's fault.

    0   1   2   3   4   5

7. What I'm resisting has long-term effects.

    0   1   2   3   4   5

8. What I'm resisting is against my values.

    0   1   2   3   4   5

9. What I'm resisting is an unknown.

    0   1   2   3   4   5

10. What I'm resisting is a surprise.

    0   1   2   3   4   5

11. What I'm resisting affects my self-esteem.

    0   1   2   3   4   5

12. What I'm resisting is wrong.

    0   1   2   3   4   5

13. What I'm resisting is out of my control.

    0   1   2   3   4   5

14. What I'm resisting is a hard decision.

    0   1   2   3   4   5

15. What I'm resisting is unexplainable.

    0   1   2   3   4   5

16. What I'm resisting is a familiar problem.

    0   1   2   3   4   5

17. What I'm resisting is a disappointment.

    0   1   2   3   4   5

18. What I'm resisting is bad.

    0   1   2   3   4   5

19. What I'm resisting is demoralizing.

    0   1   2   3   4   5

20. What I'm resisting is unwinnable.

    0   1   2   3   4   5

Add up your score:

80–100 = You have a major acceptance problem.
60–79 = You have trouble with acceptance.
40–59 = You have moderate problems with acceptance.
20–39 = You have minor problems with acceptance.
 0–19 = Acceptance should be easy.

No matter how overwhelming current reality may seem, you can accept it. Once you accept reality, you set the stage for getting better.

Likes attract likes. Acceptance creates peak experiences—peeks or glances at how you are different from others yet the same. We are all interdependent and live in one world and one universe. There is a natural progression to this realization. First, when your acceptor is working you accept yourself ("I accept the way I look"; "I love my gray hair"). When you like yourself you are free to be yourself. Second, you like what is like yourself ("I like him; he has an irreverent sense of humor, like me"; "I like this house; it has character"). When you accept others, you begin to see how similar they are to you, and you start to like them. And, third, if you can accept the differences between you and others, you move to a higher state. The feeling of connectedness with others leads to a larger cosmic sense of oneself.

Jim has seen the decision to accept other people as they are save many family relationships. In a typical family situation the parents are adamantly against drugs; their teenaged children choose to take drugs and make this their battleground with the parents. When parents are able to accept (grounding in current reality) the fact that their child is going to use drugs despite their wishes and proceed to *set limits* and keep the relationship alive, there often is a major improvement in the relationship.

Rather than feeling helpless, frustrated, and hopeless, the parents realize that they do have effective responses they can make. They cannot make a child decide not to use drugs (a decision for which only the child has response ability), but they can hold the child accountable. For example, they can limit the use of the car, make less money available, refuse to provide meals and laundry as long as the child is using drugs. They can let the child know they will not tolerate the behavior. They make it clear that if they discover drug use in the house, they will turn the child in to the police; that if they know the child is at a party where the drugs are available, they will call the police; and if they find out who provides the drugs, they will call the providers and let them know that selling to their child will put the seller at risk of being turned in to the police.

This system clarifies responsibilities. The child makes the response to take drugs. The parents accept that but let the child know that they have responses they can and will make. Once the limits are set, the child has to pay the cost of taking drugs (no meals, no money, no car, arrest). Often, as the cost goes up, the child decides to give up drugs.

When you accept something you've been resisting you may feel an immediate, acute sadness, then experience a release of painful feeling. When your stream of consciousness starts flowing again, you are happy and at one with the world. Acceptance removes the barrier between you and the world. You start having peak experiences—looking at the ocean, watching children play, being with someone you love—when you are connected to everything.

3. Acceptance: Awareness and Feeling Strategies

When General George Patton wanted something done, he told his officers exactly what he wanted and then left the "how" up to them. He said he was often surprised by the creative and effective ways his officers accomplished goals when left to their own devices.

Ends determine the means. In the choice system, the "how" question is always secondary to the "what do you want" question. What you want is to accept your current reality. Don't get hung up on the right way to do it. Your unique situation (what you want to create) determines what means will work best for you. Simply desiring acceptance helps you figure out the means to reaching it.

As there are "Fifty Ways to Leave Your Lover," according to the song, there are more than fifty ways to reach acceptance. You may already have your own personal acceptance strategies or you may be a person who enjoys making them up as you go along. You'll find many different acceptance strategies in this chapter and the next. Simply reading the two chapters is helpful. Pick strategies that appeal to you and experiment until you find what works best for you. You may find that a strategy that works one time may not work at another, so make sure you have more than one strategy in your back pocket. Agility will come with practice.

The ways to accept current reality are broken down here into awareness strategies, feeling strategies, thinking strategies, and acting strategies. In this chapter we'll consider awareness and feeling strategies; thinking and acting strategies will be dealt with in Chapter 4.

Awareness Strategies

Attempts to deny, ignore, and rationalize away reality are major obstacles to acceptance. Acceptance and awareness are directly related—increase one and you increase the other. You can use many different ways to increase your awareness of current reality. Different individuals find different ways more or less useful. Stick with those that help *you*.

Observe yourself. You become better at acceptance the more you know how it works. Step back and see how you are accepting or resisting current reality. Can you see how your images or thoughts distort what you must accept?

Know what you want. Accepting current reality is easier if you have a vision of what you want. Often you are so busy resisting that you never get around to deciding what you do want. Remember that in the creative process acceptance is not the final step but the initial step in *creating* the experiences you want.

Define what you want. A simple and easy way to resolve a conflict is to move on to something better. You increase your acceptance when you define what that "something better" is for you.

For example, if you have trouble with a person at work, decide what you want to happen ("I want to get along with people there and enjoy my job"). Deciding what you want and telling the truth about where you stand gives you direction ("I chose to resolve it") and gets you moving ("I'll act as if we are friendly and as if I enjoy my job").

Focus in on the experience you want. If you find that what you want is impossible, focus on the psychological experience you want, not on the means to get there.

PATIENT: "I want Sue to come back and love me again."
THERAPIST: "For what reason?"
PATIENT: "So I'll be happy again."
THERAPIST: "Anything else?"
PATIENT: "I want to be in a good relationship."
THERAPIST: "Okay, what you want is to be happy and be in a good love relationship. Sue is only *one* way of getting that."

Make it up. What if you don't know what you want? Robert Fritz, the founder of DMA (a course that teaches creativity), has given a profound answer to this question: *"You make it up."* Simply make up a vision of what you want, and if, after you get it, it turns out you don't like it, make up another one. Be specific about what you make up because clarity equals success. The more specific you are in your vision ("I want to be in my own one-bedroom condo near the beach") the easier your vision will be to create.

In the physical world objects exist whether you think about them or not and despite what you think of them. In your psychological world nothing exists until you create it psychologically. If you want a vision that is worthy of you, you need to make it up. Its existence is entirely dependent upon you.

In the psychological world you also make up how you achieve your vision. Suppose you want to go back to school. You make up what you want to study ("computers") and you make up how you accomplish it ("I'll go to night school").

Rediscover old strategies. You may not realize it, but you have been able to accept many past ordeals. You already have a set of skills you can use, even though you may not be aware of them.

Go back over the three disappointments you wrote about in Chapter 1 and analyze how you were able to accept them. How were you finally able to put them to rest? Jot down in your notebook what you did to achieve acceptance. This is a technique you can use in the future for deciding how to accept difficult situations.

What works for you may not work for someone else, and vice versa. For example, one of our clients, Kathy, found that talking about the death of her father with her sister Carol helped her to accept setbacks. Carol, on the other hand, found that long drives by herself were more helpful.

Go with the flow. You can reach acceptance by imitating nature. Go to the beach, a river, a lake, a forest, a park, or your backyard and observe nature. Look at the sky, the sun, the trees, the ground. Nature is powerful because nature accepts all—birth, death, and everything in between. Nature delights in acceptance. The river accepts whatever is in its way and moves on. If necessary, the river will go around mountains or under them. Nature is unconcerned with good or bad; it just keeps accepting and moving on.

Writer May Sarton has captured this spirit: "I think of the trees and how simply they let go, let fall the riches of a season, how without grief (it seems) they can let go and go deep into their roots for renewal and sleep."

When you accept, you flow with Mother Nature. If your boss at work is a tyrant, that's the way Mother Nature designed it. Given your boss's genetic, social, and psychological background, your boss is likely to be the way he or she is at the moment. Dr. Richard Feynman, a California Institute of Technology physicist and Nobel laureate, has said, "Don't keep saying to yourself, 'How can it be like that?' because you will go into a blind alley nobody has yet escaped. Nobody knows how it can be like that." Mother Nature is the way she is. By collaborating with her rather than fighting with her, you can get what you want.

Contemplate acceptance. A good way to start the day is to meditate on acceptance for ten minutes each morning when you awaken. Think about how you can be more accepting during the day. The more you reflect on acceptance, the better you are at putting it into practice. For example, you might meditate in the morning on *accepting* difficulties you foresee later in the day (an unpleasant meeting, hassles getting to work, having to get through some work you've been avoiding).

At night, review the day from an acceptance perspective. Look at how the day went. Ask yourself if you need to resolve and accept any unfinished psychological business. Practice accepting the good experiences as well as the bad ("I'll accept the fact that I had a good day"). The Greek philosophers reviewed their day each night to see what they could have done better. Having the courage to face what you dislike is a form of acceptance. But don't omit reviewing what you liked about your day and what you're looking forward to the next day. You might want to write these items in your notebook.

Read the classics. Acceptance is the theme of many classic books, such as the works of the Greek Stoics, Marcus Aurelius's *Meditations,* and the teaching stories of Saint Francis of Assisi. Acceptance is old wine in new bottles.

You can learn the intellectual side of acceptance from reading the classics, then go out and actually practice it. Later, after you have taken it to the streets, you can return to the books and to other intellectual exercises. At first the intellectual side may be easiest to grasp. If you keep going back and forth between the intellectual and experiential, however, you will eventually need less reflection and will be ready to accept current reality immediately.

See the good. You'll have an easier time with acceptance if you have a good word for every occasion. A clue: If people avoid you, your negativity may be the reason. People dislike being around someone who constantly devalues the world ("How was your visit to California?" . . . "I hate Los Angeles; the smog's terrible and the people are shallow!"). Many adults avoid the company of adolescents because they so often are contemptuous of everything.

You can easily get caught in a vicious cycle. First you feel bad because you believe you don't measure up to others. You then try to feel better by putting others down. However you attempt to make yourself more by making others less, this effort always backfires. You lessen yourself by being contemptuous and you end up feeling worse. You are usually a part of what you are putting down ("I despise the whole human species").

Notice how you describe life ("My car's a wreck, I live in a dump, and my wife is a mess"). Write one sentence using your favorite negative words ("That idiot made a stupid mistake"). Then rewrite the sentence in an objective way ("I can accept her decision, even though I disagree with it").

You may be unaware of your negativity. Ask a friend or relative about your negative labels. Friends may hear you better than you hear yourself. Listen to their feedback. Then describe the same qualities in your life using positive words ("My car is a classic, I live in a comfortable home, and my wife is the earth mother type").

Ask yourself what experience you want ("I want to enjoy work") and how you can label current reality in a way that will help you create that outcome ("Learning to fill out these forms is a way to improve my work skills").

What you give is what you get. If you label others positively, you will be more inclined to label yourself positively. Mislabeling can be costly. If someone put a skull and crossbones and wrote *Poison* on a container of helpful medicine, you probably wouldn't use that medicine, even though it could make you healthy. You want to label yourself and others in a way that is the most useful.

Spend twenty-four hours labeling reality in positive and optimistic ways—focus on what is good—*then try it for five days*. You'll find that your mind automatically will start to prefer the positive. If you catch yourself making a negative statement ("I hate picnics"), ask yourself if this is what you want to happen. If not, choose what you *do* want ("I choose to enjoy myself").

Imitate the best in others. You will accept reality better if you had good coping models in the past (important people in your life who could accept their losses successfully). If your models used denial, projection, scapegoating, and rationalization, you'll probably have trouble with acceptance.

Think of someone in your past or your present who has been good at acceptance. (Children can be as good at accepting as they are at resisting reality.) You might think of a close relative, a friend, or a distant acquaintance. Notice how the person accepted some loss. How did they see the situation? How did they label the problem? What did they do? Imagine yourself accepting a problem in a similar way.

Learn from your experience. If you look at current reality from a learning perspective ("Next time I'll do it differently") rather than a blaming perspective ("I've got to discover who's to blame"), you make the reality more acceptable. Blame hampers acceptance. When you learn from current reality, you extract the nutrients that benefit you and expand your awareness. Ask yourself, "What can I learn or take from this?"

Some people suggest that suffering is good for us. This thinking is based on the observation that people are often wiser, more compassionate, and better people after they have gone through a trauma or ordeal. But we need to understand that the suffering didn't make them better. The *acceptance* of more reality is the reason for their growth: *Their awareness has been expanded*. You don't need to suffer to grow; *you only need to accept more reality*.

Get the facts. Acceptance requires fully acknowledging current reality. Get the facts and you increase your acceptance. Acquiring data helps in all forms of emotional distress. Anxiety, for example, is eliminated in this way. Once you know something, you stop being overly impressed by it and you stop fearing it. One client discovered her child was retarded. At first she was determined to hire private tutors and therapists to make her child learn. She did not even want the word *retardation* spoken around her. Her home became increasingly stressful for her family, and she became depressed and overwhelmed by guilt. "I thought I could be the one supermom in history who really made her retarded kid normal . . . with enough love, teaching, and attention. It didn't work. I couldn't change the situation. I didn't even really understand the situation."

She found out as much as she could about mental retardation. She joined support groups in the mental retardation area. She sought out the whole truth: What, if anything, did she do directly or indirectly to bring on the retardation of her child? What else was involved? What programs were available to help retarded individuals become self-sufficient? A major obstacle to her initial acceptance was a wish to deny her child's retardation. Once she moved beyond denial and got the relevant information, she could start to accept her child's handicap.

Tom, one of Jim's clients, was depressed because his father, who had died of cancer several years earlier, refused to see him in the weeks before he died. He thought his father must have been angry or disappointed with him. Because Tom kept his fears about this to himself, Jim suggested that he get more information.

Despite his anxiety that his mother would confirm his worst fears, he talked with her about the last weeks of his father's life. She told him, "Your father had a lot of pride in his physical strength. He was a lot like you. He had a macho image and couldn't stand to have anyone see how he looked at the end. He'd lost all his hair and looked like a dried-up old man."

Tom was able to accept his father's death when he got the facts. He told me later, "Knowing what really happened is like adding water to powdered milk. I still had to swallow it, but it was easier to accept."

You can learn to face the facts:

• Look at current reality objectively ("Okay, this is how a journalist would tell the story").
• Put yourself in the other's shoes ("If I were my husband, how would I see the situation?").
• Look at current reality from different angles ("I'll play Twenty Questions with what happened").
• Ask an insightful and honest person to shed some light on the situation.
• Ask others involved what they think happened.
• Use courage to override your fear of discovering the worst.

Review the event. A simple and effective way to accept current reality is to review a situation. Ask yourself what happened and how you feel about it. Go through the review at least three times (you may have to do it even more). Each time you review the event you will find it becomes more real and thus easier to accept. You probably have done this in the past and found it useful. After a trauma or emotional upheaval, you usually want to talk or think it through and review it from different angles.

A three-year-old boy was in an automobile accident on the freeway. No one was hurt, but for several weeks after the accident, he told his parents, "Talk the accident." He asked them to describe the accident five or six times. If they left out a part he reminded them of it and he, in turn, described the accident to others. He reviewed the accident so that he could process it through his acceptor. This is a natural and normal way of processing information. If people are unable to process information, however, this type of reviewing becomes an obsessive problem.

By choosing to review an event, you actively counteract avoidance. Use this method if you don't want to think about the problem. With each review you see your situation in a larger and clearer context. As you move from the worm's eye view to the bird's eye view, you correct distortions and make current reality easier to take.

Be honest with yourself and others. The best awareness strategy is to look at current reality *as it is*. Trim off excess baggage. Don't make it worse (or better) than it is. Look realistically and honestly at what you must accept.

Christy, a magazine editor, had trouble accepting her feelings of incompetence at work. She was afraid she would be fired if she didn't do a perfect job. As a result, she took hours to finish simple projects. When she first came for therapy, she insisted that she was 50 percent incompetent at work. After she set aside her feelings and rated herself more objectively, she decided that she was about 25 percent incompetent.

Then she looked at the average level of incompetency where she worked. She admitted that everyone at the magazine was somewhat incompetent according to her perfectionist standards and that even the best workers were 10 to 15 percent incompetent. Her goal was to be as good as the best people at work. What she had to accept, then, was that she was 10 percent less competent than she wanted to be.

The surplus meaning ("I'm a loser") Christy had placed on her current reality prevented the reality from going through her acceptor. She hadn't been able to accept her 10 percent deficiency in competency because she had let her feelings add to the percentage. The real situation was harder to accept when it was exaggerated. When she cleared away the exaggerations, she had an easier time accepting the imperfections and became more efficient.

When Christy felt 50 percent incompetent, the situation seemed hopeless. Her more realistic 10 percent deficiency in competence was attackable. "That I can deal with," she said. She reorganized her office space so that it was more efficient, took breaks in order to keep her mind fresh, took a local business school course in time management, and finally felt confident enough to stop checking and rechecking her work when she had done her best.

Expand your viewpoint. Don't be fooled by the appearance of current reality. *Wisdom is knowing the difference between the container and the* *contents.* What you believe is too terrible to accept is often just the container (or appearance). When you get behind the appearance, you may find a blessing. Withhold judgment until you see the situation in a larger context. Tell yourself that you won't jump to conclusions until all of the facts are in. One client, for example, was devastated when he was passed over for a promotion. He had poured all his time and energy into reaching the top of the executive ladder. "I worked hard to get the edge over others and I wanted support from my wife," he said, "but I realized she didn't even know me. My kids were strangers." When this client looked behind the devastating appearance of his current reality (passed over for a promotion) he was able to find a blessing (a chance to slow down and invest time and energy into his family).

Look at the event from different perspectives. Take the role of a friendly observer. Ask yourself how you will look at this same situation five years from now.

Pay attention to the present. Practice describing what is happening at the moment: the color of the sky, the feel of the chair, the physical sensations in your legs, the melodious sound of your uncle's accent. Say, "Right now . . . ," then describe your current reality.

Often our awareness about the present lies in the future. You don't know until tomorrow the reason for what happened today. However, by paying attention to current reality (the *now*) you enlarge your awareness and increase your ability to create your future.

Feeling Strategies

Your life experiences consist of feelings and sensations. If you're afraid of making a fool of yourself, what you're really afraid of are feelings of shame, anxiety, and self-consciousness. For example, if you're afraid of dying in an accident, you're actually afraid of the anticipated sensation of pain and panic, of negative or uncomfortable feelings of being out of control. All you ever really have to accept, in some sense, is your feelings. Directly accepting your feelings about current reality, therefore, is often the best strategy.

Remember feelings are kinetic self-signals that something is wrong. The brain gives you an electric shock to get your attention. As long as you resist or ignore emotional signals, the brain will continue to send them. Once you accept the signals, the brain stops sending them.

Experience your feeling. A simple and effective way to accept bad feelings is to feel them purposely. Fully experience the unpleasant feeling, without trying to change it, for forty-five seconds. Get into the sensations of it. Then physically do something else (put something away, turn on a light, sweep the floor). Repeat the process until you have accepted the feeling.

One of Gary's clients was able to accept her feelings of fear by con-sciously experiencing them. Because she lived alone, she was particularly fearful at night. She allowed herself forty-five seconds to sit in a chair and be afraid. Then she made herself get up and do something. She found it helpful to work at her sewing machine or to clean house. If her fear returned, she purposely experienced it for forty-five more seconds, then made herself go back to her activity. When she accepted her fear it stopped dominating her life.

The way out of your bad feelings is through them. *You have to allow yourself to feel bad to stop feeling bad.* Once you get the hang of the process, it becomes incredibly simple to lessen your painful feelings.

Welcome your feelings. Ruth came to therapy because the man she loved returned to his wife. She vacillated between rage and grief. One evening she smashed several drinking glasses against the kitchen wall. She thought she was expressing her feelings, but her true feelings—depression, rejec-tion, loneliness—hurt so much that she resisted them. Her acting out, from tears to tantrums, was actually her way of avoiding her true feelings.

In her first therapeutic session, Ruth learned that her avoidance kept her from accepting the loss of the man she loved. She began to practice experiencing her true feelings by making a choice not to act out (throwing tantrums) and to welcome the feelings of rejection and loneliness that came when she didn't act out. She discovered that when she did so, her painful feelings lessened. She practiced acceptance at home (saying out loud, "I welcome my loneliness"; setting an extra place at the table for her loneliness); when she returned for her second session she seemed a different person. Her depression was lifting, and she was ready to go on with her life.

Rapid shifts like this are not unusual. Once people learn to use accept-ance, they can create different feelings almost immediately.

Express your feelings. You may find it helpful to express your feelings out loud ("I'm really scared"), especially if you usually repress or sit on your feelings. Exaggerate your feelings; speak about them in a dramatic way ("I feel terrible, the worst I've ever felt"). It is generally best to use this strategy while you are alone. Expressing your feelings to others can help if you *own* the feelings ("I feel" versus "You make me feel"), but if you blame your feelings on others, you create more problems than you solve. The idea is to express the emotion through its effect within you, not to manipulate others.

Your emotions go up a scale from apathy and grief, through anxiety and anger, to joy and serenity. An effective technique is to express your emotions in stages:

1. "I feel devastated by it."
2. "I feel sad about it."
3. "I'm really afraid of what this means."

4. "I'm angry at it."
5. "I'm irritated by it."
6. "I'm bored with the same old thing happening."
7. "I'll accept it."
8. "I'll get interested in doing something positive."

You can utilize this strategy alone or with others.

Your feelings move in stages along an emotional scale. If you're apathetic and down about a project, you usually have to go through fear, anger, and boredom before you get positively involved in doing it. One artist broke a sculpture he was working on. He was at first down and gave up on redoing it. He then remembered the emotional scale and decided to use it. At first he was afraid that he couldn't make it as good as it was before, but knowing his feelings would change, he went through anger, irritability, and boredom. Then as he progressed he became interested in the project. By the time he had redone the sculpture he felt elated.

Other expressive behaviors, such as demonstrating anger by throwing balloons with all your might or rolled up socks at the wall, can be helpful. However, a potential problem with all expressive behaviors is that in carrying them out you can restimulate yourself and feel worse.

Let yourself experience feelings of ambiguity. Life is a continual process of facing the unknown. We all live in a world of unknowns. Every moment is in some way new and unknown. Focusing on the uniqueness of each moment is a powerful acceptance strategy.

If you resist the ambiguity of the moment ("I need to know"), you're going to create more ambiguity. All you can count on are probabilities (most cars stop at red lights). The greater your ability to tolerate and love uncertainty, the happier and more successful you will be.

You usually react to the ambiguous situation in three ways:

1. By seeking the answer to one arbitrary but unanswerable question ("How long will it take?"). The solution is to ask a better question ("How can I best accept the unknown?") rather than asking a question that has no answer.

2. By jumping to a conclusion ("I know it'll turn out badly"). The solution is to expect the unexpected and tolerate the ambiguity and the fact that you can't know for sure.

3. By seeking constant validation that your answer is right ("I'll be okay, right?"). The solution is to experience your ambiguity and let go of your need for guarantees and constant reassurance.

Learning to accept the unknown is especially important when you're experiencing emotional distress. Your negative or fearful feelings cause you to jump to negative or fearful conclusions. When you're feeling calm, your hunches or intuitions are often right. However, emotional distress shuts off your intuition, so your emotionally based hunches or flashes of apparent intuition are nearly always wrong. For example, many, if not most, people who take an airplane trip have automatic flashes of feeling that their plane might crash. But they realize that their premonitions are unfounded and so they fly anyway.

You can increase your tolerance for uncertainty with ambiguity training. Think of times or places in which you hate ambiguity ("I can't stand not knowing where my date is taking me"). Decide to seek out and experience the unknown in precisely these areas ("Don't tell me where we're going"). Imagine yourself accepting and enjoying the ambiguity. As part of your ambiguity training, whenever you run into any ambiguity, decide to *accept and experience the feeling*. If, for example, you can't find something you believe you need at the moment but really don't ("Where did I put that book?" "What was that person's name?"), accept the ambiguity of your situation and let what you are searching for surface on its own.

Accept past losses. If you accept unresolved past losses (such as the death of a parent), you'll have an easier time accepting current reality.

For example, if you find you haven't accepted the death of a parent, you might visit the grave site in order to say good-bye; immerse yourself in memories of the parent (photo books, old scrapbooks), then write a good-bye letter; talk with someone about what the separation means to you; imagine your parent asking you to accept his or her death; make a list of reasons why your parent would want you to accept the death; make a list of reasons why you want to accept the death. Finish unfinished business such as forgiving yourself or your parent for some transgression. You may have overidentified with your parent and need to imagine saying good-bye and going your own way.

Once you have accepted the death of a parent, you will find it easier to accept your current reality, which may involve losses (the loss of a job, the loss of opportunity, the loss of the use of your car, the loss of a chance to go on a date). Unresolved past losses hinder your acceptance of current reality because they are a reminder that there is something you haven't accepted. You begin to think maybe you don't have "acceptance ability" and therefore don't have the ability to accept what is happening to you in the present. Consequently you are always at risk for depression.

Lisa, one of Gary's clients, came for therapy because she was depressed, listless, and unable to cope with the demands of ordinary living (getting dressed, brushing her teeth, making phone calls, shopping for food). She did not want to accept her current reality (that she was a single woman approaching age thirty). When Gary asked her to imagine what her feelings resembled, she recalled a time when she was in college and her fiancé quit school, ran off with another woman, and never said another word to her.

Lisa had never thrown out the pictures of her fiancé and still had the letters and gifts he had given her when they were in college. She still wore the diamond ring he gave her. Gary suggested that she accept that past loss in order to accept her current reality.

Lisa purposely imagined a phone conversation in which her fiancé called her and told her the engagement was off and she was able to say good-bye and wish him luck. She wrote him a letter (which she didn't intend to mail) and told him how the separation hurt her but that she was planning to lead a happy life because she was accepting the loss. Although she had no idea where he lived, writing the letter aided her acceptance. She threw away his pictures, saying out loud, "I accept the fact that I will never see you again, even in pictures." She took some of his gifts and mementos to a hospital thrift shop and told herself that her acceptance of the loss was helping her as well as the hospital. For three months, she worked actively at accepting the loss of her fiancé. Eventually Lisa sold the diamond ring and bought herself a year's membership in a health club. "I'm ready to be healthy, to live on my own if necessary, and to turn thirty. I don't need somebody to make me happy. I can do that for myself." Lisa's acceptance of her past loss (her fiancé) helped her to accept her current reality—turning thirty as a single woman. This freed her to start creating what she did want.

Ask yourself what earlier painful feelings your current experience resembles. Associations and images of earlier events will come to mind. Use your acceptance strategies to resolve earlier experiences. For example, say out loud, "I accept feeling bad about my parents' fights"; "I accept feeling angry because my mother liked my brother better"; "I accept feeling sad because other kids didn't like me."

Accept chains of feelings. What you resist usually comes in clusters. For example, a client had been rejected by her boyfriend and fired from her job within a few months of each other. Her feelings called up many past rejections. She listed as many feelings of rejection as she could recall and applied the acceptance methods that worked best for her. She discovered that acceptance had a cumulative effect. Acceptance of her past pains helped her accept her present ones. She also began to see that her rejections sprang from her need for people to love and approve of her. Her clingy behavior drove others off. She decided to start creating healthier relationships and took action to get them by becoming more emotionally independent. She used her savings to go back to school in order to get her teacher's certificate, a move she had always been afraid to make.

A helpful technique is to write down everything that you would like to accept. Just write, "I accept the fact that . . ." You may come up with more than a hundred items. This can range from something your parents did to you to how you feel right now.

Increase your tolerance for discomfort. To get what you want you often have to tolerate discomfort. Acceptance is never having to say, "I can't stand it." When you say, "I can't stand it," you're really saying, "I can't stand on my own in face of this feeling." You're giving the feeling power and dominion over you. Practice increasing your tolerance for discomfort. Think of experiences you feel you can't stand ("I can't stand listening to my daughter talk about her punk boyfriend"). Then, when you find yourself in the situation, purposely stay with the experience. Make yourself stand it for five minutes today, then five minutes tomorrow.

Every day you'll have many opportunities to accept discomfort. Welcome them as learning opportunities, times to stretch your acceptor and improve your ability to accept discomfort. When you run into hassles at the telephone company or at the bank, make a point of accepting them. Practice saying yes to uncomfortable experiences, such as being stuck in a traffic jam, being in a place that is too cold or too warm, having to sort out a restaurant bill with friends. Approach difficult situations—fill the car with gas, make unpleasant phone calls, open bills as soon as they come—to avoid resisting them.

Flood yourself. To approach what you are rejecting, flood yourself with images and feelings of what you are fighting. For example, if you're resisting a breakup, look at pictures of the other person, listen to "our song," smell perfume or aftershave lotions that bring on memories. If you have trouble accepting your body, look at it in the mirror. If you are resisting your financial situation, balance your checkbook, count your change, look at the balances on your bills, count the number of creditors you have.

If you can't accept the death of a child, surround yourself with memories—look at pictures, write down funny things your child said, make a memory book. Flood yourself with negative and positive memories. You may find it helpful to flood yourself with the fact of separation. Spend time at the grave site saying good-bye. Think about what you want to do with your child's toys and clothes. If you can't yet give them away, then prepare them to give away. Wash and iron the clothes, organize the toys. Find someone with whom you can talk about the separation.

If you are fighting the reality of a serious illness, flood yourself with all the fears you have about it. Read all you can about the disease. Talk with professionals about what to expect, and allow yourself to experience the feelings that arise as a result of what you hear. Allow yourself to hear the truth about current reality. If you have to, start with a symbolic gesture and face one small fact you have been avoiding. Flood yourself until you have washed out all of your resistance to current reality.

Force yourself to think of the worst. You rarely have to accept Armageddon. To reach acceptance, however, you have to be willing to do what is necessary, which often includes the willingness to accept the *possibility* of the worst happening. The plane could crash; you could get terminal cancer; your husband or wife could die in an accident. One strategy for dealing with the possibility of the worst is repeatedly to imagine the worst possibility *on purpose*. Continue imagining the possibility until you feel more comfortable with it. By doing this you take the charge off of the picture. You come to see that you are dealing with only a psychological mockup of the physical world. It doesn't exist in the real world. Once you separate the two worlds, your distress disappears.

Love the feeling. What can you love about the situation? Here is an opportunity to use the division strategy. See if you can love 1 percent of the situation. Look for something useful in it (there is always something), and love that. Is the experience a way to become wiser? A good antishame exercise? A way to eliminate your false pride?

A former prisoner of war said he was able to stand the torture of his imprisonment by learning to love the pain. Mystics have written, "Hell loved is heaven." When you love your enemies they don't stand a chance. To decide to love the experience simply because you have it often leads to acceptance. Love can solve nearly any problem, because it moves you up to a higher psychological level of functioning. Love is thus a powerful acceptance strategy.

One of Gary's clients decided to love being in debt. She had suffered from depression for years over her inability to control her spending. The more depressed she got, the more she spent. When she loved her debt, she was able to see it as a way to learn to budget not only her money but also her life. "It occurred to me that I was never willing to pay the cost for what I wanted. My debt became my teacher. If I was willing to pay the cost, I could get what I wanted." She was able to break up with an abusive boyfriend and pay the cost (living alone) in order to get what she really wanted (emotional independence and peace of mind).

Take the opposite tack. If you find it too strange to love your painful experience, then do the opposite. Develop obstinacy. Actively hate the bad experience. Refuse to accept your feelings. Exaggerate your need to change your feelings. Go way beyond your normal resistance. Forbid yourself to accept the situation ("I'll never accept this no matter what"). This strategy works because the mind is like a child and often does the opposite of what you tell it to do.

Ken, one of Gary's clients, had trouble accepting his approaching fiftieth birthday. His depression was accompanied by a desire to leave his wife, quit his job, and just have fun. He decided to consciously reject his birthday. He said, "I refuse to accept my fiftieth birthday" out loud as he drove to work, cut the day out of the calendar, and forbade his forty-ninth year ever to end. "After a while," he said, "I just accepted that I would be fifty years old. I don't know why, but it just didn't seem important any-more."

Laugh at your painful experience. Many people use humor to accept adversity. Look for the irony or absurdity in the painful situation. Draw cartoons of the situation or make a good news/bad news joke out of it. One client, when told he had choices, said, "Yeah, which wrist to slash, my left or my right." This sense of humor eventually led to flashes of acceptance and he snapped out of his month-long funk.

Laughter is one of the best ways to open a blocked acceptor. You might, for example, make a point of telling or exchanging two jokes a day. Ask people you meet if they have heard any good jokes lately. If they tell you a joke, pass it along to others. Laughter often releases you from the shame of your feelings. Because of taboos against feelings ("You shouldn't feel that way"), you feel bad about feeling bad. Being able to laugh at your feelings can start an acceptance cycle.

Be kind to yourself. People are rarely kind to themselves. When you are more self-compassionate and less self-contemptuous, you can accept adversity with more agility.

Most of the time, what you need to accept in order to get relief from emotional distress is yourself. To love yourself you must begin to treat yourself in a loving way. Instead of criticizing yourself, be sympathetic. Counterbalance complaining with giving credit. Form a psychological credit union with yourself or others. In the problem area, give yourself credit where it is due ("I took a risk rather than copping out as usual"). Instead of discounting yourself ("I'm really stupid; I can't do anything right"), honestly give yourself credit where it's due ("I am conscientious in what I do"). Develop the habit of acknowledging yourself.

The same principle applies to sticking pins in others. Be kind to people you want to accept. Instead of attacking, give your blessing. Dan had a passive-aggressive marriage. He was aggressive, Judy was passive. One of their running battles was over a messy kitchen. He decided to take the opposite tack and replaced "You always leave a mess in the kitchen" with "I enjoyed the meal you cooked." Not surprisingly, after he switched from nagging to kindness, Judy began to cooperate with him. He, in turn, felt more love and acceptance toward her in general.

A major psychological principle is "like begets like." When you treat someone with love, you start to love him or her. Self-acceptance is like that—treat yourself as you would have others treat you.

Use *acceptance* as a switch word. Become acutely aware of what acceptance feels like. Go back to the three disappointments you listed in Chapter 1. See if you can recall the moment when you reached acceptance on one or more of them.

Whenever you accept or let something go, get in touch with that feeling and say the word *acceptance* (or a similar word or phrase, such as *letting go*) to yourself. When you make *acceptance* a conditioned switch word, you can put it in your back pocket and use it when you need it.

Dan practiced pairing the switch words *letting go* with daily hassles (having to get up in the morning, fighting rush hour traffic, handling angry customers, and having to do mindless paperwork). Whenever the messy kitchen bothered him, he said the words *letting go*. The words helped him accept the mess so that he could move beyond it and create a more loving relationship with his wife.

He also learned to use *letting go* with serious problems he had to face. He would imagine the situation, then (a) draw on this feeling of acceptance, (b) say the switch words, and (c) see himself accepting whatever happened. He said, "Sometimes I imagine three screens. On one is the worst scenario. My wife says, 'Why would I want to stay with *you?*' On another screen is the best scenario. She says, 'I love you just as you are and want to spend my life with you.' On the third screen is a median between the best and the worst. I practice accepting all three."

Besides awareness and feeling strategies for achieving acceptance, you can use thinking and acting strategies. We'll describe them in the next chapter.

4. Acceptance: Thinking and Acting Strategies

B y thinking and acting in new ways, you can accept current reality. You can use many different methods to reach the same end. Hold onto your vision of acceptance of current reality and use what works for you.

Thinking Strategies

We humans despair more than any other living creatures. As a species, we alone make ourselves unhappy. On the other hand, what makes us unique is our ability to direct and correct our thinking. When your thinking is straight and clear, you accept reality better.

Your thoughts are choices in how you see reality ("This is good") and in how you act ("I'll go for it"). Thoughts do not change. You can, however, substitute or select a new thought to replace an old one. Think of a circle. Now think of a triangle. Your thoughts of what constitutes a circle didn't change. The idea or thought of what makes a circle stays the same.

Thoughts create experiences. For example, the thought "I need to be perfect" creates anxiety. While you can't change this thought, you can select a different thought ("I'll accept my imperfections"), and this will create a different experience. You can use the following methods to clarify your thinking and make new choices on how you want to think and act.

Choose acceptance. Often the simple act of choosing to accept reality is enough to clarify your thinking. Think of everything that needs to be changed for you to be happy ("I need to lose fifteen pounds"; "I need my boyfriend to come back"; "I need not to have lost money on the stock market"). Include every distressing situation, large or small. Write this list down in your notebook and underline the word *need*. Next, go through the list and, one by one, ask yourself if you can let go of the need or demand to change it. Keep in mind that you still want to create your original vision. You'll find you can let go of many of these needs for change immediately.

With an item you have trouble accepting, write down the reasons you can't accept it ("It's not right"; "It's unfair"; "It means too much"). Look at each reason and say out loud that you choose to accept it ("I accept that being robbed was unfair and wrong"). Your objections will start to disappear.

For example, Mary Ann, twenty-seven, came to Gary for therapy because she was acutely depressed. She had just failed the bar exam for the second time and was fearful of losing her job. She needed to change current reality ("I need to feel secure at my job; I need to pass the bar exam").

She was able to accept immediately that she would have to pay for another review course, study more, and retake the test, but she had more trouble with the big issues—failing the test and possibly getting fired.

In her first therapy session, Mary Ann outlined her reasons for needing reality to be different: "It's unfair. People who don't work as hard as I do passed the bar; and besides, I don't want to accept it." After Gary explained the choice system to her, she practiced accepting her objections. During the week, while driving her car, she would say out loud, "It's unfair for them to fire me, but I'll accept it if it happens. I wish it were different, but I'll accept it if it happens. I wish it were different, but I'll accept it anyway."

By the time she came for her second session, Mary Ann reported that much of her anxiety was gone. She felt almost strong enough to discuss her situation with the senior partner at her firm. The following week she did talk to him. He told her that he liked her work and had no intention of firing her. The next time the bar examination was given, Mary Ann approached it with much less anxiety and was able to pass it.

Explode negatives with exaggeration. Accept current reality by exaggerating it all out of proportion. Paradoxically, blowing up a situation enables you to accept it. If you're worried about money, imagine yourself as a bag person, living on the streets, eating from garbage cans. If you can't accept your current weight, imagine yourself to be so huge that you burst the walls of your house and need guide wires to keep you balanced.

This technique worked for Max, who was paralyzed by anxiety. Happily married for twenty years, he lived in fear that his wife would discover an affair he had carried on the year before. In his first session he said, "We married young, when she got pregnant. I was only eighteen. I thought I should be able to try to enjoy sex with someone else at least once. I started an affair with a woman at work who was being transferred to Chicago. I thought it would be safe. Then one day, I turned around and realized I might lose the woman I married."

Max then learned he would be transferred to Chicago. In the beginning he experienced a small amount of fear that his wife would find out about the other woman, but he pushed the fear away. As his transfer came closer, however, his anxiety became full blown. He couldn't concentrate at work; and his relationship with his wife became strained. He was afraid that she would find out about the affair and leave him.

Max agreed to try exaggeration. He thought of himself as the stupidest man in history, so stupid that he was written up by Ripley ("Max, who married a woman anyone would treasure, cheated on her . . . she leaves him and takes the kids").

He visualized the news being splashed on the front page of the *New York Times.* In his mind he wrote special news bulletins ("A dramatic development in a seemingly happy marriage. The truth about Max—see it on film at eleven").

Eventually, by repeatedly blowing the situation all out of proportion, Max was able to accept it. At that point he realized that he should confide in his wife. If their marriage was as good as he knew it to be, it could stand the truth. He simply told his wife about the affair.

She was devastated at first and then relieved to discover the reason for the recent marital strain. It turned out that she had suspected his affair all along. Max's anxiety vanished and the marriage continued stronger than before.

Blow up positives. Strut and brag mentally. Throw all modesty out the window. Imagine how much other people are impressed by you and how much they like you. Exaggerate the positive.

When you are distressed, you exaggerate the negative side. By exaggerating the positive side, you balance the negative and help move it through your acceptor.

Be self-accountable. In your notebook write down what you did (directly or indirectly) that caused your problem. Then *own* your actions. Max, for example, wrote down that he chose to marry his wife, chose to "mess around," chose to stay married to his wife when he realized he loved her, and chose to accept a transfer to the same city where the other woman was. He owned each one of the choices and found that he was able to move beyond his need to change the situation ("It's not fair that my success in my company depends on moving to Chicago; I wish New York had called instead") to self-accountability ("I hold myself accountable for all my choices and am willing to accept the consequences of my actions").

Self-accountability—holding yourself answerable for all of your experiences—leads to greater awareness and acceptance, and thus relief from pain and distress. Self-accountability is the opposite of blaming or making excuses.

Use the ACT Formula. Suppose you want to lose weight, but you overeat at a party. You did this for one of several reasons: You may have had a feeling of free will and chose to overeat regardless of the consequences, or you didn't have a feeling of free will and just automatically, mindlessly overate. You didn't separate your desire to feel better from your vision—to be thin.

Usually, in such situations you don't have a feeling of free will. You go into a mild trance. Your awareness contracts to the demands of the moment, and you lose your original vision. When you lose your vision, you also lose your awareness; you unconsciously eat. After the first few bites you don't even taste the food. By getting down on yourself, you keep the trance going. Blaming yourself ("Why am I blimping out?") stops the process of acceptance and keeps you tranced out. You keep eating to try to feel better and to avoid being honest with yourself about what you are doing.

You did what you did because at the time it seemed like a good idea. Given your level of constricted awareness, it was what you chose to do. A basic principle of psychology is, "People do the best they can given their level of awareness at that moment."

When you find yourself in the vicious circle of trance and blame, use the ACT Formula as soon as you can:

1. *Accept current reality.*
2. *Reaffirm where you choose to go.*
3. *Take action to get there.*

Practice tolerance. Intolerance ("All Arabs are evil"; "Baseball is stupid") prevents acceptance. Belittling anything or anyone (your wife, kids, parents, job, house, car, town, country) belittles yourself. You end up with less self-acceptance. You can use this rebound effect to your advantage. Accept others and you'll accept yourself.

For example, choose a person or circumstance you have trouble accepting. Acknowledge your bigotry ("I can't stand lazy people"). Then turn around and describe the person in an accepting way ("He's a good driver; he's good with children"). Recognize that your bigotry always takes a moralistic tone ("Rich people are all crooks") that blocks acceptance and leaves you less connected to everyone and everything.

Question yourself. Undermine your resistance by questioning your beliefs about current reality. Don't worry about the answers. The questions alone stimulate a shift in your beliefs. Write the questions you find helpful in your notebook and review them whenever you resist reality. Some helpful questions might be:

"Am I engaging in all-or-nothing thinking?"
"Do I want to spend my energy on this?"
"Can I lead my life without feeling bad about this?"
"Can I let go of the need to change this?"
"Does the physical reality (flat tire, bank account) really care about my feelings?"
"Can I love any part of this?"
"Can I act as if what I want has already happened?"
"Can I enjoy this?"
"Can I let go of others' and my own expectations?"

Your distorted thoughts about reality ("It's terrible"; "I ruined my life"; "No one will ever love me again") stop acceptance. You can use three basic questions to correct most distortions. Think of even your worst scenario, then ask yourself these three questions:

1. *What's the evidence?* ("My husband has been late before. I've no evidence he's been in a car wreck.")
2. *What's another way of looking at it?* ("He probably got talking with people and time got away from him.")
3. *So what if it's true?* ("If he has been hurt in an accident, we'll have to solve that problem and get on with our lives. Even if he's dead I'll have to handle that reality and continue with my life."

Practice these three questions to realign your perceptions of current reality. Once you put current reality in the right perspective, you can accept just about any situation you may experience.

Forgive others and yourself. If you can forgive ("I'll forgive her even though it still hurts") rather than nurse grudges ("I can remember every rotten trick my mother pulled on me"), you'll have an easier time accepting current reality.

Unforgiveness is based on your need to change the past and occurs when you blame others for your experiences. When you run your life by choice, you give the experience to whomever it belongs ("My mother chose to criticize my competence. It's a free country; I have the choice to develop competency in any area I want").

Look for the grudge in what you have trouble accepting ("I can't forgive my ex-wife for leaving me for another man"). Pinpoint how you use blame in the grudge situation, then reexamine the situation from a choice perspective ("My ex-wife did what she did. Period. I can choose to feel angry about it or let it go"). When you don't forgive, you vote to keep your pain.

Value acceptance. Often all you need in order to achieve acceptance is a desire to accept something. Start by raising your opinion of acceptance. Find ways to value and esteem it. In other words, sell yourself on acceptance.

List in your notebook all of the benefits you will enjoy once you reach acceptance. For example: "I'll have more clarity in my thinking. I'll be better able to create my own life. I'll be wiser. I'll have more confidence. I'll have more energy to reach my goal." Then, list some disadvantages of your resistance: "I won't be able to see clearly. I'll be at the mercy of my feelings. I'll be too tired to reach my goal."

Make use of daily reminders. On an appointment calendar each evening, write a belief you want to use for your next day. Do this just before you go to sleep. When you are in bed, repeat the statement and tell yourself, "I choose to believe this as I sleep." The following day, repeat the sentence to yourself. If you want, write it on a card and carry it in your pocket or purse. When you see or feel the card, repeat the sentences to yourself. Use whatever sells you on acceptance:

"I love acceptance."
"Acceptance helps me."
"Acceptance brings love."
"Acceptance brings wisdom."
"Acceptance brings clarity."
"I am an accepting person."
"I accept reality as it is."
"I accept you."
"I accept my feelings."
"Acceptance brings relief."
"Acceptance is the first step in creativity."
"Acceptance is telling the truth."
"Acceptance brings freedom."
"Acceptance is being true to myself."

You can use these sentences or make up your own. You can also use beliefs you have tailored to fit your specific problem areas. For example:

"I accept my father's coldness."
"Accepting my father's coldness helps me."
"Accepting my looks makes sense."
"Accepting my weight brings love."
"Accepting my weight sharpens my vision."
"I accept my boss's rudeness."
"Accepting my boss is helpful."
"Accepting my shame frees me."

This technique works best if you use the wording "I choose" in front of the phrase ("I choose to love acceptance" or "I choose to accept my boss's rudeness"). You can use reminders in the physical environment to prompt you to repeat your sayings, such as a date on your watch or getting in or out of bed.

Use the power of repetition. Get a box of paper clips and pour them out on a table (they come 100 to a box). As you pick each one up, say, "I accept the fact that _____" (state what you want to accept) or "Letting go of _____ will help me." You can use any kind of sentence that sells you on acceptance, either generally or specifically. You may need to run through the box of clips several times before you feel the effect. If you don't have paper clips, use matches, rubber bands, safety pins, or something similar.

Act like a salesman. If your mind is racing about a problem, sit down and make yourself come up with an ad campaign for acceptance. Use the same eye-catching words that professional ad agencies use: "Acceptance—it's all you could want . . . and more!" Come up with a campaign as if acceptance were a book ("Over 10,000 years on the best-seller list") or a movie ("Amazing! Stupendous!") or a type of gasoline ("You get more mileage out of Acceptance").

Describe acceptance using your favorite advertising words: "Acceptance—it's the real thing"; "Join the Acceptance generation"; "You only go around once—grab for all the Acceptance you can."

Using advertising descriptions can benefit you when you feel overwhelmed by your feelings. Jump right in and be a cheerleader for acceptance. The process gives you a task to focus on while making your mind use humor to sell yourself on acceptance.

Use your dreams to let go. We all accept many losses and setbacks through dreams. Enhance the process by giving yourself a clear suggestion to accept your problem while asleep ("Tonight I will accept what happened at work").

Keep track of your dreams in your notebook to determine whether you're having accepting or resisting dreams. If you wake up after a resistance dream, close your eyes and finish the dream with acceptance in your imagination. One client, for example, had dreams in which her feelings were hurt because her boss was unfairly angry at her. Before getting up, she finished her dream in her imagination and accepted her boss's anger, took his feedback constructively, stated her case clearly, and had her boss respond reasonably.

Rearrange the wording. Experiment with different wording:

"I'll choose to accept it."
"Can I accept the situation?"
"Stop fighting it."
"I can stop struggling with it."
"Can I flow with Mother Nature?"
"Let go of the need to control it."
"Need equals pain."
"I refuse to feel bad about this."
"I'll love that this happened."
"Acceptance will give me peace of mind."

Because a major block to acceptance is needing to change current reality, the phrase "Can I let go of the need to change this?" is to the point. But you'll need to experiment until you find what works for you.

Divide and accept. Patricia Carrington, a writer and noted psychologist, suggests you start by accepting a small part of the problem. As we mentioned earlier, once you get anything through the acceptor, you open it up. Try the following series of steps:

• Accept some insignificant aspect of the situation ("I accept the color of the shirt I wore when I flunked my Ph.D. oral exam").
• Accept 1 percent or even .01 percent of it ("I accept the first five minutes of the exam").
• Accept the situation for one or two seconds at a time ("I accept my failure as I count to two").

• Accept just the *feeling* of needing current reality to be different ("I accept my yearning to have passed")
• Accept something that's easy to accept ("I accept the fact that today's Tuesday"), and then return to the problem.

Develop a grace factor. In her book *Success Is the Quality of Your Journey,* Jennifer James, a keen observer of life, suggests that you develop a 10 percent grace factor in your life. Assume that you'll get cheated about 10 percent of the time, that people will be rude 10 percent of the time, that you'll pay 10 percent more than your share, that you'll lose about 10 percent of your belongings. With some people (your in-laws, your boss) and some places (foreign countries) you may need to have a 20 percent grace factor.

Develop a quota system. Ethnomethodologists (anthropologists who study ordinary life) have found that life for just about everyone in America can be put into one sentence: *Life is one damn thing after another.* The human brain is designed to find and solve problems. When one problem is solved, we find another one. Accept the reality that life is a series of obstacles or challenges.

Develop a quota system for "damn things." Most people have three or four things that go wrong each day, or a quota of 1500 to 2000 problems a year. If you want, estimate quotas for each specific problem. When some "damn thing" happens, assume that it's part of the quota. You will have a quota of, say, twenty flat tires in your life or 1500 cutting remarks from close friends. When you have a flat tire or someone cuts you down, say to yourself, "That's one more out of the way."

Some of your difficulties are almost "laws of the universe." If you drive a car, the law of the universe says that you're going to have car trouble at times. If you have a dog, you will have dog piles to clean up. People enjoy Murphy's "laws" because they contain kernels of truth. You might write in your notebook, "Life is one damn thing after another," and refer back to it from time to time.

Appreciate half a loaf. Letting go of your demands for perfection will help you move toward acceptance. You'll stop feeling chronically let down. Revise your absolute standards ("My wife must always be cheerful, efficient, intelligent, and beautiful").

Let go of excess baggage and give up your perfectionism. You may be afraid if you let it go, you'll be settling for the mediocre, but the paradox is that when you let perfectionism go you achieve more.

In the choice system you're true to your visions, which are often high. You hold on to your standards and honestly admit it when you fall short of them. However, unlike the perfectionist, you don't have to have a perfect physical world to be happy and can appreciate what you have.

Serve your vision, not your perfectionism. Keeping your eye on what you want gives you energy. Focusing on flaws and mistakes depletes your energy. When you design your own life, you can appreciate and enjoy the present because you're moving toward what you love.

Adopt a mature attitude. Young children actively resist what they dislike. They are often in the change system ("Mommy, I can't color inside the lines because you won't color with me"). An average adult may act like a baby once or twice a day, a small child ten or fifteen times a day.

Recall events of the last day or two. How many times did you "go baby"? ("Damn it, my pencil broke"; "If I can't have the last piece of cake, I'm going to bed").

Imagine yourself in the same situation responding as a mature adult. When you have trouble accepting something, ask yourself, "What is the most mature way to handle this?"

Be flexible. Physical reality is constantly changing: If you accept this rather than fight it, you'll save yourself pain and the possibility of being left behind. One client, Helen, began suffering from depression when her company, a large health laboratory, switched to computers. Helen resisted the necessity of learning how to operate the computer. Her work suffered and she slipped deeper into depression.

Helen considered switching companies but found her choices narrowly restricted by the computer boom. Most laboratories used them.

In therapy, she made the choice to flow with technology. She started learning to use a friend's VCR. The more active she became, the more flexible she grew. She took a night course in computers and stopped avoiding the laboratory computer workshops. After she mastered the computer, she loved it and couldn't remember why she had resisted it.

Industrial psychologists have found that it is not change itself that workers resent and resist but not having a say in initiating the changes. However the change is introduced to you, you must always initiate your own responses to it.

Look at your rigidity in situations. Discover ways to be more flexible. Ask yourself, "What's another way I can look at this?" "What are the other options that I have?" Then put your flexibility into practice by acting differently. Stretch your acceptor. *Think of areas where you have been able to be more flexible in the past, and transfer this attitude to your present situation.*

For example, you may think:

"I was able to move away from home to college."
"I was able to get to know my roommate, a total stranger."
"I was able to learn the social mores of my fraternity."
"I was able to learn the various whims of the professors."

"Therefore, I can":

"Adjust to this new situation (a new job) as I adjusted to college."
"Get to know my coworkers as I got to know my roommate."

"Learn the ins and outs of the business as I got to know the social mores of my fraternity."

"Relate to my supervisors as I related to my professors."

Stop why-ing. The best way to resist current reality is to ask yourself, "Why? Why did it happen? Why me?" *Why?* means "I refuse to accept this." *Why?* elicits thinking that raises unanswerable questions. To accept a situation you have to stop being a *why*-ner.

Replace the *Why?* with *Why not?* (For "Why did this accident have to happen to me?," substitute "Why not? It did happen to me"). *Why?* is another way of saying, "This shouldn't have happened." You fight with reality and bring yourself down. *Why not?*, on the other hand, allows you to collaborate with reality.

Another strategy for achieving acceptance is to replace the destructive *why?* with the constructive *where?* and *what?* ("Where am I right now and what do I want? I got a *D* on the test, and I want to get at least a *B* for the course"). "Why" questions keep you stuck. "Where" and "what" questions make you focus on current reality and your vision.

Action Strategies

Be a doer. Alfred North Whitehead, considered the greatest Western philosopher since Plato, said, "We do not think first and act afterwards; from the moment of birth we are immersed in action, and can only fitfully guide it by taking thought." In the final analysis, it's not what you think or feel that counts, but what you do. *Be a doer and keep moving toward your visions.*

Jump in, go around or over the obstacle in front of you: Make the phone call to clear up the department store bill, tell your boss you want a raise, make an appointment with the doctor about your lump. Even a false start is usually better than no start. When you just think about a problem you stand still. Once you take action you move vertically, so that you gain a better view and can see or open up new paths to your vision.

Realign yourself. Line up your images, choices, feelings, and actions and move them in concert toward acceptance. When one of the three is out of line, focus on the other two ("I feel bad, but I'll choose to feel good, imagine the best, and act *as if* I am feeling good"). Because emotional distress is a feeling, in order to create a new feeling you often need first to focus on making your images, choices, and actions move toward acceptance. To do this, *act as if* you accept current reality. Be a psychological chiropractor and realign everything toward acceptance and your vision.

Ask yourself what needs to be done behaviorally to reach acceptance—then do it. Try new activities. If you don't know something, admit it. You keep the problem unacceptable by hiding it.

Clara suffered from low self-esteem and extreme anxiety after the unexpected death of her husband, a high-powered business executive. She had never been in the work force but, with her children grown, she wanted her life to be more than shopping and soap operas.

Clara was convinced she had no marketable skills. In therapy she said, "I don't know what I want." When pressed she finally said, "What I've always wanted is to run my own business."

She loved the idea but was frightened by the prospect. She protested that although she had the financial resources, she knew nothing about business and furthermore wouldn't even know what kind of business to buy, let alone how to run it. She decided to act *as if* she were going to buy a business and to make inquiries about what might be available.

After Clara investigated various businesses, she became excited about a balloon-bouquet store that was for sale. She had already clarified her thinking as to what she wanted. Her anxiety was lessened, but she still had to act *as if* she knew what she was doing. She enrolled in an extension course on running a small business and put in a bid, which was accepted, for the balloon business. At that point she had her last therapy session. (She said she was too busy with her classes and her new business to continue the session.)

When Clara acted *as if* she were going to buy a business, she knocked down many obstacles ("How will I keep the books?" "How do I hire people?" "What if I fail?"); she just did it. Obviously, educating herself about running a small business was an important part of acting *as if.*

Make yourself decide. Often you resist reality by a refusal to act on some decision. ("Should I leave or stay?" "Should I ask the boss or not?" "Should I confront my husband or not?")

Psychologists have found that the decision you make is minimally important. What *is* important is *what you do after you make the decision.* Whether to have children or not, for example, isn't as important as what you do after you make the decision. You can have children and choose to accept or resist the interruptions, messes, and demands on your time— that's what will create your experiences.

Similarly, you can decide not to have children and choose to accept or resist the remarks of others, the change in relationship with friends who have children, and your childfree life-style. It is your actions after you make the decision that will determine your emotional experiences.

Get second opinions. You may have friends and acquaintances who support your lack of acceptance ("That's terrible"; "You should be angry about that"; "You're right, they're wrong"). Make a habit of associating with people who are objective or who have a more acceptance-oriented, action-oriented, and truth-oriented point of view.

If you have been keeping your problem a secret, you can benefit by telling others about it and that you're choosing to accept it. If, on the other hand, you have been excessively discussing your problem, you might find talking to yourself out loud more helpful.

Keep Your Attention on Your Vision

Successful people accept setbacks in stride. Disappointments rarely stop you from getting what you want—*if you don't let them.* By holding onto your vision in the face of disappointments, you also will find that more people will want to help and support you because they see you are serious. This is how you develop fans and loyalty.

• Shrug off setbacks and move on. Don't let disappointment cause you to scrap your vision.
• Accept setbacks as setbacks, not as failures or defeats.
• Keep your focus on your vision and see the setback as a friendly guidepost ("This way") to another course, one that is usually shorter and easier.
• See disappointment as the removal of obstacles to higher attainments. Project yourself into the future ("Looking back, I see it was really the best thing that could have happened to me"). Assume that retrospection will reveal a current problem to be a blessing—in fact, this is usually the case.
• Develop the self-faith and resilience to make disappointments serve you. Get knocked down six times, get up seven times.
• Go with the flow. The shortest distance between two points isn't a straight line but the line of least resistance.
• Take the setback, not as a superstitious "sign" that you won't get what you want, but as necessary feedback.
• Recover quickly from disappointments. Minimize the amount of time you are on the mat. When you wait for the full count of ten, you miss out on opportunities that current reality has to offer. You usually have "golden time" right after a disappointment, during which you can redirect your course.
• Go the extra half inch. The difference between success and failure is often very small, but that half inch can be so difficult that most people don't complete it.

For example, Tom started his own printing business and was relieved when a client from his old firm became his best account. Tom became overdependent on this one client, because the client accounted for 40 percent of the business. After Tom had been in business for six months, this client decided to take his business elsewhere. Tom sank into depression, afraid his business would go under. He came for therapy when he realized he was starting to take his thoughts of suicide seriously.

In therapy Tom said that he'd left his lucrative management position at the old firm because he wanted the challenge of "making it alone." When he clarified his vision out loud ("Making a success on my own") he sat up straight. "I wasn't making it alone. I'd talked that client into coming with me because I was afraid. I tried nothing new and innovative because I didn't have to. I was 'resting' on the client. He probably just got fed up."

Tom began to see his disappintment as feedback about current reality rather than as a sign that he had failed. After he focused on his vision—to create a successful business of his own—he started to make the moves needed to create *new* business. He eventually became enthusiastic about this side of his business.

After a setback, focus on what you can do *in the present* to bring about the desired results. Tom focused on an ad campaign and on obtaining a loan for a new piece of printing machinery that broadened the appeal of his business to artists and photographers.

Be willing to do everything you must to accept your current reality and create what you want. You don't *have* to do everything; just be willing to do everything. If you are willing to walk in every open door that you need to, follow every new path, take advantage of each opportunity, you can create what you want.

5. How to Create What You Want

To create the experiences you want, you need to connect where you are (current reality) with where you want to go (your vision). Your vision lets you know what action you should take in current reality. Your vision is the magnet that does the pulling—you simply allow it to.

Lights, camera, action. You use three steps to create what you want:

1. Acknowledge where you are (tell the truth).
2. Create an image of what you want and visualize it happening.
3. Let the "how" of going from Step One to Step Two emerge naturally. Light up where you are, picture what you want, and act on your hunches.

Make It Up

We have already covered the first step, accepting current reality. The second step is to make up what you want to create.

Exercise

A. Write in your notebook ten experiences you want to create ("I want a good relationship"; "I want a new car"). If you can't think of ten, make them up. If you have trouble with that, create a vision from what you don't like having. For example, if you dislike having a cluttered house, create a vision of a clean house and list that.

B. Make each item specific and measurable ("I want to weigh 120 pounds" instead of "I want to lose some weight").

C. Put "I choose to have" in front of each vision and say the sentence aloud ("I choose to have the experience of weighing 120 pounds").

D. Update the list as you reach your visions. You will find you automatically feel better as you move toward your vision.

Many creative people believe that we have a fixed amount of creativity. F. Scott Fitzgerald believed, for example, that each writer has only a finite amount of creativity. The mistake in this thinking is confusing the finite physical world with the infinite psychological world. Creativity belongs to the psychological realm.

Highly productive, creative people such as Pablo Picasso and Steven Spielberg know that creativity is boundless. Creativity is variation on themes, and the number of themes and variations you can come up with is limitless. As long as you know you're just making it up, you can never run dry.

Your ultimate choice is to make up what you want and then create it. In the choice system, because you choose what you want, you are able to define your visions. The more clearly and specifically you define your visions, the more likely you'll achieve them. Use the following suggestions to create visions:

Create visions, not goals. A goal is something you believe you have to do or should do. Goals usually are internalizations of parents' or social expectations. You feel pushed or driven to reach goals. A vision, on the other hand, is a picture or image of something that's important to you that you want to create out of thin air. You allow the vision to pull you to its realization.

Hold your vision and let go of expectations. Expectations are a force for failure. People in the change system often shift from positive expectations to negative ones in an attempt to ward off disappointment. Neither work. One of Murphy's laws is that negative expectations lead to negative results and positive expectations also lead to negative results.

Expectations come from reactive thinking—you put the power for achievement outside of yourself. You expect that something in the future will dictate your experience. Expectations are full of surplus meaning ("If this happens, that will mean . . .") and endless self-talk. Expectations take time and energy. And because you are so sure of what will happen, you overlook many opportunities that could help you create what you want.

Visions, on the other hand, take little or no emotional energy (contrast visualizing winning the lottery with expecting to win the lottery). Vision is creative rather than reactive.

Make the vision yours. The vision needs to be something you can create ("I feel good about my son" versus "My son has a job").

Make the vision as detailed and clear as possible. To get a clear picture, take a deep breath, relax, close your eyes, and move your eyes up to the right corners; hold them there, and let the image you want come. You access the image source by moving your eyes in this direction. As we just mentioned, be specific—the more specific the better ("I'll grade all the exams and read two of the research papers" versus "I'll catch up on some grading"). Add some specific detail to the picture ("I see myself putting the papers in my briefcase"). Visualize what attention to your visions will feel like, look like, and sound like.

Focus on the end result, not the how. Don't focus on a specific person to create your vision—for example, a relationship with a specific customer to whom you want to sell your product. When you need specific people, the tendency is to become manipulative or desperate.

Have your cake and eat it, too. Replace *either/or* with *and*. "I can take the promotion or be relaxed and calm"; "I can be married or feel free" become "I'll take the promotion *and* be relaxed and calm"; "I'll be married *and* feel free." As long as you create your visions, why not create the best case?

Write your visions down. Put your visions down in the present tense when you write them out ("I have a job that pays $50,000 a year"; "I feel good about my family").

Don't worry about vanity. In everything we do there is a degree of vanity. Don't let the vanity issue stop you from going for what you really want. Don't let your belief that getting what you want would be showing off stop you. And don't let others' opinions stop you. For example, if you've lost your job but have been offered another one at a lower salary, don't let vanity stop you from reaching your vision (to be employed).

Make your vision positive instead of negative ("I'll turn the report in Friday" versus "I don't want to turn this report in late").

Don't be stupid about your visions. If you can't swim, don't make your vision to win seven gold medals in swimming at the next Olympics. While most people underestimate what they can create, a few sabotage themselves with pie-in-the-sky daydreams.

Get in the habit of visualizing on a daily basis what you would like to see happen. In your mind, picture the accomplishment of your visions. For example, before you go to meetings, imagine the results you want. The more you practice visualization, the better you will become at it.

Develop an aim for the day. When you wake up in the morning, state one vision you would like to see happen during the day ("I will savor everything I hear today"; "I will get the paperwork done on my taxes today").

Ask. Say specifically what you want. Tell people directly what you want ("I'd like you to fill the car with gas" instead of "How's the gas situation?"). You have to ask before you can receive.

Get in touch with your intuition. Imagine your intuition as a guide or teacher, and ask the teacher what matters most to you. Then be open to what comes to you. You don't have to worry about the how because your intuition will show you what to do if you (a) hold the vision, (b) tell the truth about current reality, and (c) are open to your hunches.

Be true to yourself. Keep the *shoulds* from undercutting your *wants*. For example, you may think you *should* go to graduate school, but you really *want* to travel. Even if what you want seems inappropriate, be true to yourself and create a vision that matters to you. It is much easier to create something you really want.

Be honest. If you don't really believe you'll do something ("Sure, I'd like to share an apartment with you"), don't say you will. Be truthful about what you want and don't want.

Develop a habit of doing only what you really want to do. You do have that freedom. Gary learned about this freedom when he first started doing therapy. As a new therapist he thought it very unfair that he had to help any client he could while clients had the right to quit any time they chose to. Then he realized if he had a client who just wanted to talk about problems and not do anything about them, or one who kept coming late and breaking appointments, he could decide he didn't want the experience and recommend another therapy or therapist to the client.

Ask for what you believe you're worth. A recent study found that people who asked for a lot of money for their work usually got it, while people who asked for little got little.

About the "How"

The Past as Cause

When you're in the old, unrewarding change system, you look to the past (your parents, bad breaks, lack of education) for the cause of your present problems, and you look to the past for answers on how to create your future ("How did I do it before?"). You stir the dead ashes of the past trying to light your future.

Past "hows" rarely work, however, to create something new. You've never done the "new thing" before, so you don't know how to do it yet. You may at times develop plans along the way—if one plan doesn't work you let go of it and create another. The plan is always secondary to the result you want.

The Future as Cause

In the psychological world you're free from time constraints. You only have one time, the present, so you can play around with time. For example, you can make the future the cause of the present. You choose and envision what you want to happen in the future and let that determine what you automatically do in the present. Perhaps you envision being a lawyer. As long as you hold that "future" vision, it will become the cause of what you do in the present (apply to law school) to make it happen. After you choose the future, you're free to focus on current reality. The tension between your vision and current reality will lead you to see what needs to be done in the present to create the future.

For example, we have a vision of you reading this book. That vision becomes the cause for what we do to bring it about. We don't know exactly how it will get from the bookstore or library to you. How isn't a major concern. We focus on what needs to be done and let the how develop as we go along. We know that *somehow* the book will get to you.

Indecision often comes from needing to know how. It's the ultimate "Yes, but . . ." ("Yes, but *how?*" "How do I lose weight?" "How do I get the money?"). *How* puts the responsibility outside of you. Eliminate decision anxiety by letting the how develop spontaneously in the now.

Replace *how?* ("How will I get the money and how will I get the time to go to Europe?") with *somehow* ("Right now I don't have the time or money, but somehow I'm going to Europe"). *How?* expresses a lack of faith and increases self-doubt and undermines commitment. *Somehow* is a statement of faith and commitment. Making the "somehow" commitment generates the necessary "hows."

To create what you want, all you ever need to do is acknowledge current reality and create a current vision. This will automatically move you toward your vision. This never changes. You always have this dual focus. After you create your vision, this becomes your current reality and you then create a new vision. In this sense the creative process is always static and unchanging, because that is the nature of the psychological world.

Matthew, one of Gary's clients, found that he could achieve his athletic vision by acknowledging current reality ("I'm out of shape") and creating a vision ("I want to be able to run a marathon"). By continually acknowledging what his current reality was ("I'm out of shape"; "I'm feeling more in shape"; "I can run a mile without feeling winded"; "I can run five miles without feeling winded") and holding his vision to be a marathon runner, Matthew was able to reach his vision. After Matthew had run in his first marathon, he created a new vision that involved bettering his time.

Another of Gary's clients used the same creative process to get her taxes done. She acknowledged her current reality ("My receipts and checks are strewn all over the house") and held her vision ("Get my taxes done before April 15"). She gathered her papers together, then acknowledged her new current reality ("I don't have the proper forms"). She continued to hold her vision (taxes done on time) and called the IRS for the forms she needed. As her reality changed ("I don't know the new tax laws"; "I'm not sure how to fill out an investment credit form"), she acknowledged it. Eventually she reached her vision. She was then able to create a new vision ("Keep informed about tax regulations and keep my papers organized month by month").

Is Your Vision Hot or Cold?

The creative process works like a heat-seeking missile. Keep your vision hot and use current reality (the now) to guide you (by telling you when you're warm or cold) and you will automatically reach your vision.

When you decide what you want and then keep your vision hot until you hit it, you demonstrate on a continuing basis that you run the show. You practice creating what you want in life, one of the best ways to upgrade to the more powerful choice system.

Some Common Failure Patterns

Most people have some habitual point where they lose their vision and shoot off on a tangent away from the vision. When this happens to you, your discomfort heats up and your original vision cools off. Your primary concern becomes to feel better rather than to be true to your vision. Here are some common ways discomfort cools vision. In each of these points your focus switches away from vision toward some self-defeating belief. See if you recognize your own self-defeating beliefs in these comparisons with members of the bird world.

The lovebird. You believe you need others' love and approval to feel worthy. You look for love in all the wrong places. You forget your vision and start trying to woo others' love and approval. If everyone likes you, you're probably not getting what you want—you're giving everybody else all that they want. You need more vision and less focus on others' approval.

The peacock. You want to be the star. You believe you need others' attention. Your showing off throws you off course. Go for more vision and less image. Win the race rather than show off your new jogging suit. Become freer and more successful by destroying your image ("I'll be uncool and do what I really want"; "I'll make a fool of myself and admit I don't know"; "I'll pay the price of initially looking inept in order to gain the skill").

The hatchling. Your underlying belief is that you're not capable of doing it on your own. You believe father and mother know best. You open your mouth to let them feed you because you believe you need their nurturing. You do what they want you to do so that they'll keep feeding you. You need more vision and less permission. Become your own authority. Decide what you want and let that guide you.

The hawk. You believe you know what is morally right for everyone. You get hung up on the principle of the matter ("I have to do it according to the book"), and your original vision gets lost in the shuffle. Go for the vision, not the principle.

The whooping crane. Your self-defeating belief is that you can't trust others. The problem is that you don't trust yourself either, so you have to seek others out. Being able to whoop about being taken advantage of becomes the focus, rather than getting what you want. You set the situation up (although unwittingly) so that you'll be mistreated. For example, your vision may be a successful relationship but you continue to relate to abusive men ("I told you I couldn't trust men. See, I was right"). You need less whooping about mistrust and more vision about the kind of relationship you want to create. Accept your feelings of mistrust and go for your vision. Trust is a side issue that takes you away from your vision. Instead of worrying about trust, go for what you want.

The condor. You circle around what you want until you become extinct. You believe you have to be perfect. While you circle you give yourself and others plenty of time to shoot down your ideas. Planning and preparing become more important than doing. For example, Rob, a client, spent hundreds of dollars on time management programs. He wanted to start a business and spent six months just looking for the right logo. He wrote in one planner when to write in his other planners. Eventually Rob learned to throw away his planners and do what needed to be done. He stopped circling and went for his target.

The chicken. You give your vision away on the installment plan because you believe you're not good enough to get what you want. You undervalue yourself and overvalue others. You're quick to compromise your vision because you're afraid you'll lose everything if you don't ("I'll settle for this relationship because at least it's something"). You settle for the lesser of two evils until you have nothing left. You must stay true to what you really want if you're ever to get it.

The ostrich. You believe that you can't develop the skills you need, so you use diversions and smoke screens to avoid the growing suspicion that you don't know what you're doing. You're afraid of current reality ("I really don't know how to run this business"), so you stick your head deeper into the sand, your backside waving in the wind. Go for a deeper level of honesty about what you can and can't do. If you lack the skills you need, admit it; choose to believe you can develop them—and do so. If you think you lack the skill to ask someone for a date, choose to get the skill rather than try to pretend you have it ("I will ask someone out someday"). Ask a relative or friend to role play; use video equipment to practice; admit your hesitancy to the person you want to ask out; read books on how to relate to people.

The rooster. You're more interested in being the boss than in getting what you want ("If I can't rule the roost, I'll leave"). You spend all your energy trying to be in control and lose sight of what you want. You get in control by putting yourself on tough regimens; you then feel controlled by the regimens and rebel. One client, Joanne, wanted to become healthy and decided to go on an extremely strict eating regimen. She thought the only way to get her vision (health) was to maintain strict control. She wouldn't give up the control even when her health began to deteriorate further. When Joanne realized that she wanted to be healthy more than be in control, she chose to give up control and to pay the price of feeling temporarily out of control (giving up her weird diet and being tempted by junk food). She was then able to choose a more sane diet. She had to let go of control to create her vision.

The magpie. You sit on the fence and say what you could have done if you'd wanted to. Your core belief, however, is that you don't have what it takes. Because you don't want to fail, you only do what you can do well. You quit before you can fail ("I wasn't serious about doing it anyway"), and you rationalize away your failure ("I didn't really want to do it"; "I learned a lot and that's what's important"). You seldom lose, but you rarely win. To win, you have to be willing to lose status and accept the possibility of failure.

The bat (Yes, we know a bat is not a bird, but the comparison is apt). You become hung up on your belief there is one right way to do something and blind yourself to other ways. Your purpose becomes showing that you have the truth rather than getting to your vision. You need to get off your premise and do whatever is necessary to reach your vision.

Jonathan Livingston Seagull. You become overconcerned with whether or not you belong. Your basic belief is that you don't belong. You feel odd person out when you're with others. You go off by yourself to avoid this discomfort. Everyone needs a sense of independence and self-determination, but you have an excess. As a result you sacrifice collaboration and cooperation. Accept your feelings of discomfort and be willing to cooperate to get what you want.

EXERCISE

Look at the three disappointment experiences you first listed in Chapter 1. What kind of a bird were you? Was it the same in each case? Do you recognize how your habitual pattern got in the way of what you wanted to create? This pattern is probably your habitual way of failing. Become aware of your underlying belief and catch yourself when you are about to go off course.

Your self-defeating beliefs are like brain grooves. You repeat them thousands of times until they become conditioned, habitual ways of responding to specific cues. Writer Eknath Easwaran compares our beliefs to channels in the mind. Each time you react to a belief, you dig the corresponding channel a little deeper. In the book *Dialogue with Death*, Easwaran says, "It is almost neurological; we are conditioning the patterns of thinking within the brain. And finally there is a huge Grand Canal in the mind. Then anything at all is enough to provoke a conditioned response. Conscious pours down the sluice of least resistance."

Your automatic reaction is like going into a kind of trance. You overlook the actual current reality and get lost in your own version of current reality. You can probably recognize the feeling and the corresponding thoughts ("I have to control this"; "I'll show them"; "Do they like me?"). Use these four steps when you catch yourself falling into these patterns:

1. *Acknowledge your trance state.* Accept and love it. Experience it for forty-five seconds and let it go ("I am in a trance state, wanting to

control the situation, and I'll just acknowledge it and experience my feelings").

2. *Refocus on your vision* ("What do I want here?"). Choose your vision ("I choose to create it").

3. *Let go of all your demands*—good and bad. Keep your expectations few and your vision hot ("My vision is to feel good about myself at the party. I'm not expecting anything—that people will laugh at my jokes, that men/women will fall all over me, that I'll control my drinking—to happen or not happen").

4. *Tune into the physical world*. Look, touch, listen, do something. When you're in your trance, you're out of it (the physical world). Bring some real-world input into your system. Look at the world around you as if you're seeing it for the first time. Do something, anything. Get up, move around, talk to someone, smell a favorite cologne, touch a tweedy fabric or the arms of your chair.

Birds of a feather. You probably find you are attracted to or attract people who reinforce your failure habit. If you believe you have to be the star, you'll find people who "one-up" you or who will cater to your vanity. If you are overconcerned with others' approval, you'll find people who stroke you or reject you.

Don't Take Success Personally

Most of us are highly vulnerable to going off course after some success or movement toward our vision. People frequently take success personally ("I am a star"; "I am in control"; "I am lovable"), lose sight of their vision, and stop their forward progress.

Keep your vision pure. Serve the vision, not your beliefs ("I want a new car just to have a new car, not to prove that I'm a worthy, powerful, and successful person"). Keep your motivation at the highest possible level. Create your vision for the joy of it, the love of it, the beauty of it, or the truth of it, rather than to show others or yourself that you aren't a loser. When your motivation is based on a disfunctional belief, you end up strengthening that belief, not dispelling it.

When you are moving toward creating what you want, you'll generally feel good, interested, and enthusiastic. When your mood jumps up to exhilaration, however, you need to make sure you haven't lost sight of current reality and gone into a trance. You may need to reground yourself in physical reality.

If you're successful, it is *because of what you're doing*, not because of who you are. When you go off on side issues, you not only lose your vision but you reinforce the false beliefs that cause your failures and emotional distress.

When Paul, thirty-two, first came to see Gary for therapy, he was depressed about his inability to get what he wanted in life. He was constantly fatigued and depressed. In particular, he found himself constantly ruminating about his inability to buy a house. He and his wife, Sue, both high school teachers, had married and entered the work force two years after housing costs had begun to skyrocket. When they were unable to buy a house in Los Angeles, Paul automatically assumed they were out of luck.

"Everytime I turn around," he said, "someone slams another door in my face." His fixed idea or psychological set blinded him to other options that were available to him. He was bitter and resentful because he believed that he was controlled by events ("The land developers and banks have all the power").

The idea of control, like change, is confusing because control does happen to operate in many situations in the physical world (for example, the carburetor controls the flow of gas in your car). But in the psychological world, your opportunities for choice are in flux, constantly increasing and decreasing. Sometimes choices are available and at other times they are unavailable. If your boss refuses to give you time off, he is not controlling you; he has merely taken away one of your choices (your choice to leave with his permission—you still have the choice to leave without his permission and accept the consequences).

Look for transfers. Once you move into the choice system, options begin to appear that you never suspected you had. But remember—the choice system is not magic. Rarely do you have one clear path to get what you want. You usually need to use several avenues to get where you want to go. If you're willing to take only a nonstop flight to Nome, Alaska, from Little Rock, Arkansas, you'll probably never get there. Rarely do you have perfect solutions or one-way flights; more often you have a series of partial solutions that eventually get you what you want.

Once Paul accepted the housing situation in Los Angeles and reaffirmed what he wanted ("I want to own my own house"), he started to see other choices ("I can buy a smaller fixer-upper in a less expensive neighborhood; I can learn more about real estate so that I can find myself the best possible deal; I can buy into a co-op; I can move to another city where houses are cheaper").

Substitute vision makers for vision killers. Paul's case is a good example of how the creative process works. First, instead of following his habitual thinking pattern ("Someone will slam a door in my face") he decided to keep his commitment to own his home. Commitment is *valuing your vision enough to make it happen.* Its opposite is contempt, a vision killer. Contempt is *devaluing your vision to make yourself feel better.*

Devaluing your vision ("Who wants to own a house?" "Houses are too much trouble") throws you off course. Similarly, because you are always part of your vision, devaluing yourself ("I was too stupid to buy a house when the market was good") destroys your vision. The old Groucho Marx joke about not wanting to join a club that would accept him illustrates a subtle way to devalue yourself: "I wouldn't want someone or something (a job, mate, or house) that would have me." The moral: Stay away from contempt.

Be on the lookout for the three other *vision killers:*

• *Why?*—"Why do I want the aggravation and responsibility of owning a house?"
• *What if?*—"What if Sue or I lose our jobs and can't make the payments?"
• *How?*—"How will we ever find a house we can afford?"

Paul learned to replace the three deadly vision breakers with three *vision makers:*

• *Why not?*—"Why not buy a house? It's what I want." A character in one of George Bernard Shaw's plays said, "Some people look at what is and say, 'Why?' I look at what might be and say, 'Why not?'"
• *So what?*—"So what if one of us loses our job? We'll get another one." *So what?* is accepting and thereby freeing yourself to get what you want.
• *Somehow*—"Somehow we'll find a house we can afford." *How?* is doubt; *somehow* is faith. Faith and patience are important because you use them while you hold on to your vision.

Paul had previously kept quiet about wanting to own a house. He was afraid that people would ask the "why," "what if," and "how" questions and that he would then become discouraged or look foolish if he didn't succeed.

The benefits of telling others what you want outweigh the disadvantages. Saying what you want reaffirms your commitment and increases your resources. You find that other people are a gold mine of information. Paul's college roommate, a clergyman in Tulsa, Oklahoma, suggested Paul and Sue move to Oklahoma, where houses were a third of the price of California. They followed his advice and moved to Tulsa. Both got jobs in the school system there, and three months later they bought a home.

But don't use public opinion to shame you into completing a task. Over the long run this will backfire by making others' opinions more important than your own. Take the suggestions of others only if they are compatible with what *you* want.

Avoid the cosmic myth. A frequent stumbling block when you start to create your own life is the belief that the universe will automatically provide you with what you need. The reasoning is that if you just picture what you want and release it to the cosmos, universal forces will automatically manifest what you want in your life. This is magical thinking, the type of thinking children often engage in. When what you wish for doesn't appear, you go to the opposite extreme and believe you can't create anything.

To create what you want, you are the one who must make it happen. You have to create a vision, choose to have it, *and do whatever is necessary to make it happen.* As you become better at this process, you will be able to make your visions happen earlier and more easily. At times, achieving your visions may seem magical because you don't know how it happens or why. The right opportunities begin to appear at the perfect time. The reason is that, as your awareness expands, you'll be able to see more of the choices and opportunities that were always there.

The rich get richer. As you become familiar with the psychological principles of self-creation, you will have an accelerating rate of success.

Rock Bottom Change Versus Rock Bottom Choice

As you move toward your vision, you will nearly always encounter some setbacks and obstacles. In the choice system, setbacks are creative forces that propel you toward your vision. Setbacks are opportunities to reaffirm your vision and to be true to yourself.

Rock bottom is where you think you have to hit before you can start to get better. Many people say they have to "hit rock bottom" before they can bounce back. In the change system you free-fall to rock bottom. You have to wait until your life is a total mess before you decide to quit drinking. You know that you will hit—but where? And when? In the choice system *you* define your rock bottom. To hit rock bottom, simply accept current reality.

One of the ways Paul helped himself when he was depressed about the cost of a house was to define his own rock bottom. Each time real estate prices had gone up, Paul had gone deeper into depression. In therapy Paul said he was afraid to read the newspapers because he didn't know where the price spiral would end. Because he felt as if events controlled him, he thought events dictated how depressed he would grow. "I don't know where I'm going to hit," he said, "and it frightens me. What if I get so upset I do something I regret?"

When Paul realized that he could determine rock bottom himself, he said he felt as though a ton of emotional baggage had been lifted from him. He was able to choose his rock bottom by accepting the truth about his current situation. When he accepted it ("Okay, this is the way it is. I'll accept that and I'll look for another route to my vision"), he switched out of his depression.

ACT, don't react. Paul accepted the darkness and coldness of the moment (rock bottom), and this freed him to envision and choose what he wanted to happen—to see the light at the end of the tunnel. He used the ACT Formula:

1. "*I accept* that I feel depressed about not being about to buy a house."
2. "*I choose* to envision myself living in my own house."
3. "*I will take action* to achieve that vision."

Robert Fritz, in his book *Path of Least Resistance,* teaches that "structural tension"—focusing on both current reality and your vision at the same time—is necessary for you to create what you want. Accept where you are and go for what you want. The vision you choose (being successful at your job, having a successful relationship) feeds back on current reality and makes the reality lighter, warmer, easier to accept. Taking action to create your vision helps to complete the acceptance process and reinforces your commitment to your vision by reaffirming its value.

Making a Critical Choice

With patience, you will start to make more critical choices—choices that more quickly create the experience you want. For example, Larry's business had run smoothly for years but started to lose money after he promoted his brother-in-law to the post of general manager. Because he felt responsible for his brother-in-law's feelings, Larry tried different solutions (increasing advertising, hiring a new salesman) to turn the business around, but his attempts were unsuccessful. He then told himself the truth and decided he wanted to save his business. He replaced his brother-in-law with a more aggressive manager, and his business began to make money again. Because Larry accepted current reality and held to his vision (saving his business), he was able to make his critical choice (replace his brother-in-law) and pay the cost (possible hard feelings within the family).

Mess it up to break your failure pattern. If you want to bake a cake that tastes good, you have to follow the right recipe. If you keep baking a cake that fails, something's wrong with the recipe; you have to modify it. You might have to add more eggs or put in less flour. In life, people often keep using the same recipe (failure pattern) and are surprised and upset when the cake keeps coming out in the same distasteful way. You need to alter the recipe (your choices) to have your cake come out the way you want. If you can't think of anything to alter, mess up the recipe—do *something* different. You're bound to get a different outcome.

The critical choice for one person's happiness may be to leave a job; for another, the critical choice may be to stay. When you use the ACT Formula, critical choices start to appear. Often you have to start moving before a critical choice becomes clear. The ACT Formula gets you moving:

1. *Accept* your current reality.
2. *Choose* to envision what you want to create in your life.
3. *Take action* to get it.

Get started, keep going, and finish. Review your three disappointments and pinpoint where you had trouble—the beginning, middle, or end stage. For example, you may have taken so long to get started that what you wanted was already gone (someone else applied for the job and got it). Maybe you started a project (a novel) and got most of the way through it but never finished.

Once you have pinpointed your pattern, decide to correct that characteristic on a daily basis. If you are a slow starter, practice jumping in and making something happen. When you wake up, get up. When you get up, do something. If you lose interest in the middle of a project, keep going anyway. Do what needs to be done. Visions are born in the joy of inspiration; they are accomplished with persistent patience. If you have trouble with endings, practice finishing what you start (put the last of the dishes away, complete the paper that's due at school, mail off the letter you wrote, finish repainting the bedroom, make the follow-up call to your client).

Farsighted Creativity

If you're temperamentally farsighted, you're probably great at fantasy and at coming up with brilliant ideas. You have trouble with the details, however, and don't see the obstacles that are in front of you. When you run into difficulties, you forget your original vision because it's more fun to conjure up a new vision. To strengthen your near vision:

Hold one vision at a time. Once you start a project (cleaning the garage), don't start anything else until you have finished it.

Pay attention to current reality. Develop the habit of describing where you are now—the sights, sounds, smell, and sensations of the moment. If you are stopped in rush hour traffic in the middle of the freeway, for example, take a moment to describe the physical reality to yourself ("I smell the gasoline exhaust; I feel the smooth plastic of the steering wheel; I hear music on the tape deck").

Focus on what you're doing when you're doing it. When you get gas for your car, turn all your thoughts toward getting gas. Think about each step as you do it (turn the pump on, fill the tank, replace the hose and cap).

Take the frontal position. Face what you fear. Move toward what you want to avoid. If you have important phone calls to make, make the one you dread the most first.

Act more and think less. Spend less time thinking about what you are going to do and do it instead.

Talk less and do more. Talk can lull you into thinking you're taking action.

Sell yourself on the value of taking care of details. Stop putting down people you consider to be "plodders" or "grinds." Begin to value them instead. Look at the results they create by paying attention to detail. Notice how they use detail to get them to what they want (as opposed to using detail for its own sake).

Imagine less and see more. Focus more on your surroundings and on the task at hand than on your succession of great ideas. Tune in more to the physical world and less to the psychological.

Nearsighted Creativity

Your problem may be the opposite—you get cemented in current reality. You see so many potential problems in getting started that you never do begin. Your feet are so firmly planted on the ground that you can't lift them. All you can see is what's around you. You have no vision to pull you forward. You may also have trouble finishing because that would mean you would have to start a new project.

Practice the following methods to improve your far vision:

Imagine more and think less. Practice imagining the ideal way you would like your vision to turn out. If you're working on a project, hold a vision of its completion. Don't visualize the worst and try to overcome it with self-discipline, because this method depletes energy. When you visualize the worst, you spend energy on worry, anxiety, and fear. Even the most ardent self-discipline can't produce results from fatigue and stress.

Take more risks. Jump in and see what happens. Try things out. Err on the side of inclusion. Better to make a fool of yourself than to miss an opportunity to get what you want.

Develop more faith. Assume that you will reach your vision. Don't worry about how, just begin to take action in faith. If you're working hard toward your vision, you're probably doing something wrong. You can always correct your course as you go along. If you don't like your course, you can always let go of it and try something else.

Sell yourself on visualizing. Look at great "imaginers" in our culture (Walt Disney, George Lucas, Dr. Martin Luther King, Jr., Lee Iacocca) and see what they've accomplished.

Look at people who succeeded rather than at those who failed. Find success stories to read. Go to success movies about people who don't let current reality block their visions (*Rocky, Gandhi,* and *Chariots of Fire,* for example).

Take time to daydream. As you start, ask yourself, "What do I want?" or "What would I like to see happen?"

Practice making starts at imperfect times. Rather than starting to create a thin body on Monday morning, begin it in the middle of a gourmet meal. Start your book before you have the word processor. Teach yourself that everything in your environment doesn't have to be perfect for you to begin.

How to Achieve 20/20 Vision

You need both far and near vision to create what you want. You need to be a visionary and a detailist. Keep your broad perspective and improve your focusing ability. If you find yourself giving too much attention to either your near or your far vision, use the techniques in this chapter to balance your vision.

Willpower—You Pay a High Price for It   In the change system you create negative feelings ("They are making me go to the meeting and I don't want to go"), then you use your will to overcome these bad feelings ("I'll force myself to go"). Lack of willpower is a common cause for blame in the change system ("I'm just lazy"; "He lacks willpower").

In the change system you continually have to inject yourself with willpower to overcome your internal resistances. Willpower may work for you, but you pay a high price. You lose your spontaneity and sense of fun, and you develop third-degree burnout.

A common mistake is to run an event through the "worst case" machine ("I'll get cancer"). You do this to generate some anxiety so that you will be motivated to react and avoid the worst case ("I have to stop smoking"). This strategy seldom works because you can't keep up the steady flow of negative images.

Imagination is more powerful than willpower. The image ("Wouldn't a cigarette taste good?") wins out over the willpower to stop smoking. To stop the conflict within yourself, imagine what you want to have ("I imagine healthy lungs and deep breaths"), then decide that you'll create it.

Big and Small Choices   The big choice is to have a clear desk; the small choice is to take some action to clean it (throw out old message slips, put paper clips away). Once you make the big choices, priorities are set. Once you make the big choice, the smaller ones that support it become easier to make. Your big choice will guide you. The trick is to keep your eye on current reality and on where you want to go.

Manage Your Focus   Negative feelings become ingrained when you give in to them and you stop knowing what you want. You can develop your ability to shift your attention to what you want:

Get to know your focus. Watch for times when you are able to direct your focus ("I'm tired and I'm choosing to get my homework done").

Use positive language. Start describing your visions in "choice" terms:

"I choose to finish it" versus "I'll try."
"I choose to" versus "I can."
"I choose not to do it" versus "I can't."

Accept discomfort. Whenever you find yourself in an uncomfortable situation (anxiety, fatigue, physical pain), choose to accept it and to put your focus on the experience you want. If you feel anxious about going to a party, accept your anxiety, then focus on the experience you want to have ("I'm anxious, but I am going to think about having a good time"). If you want to get your midterm paper done but have a roaring headache, turn your focus to the experience you want ("I accept that I have a headache, but I'm going to focus on getting the paper done").

Despite recurring headaches, one of Gary's clients was able to complete her doctoral dissertation in just this way. "I would simply say to myself that, despite the fact I had a headache, what I wanted was to get my dissertation done. Then I took action to get it done. Whenever I found myself thinking about how much my head hurt or how I wished I felt better, I focused on how I wanted the finished dissertation to look." It worked for her. Using this approach, she finished her dissertation in two months time. The more she focused on the job at hand, the fewer headaches she suffered.

Start a program. Start a systematic program such as aerobics or meditation. Structured programs can help develop your ability to direct your focus to your big choice.

Stretch. Stretch your image of what you can accomplish ("I will give the talk"; "I will take a trip on my own"). In golf, if you always putt short, you never make your shot. If you putt long, you *sometimes* make it.

Do what you fear. If you want to avoid some activity or person because of fear, step over the fear instead of bowing down to it. Focus your attention on what you want, even though you fear the process of getting there.

"I'm afraid to drive but I am going to focus on going to the grocery store to get what I want without having to rely on my neighbor."

"I'm afraid to ask for a raise but I'm going to focus on the raise I want."

"I'm afraid of being alone tonight but I am going to focus on creating a good evening when I can to enjoy a good book and a cup of hot chocolate."

Drop tasks to train your focus. When you're doing something and your husband, wife, or child asks you to do something else, stop and do it. Instead of saying, "Just a minute, I want to finish this," drop your task and do his or hers. When you have to hold your focus on a dropped task until you get back to it, you practice directing your focus to what you want.

Practice focused listening. Whenever anyone talks to you—your family, your clients, sales people—focus attentively on what they are saying. Attentive listening not only will help you improve your focus but is a success force in its own right. People are attracted to people who genuinely listen to them.

Keep your vows. Make fewer promises to yourself and others, and keep those you *do* make. If you decide to finish a project, finish it even though you've lost your motivation for it. Breaking your word, even to yourself, erodes your ability to hold your vision.

Use self-exams. If you listen to your secretary with only one ear, be honest to yourself about your inattentiveness. If you really read magazines in your office all day, don't tell people how hard you worked on preparing next year's budget.

People who are extraordinary in any field usually have the ability to slow down their mind enough to focus on what is in front of them. They can concentrate. The star tennis player sees the ball at about half the speed others do. When you use your focus to create what you want, you slow your mind down in the same way.

Practice Directing Your Focus With practice you're able to create your vision more quickly. When you make choices and act on them, you become smarter—you develop "tacit" knowledge that you can bring to new situations.

Robert Sternberg, a psychologist at Yale, has been looking at intelligence in new ways. To him, intelligence is getting what you want and it depends on "tacit" knowledge, knowledge that has never explicitly been taught. Most of the knowledge that you need to succeed on your job, for example, you pick up on your own. Promotions and raises often depend on how well you've picked it up. People are successful in making friends or producing hit records because they have tacit knowledge to draw upon. With practice, you can develop tacit knowledge in any area.

Imagine that you stop by the bakery to get a chocolate chip cookie every night. One day you decide to make a big choice to weigh less and a small choice to stop eating your nightly cookie. The first time you walk by the bakery, accept the reality that you're hungry and are choosing to go by without getting a cookie. You may be uncomfortable, but the next time will be a little less difficult because you gained tacit knowledge the first time. After you have practiced directing your focus for a year and have walked by the bakery 250 times, you probably will find it more difficult to buy a cookie than to pass it by. Practice makes creating new experiences easier, even if you have relapses in between.

Relationships often develop through tacit knowledge. You learn what it is that people like and dislike by being with them and paying attention to them. You can't learn from a book that a certain man or woman disapproves of off-color jokes, but if you spend time with that person, you learn about that particular characteristic. If you accept that you are afraid to develop relationships and then take actions to be with people anyway, you will learn the tacit knowledge that will help you develop relationships. Like learning to walk by a bakery without buying the cookie, it becomes easier and easier with practice. The more you practice being with people, the easier it becomes to relate to all people.

Enjoy yourself. Remember, the idea was to enjoy yourself. You chose your job, mate, and the place where you live to create more enjoyment for yourself. Creating what you want isn't a chore. If you're working hard and deriving no pleasure from it, you're doing something wrong. Instead of seeing your vision at the top of a mountain you must struggle to climb, see your vision downstream, and enjoy the float down to it. Avoid putting too many time and other demands on yourself. Periodically remind yourself to enjoy the process. *Creating your own life is an ongoing process, not a series of life events.*

Be true to your vision. Use the strategies you need to keep your vision hot and your sight clear. Some will work better than others for you, but practice always works. Your path from current reality to your vision is paved with action, the subject of the next chapter.

6. Take Action!

You can wait or you can act. You can wait to study for the bar when your virus is gone, or you can study despite your virus. You can wait to have a home until you find a husband or wife, or you can create a home as a one-person family. You can wait to go to the movie until someone asks you, or you can ask someone to go.

Don't Wait—
Create Your Happiness Now

Waiting shoves action to the future—when your headache is gone or you're married or you're made happy by someone else. Waiting robs the present of the creative possibilities. To create the moments that you want, you have to act *in* the moment, not in the future.

Alice Koller, a Ph.D. in philosophy from Harvard, spent the first thirty-seven years of her life waiting. She became sick of her life-style and decided to spend a winter alone in Nantucket, searching for the source of her unhappiness. In her journal, *The Unknown Woman,* she meticulously recorded her discoveries.

> Waiting? Why? The stupendous thing I used to wait for was something that was going to be done *to* me, or *for* me: to be initiated by someone else, independently of my choice. But there isn't a someone else to make things happen to me: I'm the only person who can do what I decide needs to be done. And besides, there is no *reason* for anyone else to do anything at all for me, particularly something as glorious as that thing I expected.
>
> So on two counts waiting is irrelevant. Nothing to wait for, because I'll initiate what happens to me. Nothing to wait for, because these minutes now passing *are* my life. They are the minutes in which my living is to be done. Whatever I do, I'll do in my own time and *I* will do it. . . .
>
> I don't have to wait to get married to have a home: I'll make my own. . . . I don't have to wait for someone to give me a sense of continuity: I'll carry my continuity within myself. I'll belong wherever I am. I'll institute my own permanence.

Waiting is part of the unrewarding change system. When you want something to change (your feelings, your job, the weather, the lonely weekend, your parents, your spouse, your life), you wait. You wait for the curtain to open and your life to begin. You believe something or someone will come along and make you happy. And so, you wait.

Future Modes: Worry and Hope

When you wait (put off action), you spend your "waiting time" thinking about the future. You either worry or you hope. Although worry seems bad and hope seems good, neither will get you what you want if you don't take action in the present. Surprisingly, worry and hope feed on one another. You worry that what you hope for won't happen, and you hope that what you worry about won't happen.

Worry-mobiles

In the change system, you drive a worry-mobile. You have a worry of the day, worry of the week, worry of the year, and worry of a lifetime. You operate on worry fuel. When you run low, you fill your tank with more ("There must be some ominous reason why things are going so well"). Sometimes you have so much worry you need a trailer to haul it around. You may ask others to take a spin in your worry-mobile ("Don't you think it's a bit odd everything seems to be going so smoothly?").

You create worry through internal combustion. You imagine the worst ("I could go bankrupt") and then react to this image ("That would be terrible"; "I couldn't stand that"). The resulting clash between your images and your reactions creates worry and anxiety. Once you crank up enough worry, you become motivated to do something about the problem ("I'd better go out and make a sale") to get rid of the worry.

In the change system, you have to stay upset in order to keep your motivation up. Once you stop worrying (imagining the worst), you lose your motivation. You may achieve some success with worry, because it is a powerful motivator. But the cost per mile is high.

Sandra came to Gary for therapy after years of worry-motivated success. In her early thirties, she had already risen to the top of her company's sales force. She and her husband, a school administrator, lived in a comfortable neighborhood among other professional couples. Their two children were in private school, and the family was able to afford almost anything they wanted, including a yearly vacation abroad.

After Sandra had been promoted to national supervisor of sales, she began to feel weary. She found it increasingly difficult to get up in the morning and to stay awake in the evening long enough to enjoy her family after work. Her marriage began to suffer, and Sandra became depressed.

"I've always loved selling," Sandra said in her first session, "from the first time I went out to sell candy in high school to support the pep club.

And I always wanted to work for a company like mine. In college I made myself study by imagining I wouldn't get a job if my grades were low. When this company hired me, I imagined that I would lose my job if I didn't make a sale. Once we bought the house, I imagined that I would lose the house if I didn't make more sales than anyone else. And it worked. At least I think it did. Look where I got."

Sandra had achieved much success, but within the past six months of work, she said, she had slackened off considerably in her activity on the job. She had called in sick half a dozen times when she couldn't get out of bed. She had let important papers sit on her desk. She said, "I just couldn't get my hand to pick them up." After motivating herself for years with worry, Sandra was horrified to find her worst fears coming true.

Because she was open to new ideas, Sandra was able to grasp the essential difference between the change system ("I'll force myself to change my situation by worrying about the future") and the choice system ("I'll make different choices to create the experiences in my life I want"). Within a month she was functioning at her peak again. She used the ACT Formula to teach herself to create the experiences she wanted:

1. *"I accept* the fact that I love selling and have great ambitions."
2. *"I choose* to be a success in sales and imagine myself doing that."
3. *"I take action* by going out and making sales."

Sandra also realized that she didn't want to be national supervisor of sales because it took her out of direct selling (where she could actually make more money). She decided to return to the sales force.

She ended up creating what she wanted by acting in the present rather than manipulating herself with worry. She held a vision of what she wanted (to be successful in sales) and took action to get it. Worry didn't sap her energy any longer. On the contrary, she felt a tremendous release of energy. She became motivated by creative energy—energy not only to create what she wanted but also to enjoy and savor what she produced.

Hope-mobiles

If you wait instead of act, you have another car in the garage alongside your worry-mobile. This car seems more desirable because it's a hope-mobile, but it, too, can keep you from acting in the present.

The hope-mobile is fueled by "it"—the perfect mate, the big break, the right job, the smaller dress size, the ultimate date. Hope is waiting for "it."

Your life is based on the illusion that when you get "it" you will be happy. Workaholics, for example, have the illusion that when they finish their last project they will be free. The idea of freedom is the "it" that fuels their hope-mobile. Rather than making a choice to work or a choice to be free, they overwork to get freedom, which is always just out of their reach.

How Goals Rip You Off   Waiting for "it" is how you get ripped off by goals ("When I'm out of school [or in school] I'll be happy"). You give the goal the power to dictate your feelings. If you don't reach the goal, if it's less than what you thought, or if you realize that you're still the same person you were before you reached it, the goal you set makes you unhappy. It rips you off. It promises but doesn't deliver.

You may think you won't be happy until you find your identity, so you spend years looking for it. You conclude you won't feel fulfilled until you know your true calling, so you live each minute looking for it.

In the choice system, you have visions, but you don't make the visions responsible for your feelings. You don't hope for something that might or might not occur to make you happy. You simply decide what you want (to be in graduate school) and take action to achieve it (work nights to earn tuition, study German to get a jump on the Ph.D. requirements, apply to schools you can afford, visit each school to find out about financial aid and work-study grants). You are already doing what you need to do to get what you want. You are a master practicing, not practicing to be a master.

Gary recently talked to Tony, a despondent graduate student. Tony had been unable to start his dissertation research. He said he had been looking for a research topic for more than a year but hadn't found one. He wanted to know if Gary knew of a topic.

Gary told him, "You can look for another ten years and you won't find a topic. You don't find research topics, you make them up. You might get someone to make one up for you, but there is no research topic out there with your name on it. You have to make one up and then put your name on it."

After You Make It Up, Create It

In the choice system, rather than looking for "it," you "make it up" (what you want) and then create it ("Instead of looking for a job, I'll create one"). If you don't like your first creation, you make up something else. For example, you may have created a vision of establishing a successful relationship with a particular person, but then you find the other person isn't interested in you. So you discard this specific vision and develop a vision of having a relationship where you receive love as well as give love.

However, a vision is not something you discard lightly. If you keep discarding your vision, usually when you meet obstacles, you will never get what you want. *You design your own life.* Rather than looking for the right path for you, decide what you want and build your own path to it.

Waiting Is Passive

When you wait for other people to act, you put your life on hold. You give the other person (or situation) power over you. A client who is an actor said that he spent so much time waiting for his big break that he had come to regard the "big break" as a kind of doctor that would finally give him life. "I know it sounds strange," he said, "but it's like I'm waiting for that big break to make a house call and save me."

A couple who came to see Jim had spent the fifty years of their married life locked in passive combat, each trying to change the other so that they could be happy. The wife was miserable because her husband had a habit of leaving tools and clothes around the house and then became angry with her when she would not help him find an item he wanted. He, on the other hand, was angry at his wife because she was always straightening up, and he felt there was no real place for him in the house. She said that his complaints made her feel criticized and a failure.

Each had a list of ten or fifteen ways the other person could "solve the problem." When Jim asked them what each could do for themselves to get what they wanted, neither had even a single idea.

Most of the therapy hour was spent helping them look at how each could get what they wanted. The husband decided that if he were more careful about where he put his belongings and did not ask his wife to help him find them, it would both eliminate most of his anger at her and greatly reduce his own frustration. His wife came to the conclusion that if she let her husband clean up one room of the house the way he wanted, it would probably lead to less criticism from him; that, in turn, would help her feel less of a failure.

When they returned a week later they told Jim that they each had been taking care of his or her own part of the plan and that, for the first time in fifty years, they had gone through a week without fighting with each other.

Waiting Is Painful

The Supreme Court ruled that it is humane to execute a criminal but cruel and unusual punishment to make that person *wait* to be executed.

Because waiting is aversive, you try to ignore all of the waiting you do. Silent resentment builds up. You resent your boss, your situation, or your husband or wife, so you become aggressive to get rid of the resentment. You may use waiting as a weapon. You make them wait the way you had to wait.

Sometimes Waiting Is Manipulation

John came to Gary for counseling because of his passive-aggressive feelings. He said he felt defeated by a mixture of anger and resentment. "I'm angry at my wife," he said, "but I feel so helpless most of the time." John and his wife, Sally, owned a large kennel that she had inherited from her father. Before John met her, he had been a dog trainer, and initially they were excited at the prospect of combining their skills to make a thriving business.

After their marriage John waited for Sally to make decisions about the business. Instead of talking with Sally about a division of labor, he assumed that she would want to do certain jobs, waited for her to do them, then became angry when she didn't. Within a short time Sally had built up a resentment at John's passiveness about business decisions. She stopped hustling for new business altogether, hoping to force John to do it.

A standoff developed. They went months without hiring an employee they needed. Both were overworked and tired by the time John came for counseling; they had been doing all the work caring for the animals and spending energy on silent resentment.

At his second session Gary asked John, "Are the costs worth the wait?" John admitted that the costs were high and decided to give the choice system a try. He accepted current reality ("I'm afraid of stepping in on Sally's business and creating problems in our relationship"), then chose and imagined what he wanted ("To have a good relationship with Sally and a successful business") and took action to get it ("I'll be more honest with Sally"; "I'll hire a custodian and make calls about the contracts on my desk").

Once John had switched into the choice system, Sally did, too. She stopped trying to make him do tasks by refusing to do them herself. They decided to talk freely and openly about the business and to state honestly what they liked and disliked doing. As a result, they were able to divide the labor in a way they both thought was fair.

A Waiting Inventory

Answer the following questions to see how much time you spend waiting. Use the following scoring system:

0 = Almost never
1 = Seldom
2 = Often
3 = Most of the time
4 = Always

1. You're on time but the other person is twenty-five minutes late. Do you wait?

0   1   2   3   4

2. You call a large company and a secretary says, "Please hold." Minutes pass. Do you continue to wait?

0   1   2   3   4

3. You have asked to be seated at a restaurant because your friend "should be here any minute." Fifteen minutes go by and the waitress would like to take your order. Do you insist on waiting?

0   1   2   3   4

4. You have not heard from a friend for several weeks. Do you wait for the friend to call you?

0   1   2   3   4

5. You would like to get to know someone better. Do you wait for them to ask you out?

0   1   2   3   4

6. You're out with friends at a night club. Do you wait to be asked to dance?

0   1   2   3   4

7. You have new neighbors. Do you wait for them to introduce themselves?

0   1   2   3   4

8. Do you wait for others to say good morning before you do?

0   1   2   3   4

9. You have been told that your new dishwasher will be delivered before noon. It's now 1:00 P.M. Do you wait?

0   1   2   3   4

10. You like the actors and the story sounds interesting, but you have not seen the reviews for a new movie. Do you wait for the reviews before seeing the movie?

0   1   2   3   4

11. Someone with important information says he will call you "sometime tomorrow." Do you wait around for the call?

0   1   2   3   4

12. An interesting museum exhibition is in town. A friend wants to see it with you but keeps postponing the date. Do you wait to attend the exhibit?

0   1   2   3   4

13. You ask your partner to do something twice and each time are told, "Wait a minute." Assuming you can do the task yourself, do you wait?

0   1   2   3   4

14. Friends tell you they don't know yet whether they have the time to go out with you. Do you wait for their answer?

0   1   2   3   4

15. You would like to have some friends over, but your partner keeps giving some excuse why this isn't the right time. Do you keep waiting?

0   1   2   3   4

16. You have finished an important project (for example, school application, sales presentation). Do you put your life on hold while you wait for a response to it?

0   1   2   3   4

17. You wait for someone you care about to make up his/her mind if he/she wants to be with you or not.

0   1   2   3   4

18. You spend your time thinking about what will occur in the future (the weekend, your vacation, your retirement).

0   1   2   3   4

19. You wait until everything (weather, health, financial situation) is just right before taking a vacation.

0   1   2   3   4

20. You make your goals and when you are going to achieve them vague ("Someday I'm going to travel").

0   1   2   3   4

21. You've called a meeting and several people are late. Instead of starting, you wait for them.

0   1   2   3   4

Add up your score:

  1–10 = Waiting is not a problem.
11–20 = Waiting is a moderate problem.
21–30 = Waiting is a significant problem.

Watch Your Waiting

You will find it helpful to become aware of your waiting moments. In your notebook, make a list of all the waiting you do in one day. For example, your list might look like this.

"I woke up early but didn't get up until the alarm went off."
"I turned on the water and waited for it to get hot."
"I put the coffee on and waited for it to perk."
"I turned up the furnace and waited for the room to warm up before dressing."
"I waited to hear the weather report before choosing which jacket to wear."
"I waited for my boyfriend/girlfriend to call about our date on Friday."
"I waited till my headache was gone before I answered a letter."

Choosing Versus Waiting

Another way to become aware of waiting is to compare what you *think* you're waiting for with what you're really waiting for.

EXERCISE

Make two columns in your notebook. Label Column One "What I think I'm waiting for" and Column Two "What I'm *really* waiting for." Take your time in making up your lists and evaluating them in order to see what waiting means to you.

One of Jim's clients, Kim, was depressed because she wanted to be a successful writer, but because she'd never published anything she considered herself a failure. Her list looked like this:

What I think I'm waiting for	*What I'm really waiting for*
To be considered a great writer	To respect myself
An agent to represent me	A belief in myself that I really am a writer even if I'm not published
Success so men will notice me	Self-esteem

Make a choice to skip Column One in your life and take care of Column Two.

Usually you have little say over what you think you are waiting for. It happens (or doesn't happen) in its own good time. Column Two, however, usually contains experiences you can create. Kim, for example, could choose to respect her work independent of public opinion. She had little influence over whether she would be thought a great writer. That was in the hands of critics, reviewers, public taste, and the place of her work in the historical movement of literature. She could, however, take action to respect herself. She could choose a project, work on it every day, complete it, and get it to a publisher, as writers throughout the history of literature have done.

White Balls/Black Balls   Waiting is caused by focusing on what you *can't do* ("Make an agent like my work") and overlooking what you *can do* ("Choose to acknowledge myself because I write every day"). Success comes when your believed choices are your actual choices.

You have many actual choices of which you are unaware. Kim was unaware that by attending writers' workshops and conferences she could meet writers and publishers who might introduce her to an agent.

You also have many pseudo-choices or illusions. Kim couldn't force an agent to accept her writing and take her on as a client no matter how long she waited.

When you are aware of a real choice, you can create success, because that is where you have response ability.

To clarify, call your unaware actual choices white balls. Call your illusionary choices black balls.

When you're trying to change something, you focus on black balls (past and future) and ignore the white ones (the present). You believe you should be able to do what you can't ("I need to turn the clock back"), and you believe you can't do what you can ("I can't accept that").

By operating from choice, you increase the white balls (make a phone call, talk to your boss, learn about the housing situation). You merge believed choices—what you believe you can do—with actual choices. In other words, you see and accept more current reality.

Divide and act. As you raise your awareness of waiting, it's helpful to separate white balls from black ones. If you want a specific person to marry you and the person doesn't want to, label that a black ball and throw it away.

Ask yourself what your white balls are—join a singles group, join a travel club, get on a coed softball team, join a choir. You can't choose to have someone propose to you. You *can* dress nicely, talk to people of the opposite sex, and ask someone out. Whether that person agrees is his or her choice (black ball), but you can choose to ask (white ball).

You Can Eliminate Waiting

Suppose you are in a long supermarket line. If you're in the unrewarding change system, you wait and make yourself uncomfortable ("Won't this line ever speed up?" "Oh no, that lady has a lot of coupons"; "Stupid checker can't even push the keys right!"). Waiting is a self-generated, uncomfortable psychological experience.

You can replace your uncomfortable psychological experience of waiting by taking action in the present. You do this by using the ACT Formula:

1. *You accept* current reality ("I am uncomfortable and in a long, slow line").
2. *You choose* and envision the experience you want ("I'll enjoy myself and get checked out as quickly as possible").
3. *You take action* to create your vision. Your actions will depend on the current reality.

To take action in the present, you might:

• Look for a shorter line.
• Leave the store and come back when it's not so busy.
• If you have a few items, ask if you could move ahead of the person with two big baskets.
• Ask the manager to open another cash register.
• Tune into your surroundings and observe people.
• Strike up a conversation with someone in the line.
• Balance your checkbook.
• Read the magazines and newspapers at the checkout counter until your turn comes.

The action you take will often be largely unconscious. After you accept where you are and choose your vision, you do what seems right. You may have the ability to rearrange the physical world (move to an express aisle, ask the manager to open a new aisle), but at times you will be in a situation in which all the lines are six deep. Being in the choice system doesn't necessarily mean you get checked out any faster. You can, however, always create a different psychological experience for yourself.

Appreciate the moment. Because you create your own experiences, you can be patient. You can enjoy and savor all of your moments. Matthew Fox, a writer and scholar, advocates a self-creating and blessing philosophy in his book *Original Blessing.* "If we savored more, we would buy less. We would be less compulsive, less unsatisfied. We would also work less and play more. If we savored more we would communicate more deeply, relate more fully, compete less regularly and celebrate more authentically. We would be relating more deeply to ourselves, to creation in all its blessedness, to history past and future, to the Now."

Strategies for Taking Action

When all is said and done about most therapies and most self-help books, much is said and little is done. To reap the rewards of the rapid relief principles, you have to put them into action.

Be in the moment. Pay attention to what you are doing as you do it. Don't wait for what you believe is making you unhappy to go away or for what you believe will make you happy to come. Attend to and savor the job in front of you.

Once you stop overidentifying with the physical world ("I lost my job so I *have* to feel bad"), you can start to connect with the energy in the physical world ("I lost my job, but I will take action to feel good by paying attention to each task at hand in the present"). When you rake your lawn or wash your car, you can experience energy coming to you—if you choose to be open, tune in, and focus on the job. By seeing and touching the physical world, you eliminate your painful psychological self-absorption. Whenever you feel bad, focus on current reality for a few moments.

If you are doing the dishes, savor the feel of the suds on a plate, the warmth of the water on your hands, the steam against your face. If you are writing out bills, listen to the sound of your checks as you rip them out. Taste the glue of the envelope and the stamps. Your five senses tell you about the *now,* your current reality. Tune in to them and savor what they tell you.

Jump in and take a risk. Behind your fear of taking a risk is usually the fear of being blamed—by yourself and others.

When you take a risk, you step out from the crowd and are an easy target for blame. A new Yellow Cab driver asked one of the seasoned drivers if he had any advice for him. The old-timer said, "I have only one piece of advice. If you see an accident, no matter what, don't stop." The new driver asked why. The old-timer said, "The only thing the witnesses will remember seeing is a Yellow Cab." People who take risks are like Yellow Cabs.

You cannot escape blame. If you don't start the business, people will blame you ("You never follow through"); if you start the business, they will blame you; if it is a failure, they say, "You should have known better"; and if it's successful, they say, "You're just money hungry."

When you're in the choice system, the fear of blame doesn't stop you. Use the ACT Formula, if necessary, to get started:

1. *Accept* your current reality ("I accept the fact that I'm afraid people will blame me if I make the wrong decisions").
2. *Choose* what you want and visualize it ("I see this working out great").
3. *Take action* ("I'll do it this way").

Nancy, a personnel director in a large company, used the ACT Formula to help her make hiring decisions. One bad judgment in the past (an employee she'd recommended had stolen a large sum of money from the company) made her afraid of making the same mistake again. By repeatedly using the ACT Formula to make personnel decisions, she regained her confidence.

Create and correct. You may be waiting until everything is perfect before you start moving toward your vision. You could wait forever. Start creating what you want, and correct your course as you go along. Act and adjust.

Earlier in this chapter we talked about making up a vision that truly matters to you. When you have a vision that works for you (for example, developing a successful relationship), you will reach it more quickly if you are willing to make adjustments along the way (joining a health club didn't work because everyone was too busy to talk, so you join a literary club instead).

You rarely create anything without some adjustments along the way. Don't worry beforehand about how you will make the corrections—that's a detail. What you'll need to know will occur spontaneously, according to the demands of current reality. Maxwell Maltz, in his classic book *Psycho-Cybernetics,* says you have to trust the creative process. Don't jam it by worrying whether or not it will work or by trying to force it. He says, "You must 'let it' work rather than 'make it' work. This trust is necessary because your creative mechanism operates below the level of consciousness and you cannot 'know' what is going on beneath the surface."

"Create and correct" is a letting-go process. You have to let go of what isn't true to your vision. In a study of young artists, researchers found that the artists who were open to correcting their work were still artists twenty-five years later. Those who would not adjust their work after feedback eventually left the field of art altogether.

A successful screenwriter in Hollywood has one word on the license plate of his expensive Mercedes—*REWROTE.* Write your script and be willing to rewrite when current reality demands it. Forget the perfect moment. Start taking action and adjust along the way.

Stop on a dime. In his book *Constructive Living*, innovative psycho-therapist David Reynolds says, "Run to the edge of the cliff and stop on a dime." This sentence contains all the advice you need to eliminate waiting for some uncontrollable event. You "run" (you become active and do what needs to be done) "to the edge of the cliff" (you extend yourself to your potential) "and you stop on a dime" (after you have done all that you are going to do, you release the situation and let it go). Then move on to your next project.

Use timers to help you "stop on a dime." For example, if you are waiting for dinner to cook, set a timer. Then focus on what you are doing until you hear the timer go off. If you are waiting to hear about a project, set up a mental timer or mark it on your calendar ("If I don't hear from them in two weeks, I'll call them"), and then let your thinking about it go.

Alice, a free-lance photographer, spent so much energy anxiously wait-ing for responses to her submissions that she had little energy left for photography. "I wish I could flood the market with submissions, but once I send something in, I start hoping and worrying and hanging around the mailbox." She bought an engagement calendar, entered the date she would probably hear from a publication about her photos, then put the submission out of her mind. For example, if the market information was "reports in 3–6 weeks," she skipped ahead six weeks in the calendar and wrote, "Drop note to _____ to inquire if they received submis-sion." Alice also went one step further. She decided to try to fill up as many dates in the calendar as possible. She "stopped on a dime" when she'd done all she could. By not wasting energy on waiting she released energy to "flood the market."

Do it now. You may be waiting because you believe you have a thousand years in which to accomplish your dreams. Buddha said, "There are those who forget death will come to all. For those who remember, quarrels come to an end." If you keep in mind how short life is, you'll *stop quarreling* with current reality and waiting for it to change and *start creating* the life you want.

Decide what is important and start doing it. Don't wait until you have enough time, money, or confidence to do it.

Tell the truth quickly. State what you want. Ask questions if you need to clear up a confusion. Being honest is the antidote for passive-aggressive waiting, whether you are the victim or the victimizer:

"You told me you would call me last week and you didn't. What's the story?"

"I didn't finish the annual report on time because I was angry about being passed over for the promotion."

"You told me you wanted to see me again, then you didn't invite me to your party. What's the reason?"

"I came on strong at the meeting because I felt intimidated by the office manager, and I didn't want it to show."

Keep your word. People may keep you waiting because in the past you have kept them waiting. What you give is what you get. Make a commitment to keep your commitments. If you tell someone you will call in the morning, do it. If you promise to send a snapshot, do it. If you tell your boss you'll be on time, do it. You not only influence others to keep their agreements with you, you also influence yourself because you demonstrate on a continuing basis that you are a person true to your word.

Focus on can-do's. You usually have choices, even if you don't have the precise choice you want. Focus on what you *can* do, and you will find that other choices will start to appear.

In therapy, Ken was at first confused about the difference between "change" and "choice" because, unless he had the particular choice he wanted, he was unwilling to consider other choices ("If I can't have what I want, I don't want anything").

He experienced a breakthrough in his thinking while on a date. The woman he took out was an avid talker, and halfway through the evening Ken became depressed. He wished he were with someone else. Then it hit him that what he really wanted was to have a good time. He immediately used the ACT Formula: *He accepted* the current reality that he was on a date with a woman who talked a blue streak. *He then chose* to have a good time, and *he started acting* as if he were. He concentrated on his date's stories as if she were a talk show guest.

At first he had to pretend, but when he acted *as if* he were having a good time, he actually started to have a good time. He laughed at some of his date's stories, liked the way she danced to big band music, and enjoyed the taste of his food. He didn't plan to ask her out again, but he enjoyed the evening. Ken created the experience he wanted because he focused on the white balls (actual choices—to enjoy the evening) rather than on the black balls (illusory choices—to be on a date with a different woman).

Forget Square One. Square One is another name for the change system. Relapses (stepping back into the change system) grow out of the illusion that you (or others) change. "I've fallen back to Square One" is a common expression of discouragement when your expectations are unmet. But "Square One" implies that you must struggle up through Square Two, Square Three, Square Four, and so on until you're back to where you started—and *then* you can start for your vision. *But there is no Square One,* and there aren't any other squares through which you have to struggle either. When you think you have fallen back into Square One, you have simply slipped back into needing to change the world.

Either you think the world needs to change for you to be happy or you know that you create your own life by choices. You don't have to struggle from Square One to Square Two and on up through square after square to get where you want. You simply switch your focus from change to choice. When you do you are already moving toward your vision. Once you become aware of going in and out of the change system, you can use your relapse experiences as a way to become wiser and a way to avoid the change trap next time.

So What—Keep Going

One of Gary's clients, Richard, was able to distill the essence of the choice system down to one phrase: "So what—keep going!" The "so what" gets you into acceptance, and the "keep going" makes you act and moves you toward your vision.

When Richard caught himself complaining about having to go to work, he told himself, "So what—keep going." He got out of bed and went to work. If he wanted to approach a woman for a date and was afraid of rejection, he told himself, "So what—keep going." He went up and introduced himself. If he caught himself ruminating on his rotten childhood, he would tell himself, "So what—keep going," and he would start doing something that he wanted to get done.

"So what" is effective because it keeps your feelings from having power over you. "Keep going" is a self-direction to act. Remember, your feelings change from moment to moment and have little to do with what you want.

"So what—keep going" keeps you moving to your vision. You might get bogged down in the middle of the journey. You may feel that you're farther from the vision than when you started. If you tell yourself, "So what," and keep going, you will find you move closer to creating your vision—and you will start feeling good again.

If you get so discouraged that you stop altogether, you'll never get there. But if you tell yourself, "I bogged down for a while. So what—keep going," you will eventually create your objective.

A variation of "So what—keep going" is "So what—do it anyway." No matter what your current reality (a headache, depression, a tyrannical boss, memories of an abusive childhood), do what you have to do. For example, "I'm afraid I'll be rejected if I apply for this job": So what—do it anyway. "I hate to write out bills": So what—do it anyway. "I can't study when I have a cold": So what—do it anyway. "When the boss is tyrannical I get so depressed I can't make myself work": So what—do it anyway.

"So what" gives you choices to create the experiences you want *despite* your current reality. "Keep going" (or "do it anyway") moves you toward your vision. "So what—keep going" captures the essence of the choice system. It keeps you from putting your life on hold while you wait, worry, and hope.

II. HOW TO APPLY THE CHOICE SYSTEM

7. Let Go of Anxiety and Create Self-Faith

A million years ago, when humans stepped from their caves, anxiety was a good friend. Armed with nothing more than a brain, these fangless, clawless, relatively weak creatures survived because their alarm systems told them when to get out of the way, when to pick up a rock and fight, or when to freeze and not move a muscle. They triumphed over wild beasts, unpredictable weather, and antisocial enemies within their own species because anxiety warned them of danger and signaled what to do.

Our Oversensitive Alarm System

We are descended from the survivors—those with the anxious genes, the sensitive alarm systems. That's the price we pay for survival. We often live at "red alert." However, most of our survival mechanisms are actually vestiges of the past—no longer useful and often more hindrance than help. Our anxiety system is too sensitive, much like an auto burglar alarm that goes off even when no one is close to the car. We constantly overmobilize ourselves for action when there is no real danger.

Anxiety is your emotional reaction to your distorted and unrealistic appraisal of a situation. You overestimate the danger of a situation and underestimate your ability to handle it. Anxiety is acting as if ("What if?") something bad is going to happen to you.

You act as if something outside of you is responsible for your feelings and you're helpless to do anything about it. You treat "what if" ideas ("What if I fail the test?") as if they were real and concrete. You think, feel, and act *as if* the feared event were occurring in the present. When you panic, you don't have an awareness that the event is fictional. You believe the walls are actually closing in on you in a crowded room or that you will jump if you get near a window. You react as if your imagined dangers are real. If you know you're acting as if, you worry. If you forget you're acting as if, you panic.

When you know that you create your own experiences, nothing outside of you "makes" you anxious. You accept responsibility for how you feel and don't blame your anxiety on anything or anyone.

EXERCISE

Look at your list of three disappointments. Reflect on the fear you had with each one. Then try to discover how your need to change something or someone led to the fear.

Here are examples of how needing change can lead to fear:

"My boss is to blame for my feelings, and I'm afraid I won't be able to make him like me (change him)."

"I'm responsible for others having a good time at my party, and I'm afraid I won't be able to get them to (change them)."

"All the people in this store are staring at me and making me nervous, and I'm afraid I won't be able to stand it (keep myself from fainting in public)."

"If I get fired, I won't be able to change how humiliated I will feel, and then I might kill myself."

"My failure to get a job is to blame for my bad feelings, and I'm afraid I'll never change this (get a job)."

"The chance of getting herpes is to blame for my anxiety about sex, and I'm afraid I'll never be able to change this (have an enjoyable sex life)."

Dealing with Loss of Choice

You are a total, interrelated organism; everything feeds back on itself. The cause creates the symptoms, and the symptoms feed back and further energize the cause. You create your anxiety by fearing your choices will be limited, and your anxiety then actually limits your choices by narrowing your awareness. By acting *as if* what you fear is true, you often bring it about. A good example is the often-told story of the salesman and his missing jack.

A salesman had a flat tire on a deserted highway and discovered that his jack was missing. He saw a lighted farmhouse in the distance and, thinking the farmer might have a jack, he set out for the farmhouse. As he was walking, he began to imagine that the farmer was hostile and would refuse to lend him the jack ("What if he slams the door in my face?"). The more he thought about the farmer, the more anxious he became. He then started getting angry at the farmer. By the time he got to the farmhouse, he was enraged. When the farmer answered the door, the salesman punched him in the mouth without saying a word.

Overcome Anxiety with Choice

The elegant way to overcome anxiety is to switch into creating your life by choice. Instead of focusing on unavailable choices or a fear of limited choices, you focus on what you want. You take responsibility for your feelings and accept the concept that, even if some future choices might be limited, you have all the choices you need to be happy and get what you want.

However, there will be times when the choice to switch out of your anxiety may be unavailable. Your primary fears ("I'll make a fool of myself") may be physically or neurologically rooted and difficult to move. Your feelings are a combination of the psychological and physical worlds. You often can't do anything directly to alter the physical reaction, or vibrations, of the emotions. Your mind is telling your body there is danger, and your body is reacting with the old survival mechanism of anxiety. Anxiety involves physical reactions (sweaty palms, racing heart, fainting, running away) that you may not be able immediately to alter simply by choosing not to be anxious. Our clients have found the AWAKE Strategy an effective method of breaking their anxiety trance.

AWAKE and Break the Trance

AWAKE consists of five steps, each one crucial to managing your anxiety:

1. Accept your anxiety.
2. Watch your anxiety.
3. Act as if you are not anxious.
4. Keep repeating these three steps until the anxiety starts to diminish.
5. Expect the unexpected and visualize what you want.

These five steps can release you from the grip of your anxiety trance.

1. Accept Your Anxiety

You can let your brain know it can turn off the red lights and silence the sirens by telling it, "Okay, I've got the message." That's acceptance. Emotions, such as your fear, are merely self-signals—messages from yourself to yourself. If you don't accept the message, the signal is intensified. If you accept the message, the signal, having served its purpose, goes away.

Needing to control what you can't control (your physical reactions) makes you feel more out of control. You escape this trap by letting go of your need to control the physical reactions. If you do this, they will soon return to their normal state. Remember, your feelings are constantly changing on their own—your attempts to change or control negative feelings prolong them.

Don't be alarmed by your anxiety. If you have not been bothered by strong anxiety before or if you have not had any anxiety for a while, the anxiety may seem more dangerous to you. This is due to the sharp contrast between the anxiety state and an anxiety-free state. Just decide to accept the feelings, no matter how strange or scary they may feel.

Acceptance helps break a common anxiety spiral. Shame over showing anxiety will create more anxiety to be ashamed of showing. To break this shame-anxiety trap, expose your anxiety ("I'm nervous right now") instead of trying to hide it.

2. Watch Your Anxiety

Awareness of your anxiety destroys it. Anxiety exists to make you aware, so that you heed the danger and take notice of the situation. Become aware and the anxiety has fulfilled its purpose; there is no longer a reason for its existence.

When you are in the middle of an anxiety trance, your awareness is constricted. You don't see current reality in its proper perspective. Something small ("The boss didn't speak to me") distorts to something big ("The boss hates me. He'll fire me and I'll end up on skid row"). An aerial view would give a true picture of the situation ("The boss didn't speak to anyone in the office today").

Self-awareness is the major characteristic of your psychological world. Being able to step back and look at yourself objectively and also look at your situation objectively is one way you can separate the physical world (events and other people) from your psychological experiences.

When you watch your anxiety ("I am watching my anxiety about my boss's reaction to me this morning. My palms are sweaty; my mind is making up things that might happen to me; my cheeks feel flushed") you avoid getting caught up in the subjective drama of it. You bring yourself back to the present, away from an invented threatening future ("The boss is going to fire me"). When you are in the present, you are able to see available choices ("My mind is racing at this moment, but I can choose to focus on my job and do what needs to be done"; "I am aware of my anxiety and how my heart and head feel; I can choose to ask my coworker to cover the phones for me while I take a ten-minute break to relax").

Awareness of your thoughts, feelings, and actions allows you to detach, or distance, yourself from them. You create a greater sense of mastery over current reality. You can use numerous methods to improve your ability to watch your anxiety.

Watch yourself watching yourself. In extreme anxiety you do this involuntarily. It is called dissociation. Paradoxically, when you choose to do this purposefully, you can lower your anxiety. For example, imagine you are sitting on the file cabinet looking at yourself as you sit at your desk ("I am watching myself as I become aware of my pulse, my racing heart, my feelings of dizziness"). Be *outside* of yourself and watch how you are performing even though you are anxious. Make your observations positive and objective ("She's putting the papers away and is taking care of business in an orderly way").

Put your self-instructions in positive terms. Replace *beware* with *be aware*. When you are anxious, tell yourself, "Be alert" or "Be awake" rather than "Don't be anxious." *Focus on what you can do,* and you will be able to decrease your sense of helplessness.

Practice self-awareness when you're feeling good. Practice prepares you for times when anxiety does occur. Tune in to your current reality as often as you can. ("Right now I'm sitting in my office chair, listening to Springsteen music, and feeling warm and comfortable").

Graph the duration of your anxiety. This information can counter your tendency to think, when in the midst of an anxiety trance, that the anxiety will go on forever.

Exercise

Rate the intensity of your units of anxiety (from 0 to 100) on one axis, and in half-hour intervals, place time on the other axis. You can also record places and precipitating events.

FIGURE 2

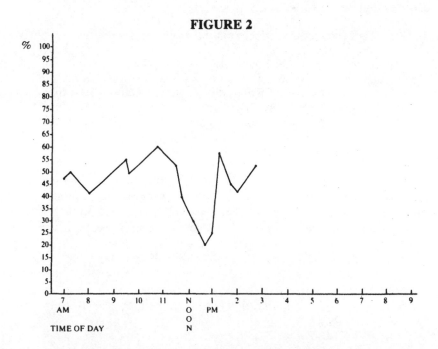

The graph will show you that *anxiety is time-limited,* is generally triggered by external situations, and is not something mysterious in itself. This will help you learn to avoid overgeneralizing and jumping to conclusions ("This terrible feeling will go on forever"; "I'm highly anxious"). When you have objective information about your anxiety and its limits, you are better able to deal with it.

When you observe your anxiety, you realize that your "peak period" lasts only so long. You may not be able to stand an anxiety that lasts forever, but you certainly can take an anxiety that is time-limited. When you know your anxiety period has a time limit, you relax. Your anxiety is automatically lessened.

Keep a diary. Record the times you choose to face situations that you previously avoided. Note the situation, your degree of anxiety in the beginning, the length of time spent in the situation, and the degree of anxiety at the end. Self-monitoring so that you acquire data about your anxious periods helps you develop a greater sense of mastery over your anxiety.

3. Act As If You Are Not Anxious

Your current reality responds to what you do, not to what you say, feel, or think. *When you are willing to do what is necessary, you can usually create what you want.* In this third step, focus on current reality and ask yourself what needs to be done to create your vision. Feel what you feel and do what needs to be done.

> "I accept the fact that I feel anxious. My vision is to go to the party, so I am going to get dressed to go."
> "I accept the fact that I feel panicked. My vision is to go to the party, so I am going to call my friend to pick me up and drive me there."
> "I accept the fact that I feel as if I am going to faint. My vision is to go to the party, so I am going to get into my friend's car."
> "I accept the fact that I feel as if I am going to faint. My vision is to go to the party, so I am going to thank my friend for the ride, get out of the car, walk up the walk, and ring the doorbell."

When you are in the middle of an anxiety trance, you often feel out of control. Your emotions and racing thoughts seem to have minds of their own. You do, however, have a say in how you move your body. No matter how anxious you are, you can still direct the long muscles in your arms and legs.

Action is the method you use to develop self-confidence and self-faith. Faith is the tool you use to deal effectively with the unknown on your way to your desired vision.

Because you focus on what needs to be done (get gas, make the list of phone calls, write the memo), you indirectly switch your attention from your anxiety and indirectly affect your feelings. When you do the job that is in front of you, your attention shifts from "what if" to "what is." Paying attention to *what is* (the job at hand) helps you eliminate anxiety.

To accept your feelings as being true and to act as if they are not is one of the secrets of creating what you want. Accept the fact that you are anxious; act as if you are not, doing what is necessary to do in the situation. Not surprisingly, the action helps to relieve your anxiety.

Dick, a client, accepted the truth that he was afraid to give a talk but acted as if he were highly confident about speaking in public. He gave the talk and it came off well. He then accepted the truth that he was afraid to ask a certain woman for a date but acted as if he enjoyed doing so. When he asked her, she said yes.

If you run, your anxiety will go down temporarily, but your primary fear will go up. If you stay and face the lion, both your anxiety and your fear will go down.

You do not have to perform perfectly, *just perform*—in spite of the anxiety. Slow down, if you have to, but keep going. If you are talking, finish your sentences; if you are reading, continue reading; if you are driving, drive; if you are working, work. Although you may act imperfectly, self-consciously, and awkwardly, keep acting.

4. Keep Repeating the First Three Steps

Each time you become anxious you have another chance to break the trance and practice the procedures:

1. Accept your anxiety.
2. Watch your anxiety.
3. Act as if you were anxiety-free.

In other words, you keep repeating the first three steps until your anxiety goes down.

This particular step in the AWAKE Strategy reminds you to develop tolerance for your anxiety. Increasing your tolerance decreases your anxiety about anxiety. By practicing, you inoculate yourself against future anxiety. People with allergies can be inoculated over and over with toxic pollens. In this way, they build tolerance in their bodies for the pollens.

Each time you experience anxiety and confront it with the first three steps of the AWAKE Strategy, you inoculate yourslf. When you see, through practice, that you can tolerate high levels of anxiety, you experience a sense of confidence—an antidote for anxiety.

Increase your tolerance by increasing the time lapse between feeling anxious and yielding to your habitual excape mechanisms (oversleeping, overeating, smoking, taking tranquilizers, or excessive drinking). Each anxiety experience you have serves to desensitize yourself to it. Keep in mind, as you practice the first three steps of the AWAKE Strategy, that *anxiety is always time-limited and will pass more quickly if you flow with it instead of fight it.*

5. Expect the Unexpected and Focus on What You Want

The worst seldom happens. This is not to say that the worst cannot happen, just that it usually doesn't. Your husband is not killed in a car accident; your son does not have leukemia; you do not have a brain tumor; you are not fired; you do not end up a homeless person. Often what happens is something you didn't count on—in terms of the everyday irrational fears that so often plague us, reality is usually friendlier than we give it credit for. People survive. If this were not true, we would not have a world population of over 4 billion people. In nearly every case, the worst does not happen.

Gary often bets a dollar about the imminence of catastrophes with his clients, and the top drawer of his desk is full of dollar bills. Gary wins because most often his clients are convinced that something awful is going to happen—but it doesn't. Over 95 percent of what you worry about never happens.

You may believe that your worrying is what prevents the feared event from happening. On the contrary, worrying is unnecessary and unproductive thinking; it is superstition. Many people even become worried because they "aren't worried." But, whatever is going to happen is going to happen whether you are worrying about it or not.

You can test this out for yourself. The next time you are worried about something, write a description of your worry in your notebook, then refuse to worry about it. When the worry returns strongly, tell yourself, "This is an experiment in living worry-free. I refuse to worry about it." Later check out your predictions. You'll find that nearly all of them don't come true. Had you allowed yourself to worry, you would have worried about nothing. Eventually you will come to realize that you don't need to worry in order to ward off bad events.

Focus on What You Want to Happen

Suppose you are anxious about an upcoming exam. You can worry continuously before you take the test, then worry during the test and until you get the results back. "I know I failed," you tell yourself. "I couldn't even understand some of the questions. Everyone else finished sooner than I did." If you end up passing the test, you've made yourself miserable for nothing. If you do fail the test, you would have failed it regardless of whether you had worried or not. Worrying did nothing to help you pass the test. If you visualize what you want (passing the test), your positive attitude can, at the very least, somewhat improve your performance because you are more relaxed.

When you visualize what you want, you can then focus on what needs to be done in the present. And if you fail, you fail not because you didn't worry but because you didn't study or because the exam was too advanced for your knowledge.

Further, it is nearly impossible to tell if an apparent setback is really a setback. Time is an important ingredient in seeing the whole picture. You cannot see the future. But you can more fully enjoy the present if you accept current reality and focus on what you want to see happen.

Create Self-Faith

To avoid anxiety completely you would never do anything for the first time. But life, by its nature, consists of one first-time event after another. You're constantly faced with risks, newness, and the unknown. You could develop a life-style of few risks and little uncertainty, and you would have less anxiety. But you would be bored. To enjoy life and be in the flow, you need a certain amount of uncertainty. Without some uncertainty life becomes flat and monotonous.

Explorers face the unknown as a way of life. They have no idea what lies beyond the ocean, over the mountain, across the river, or beyond the sun. But they have faith in themselves and in their abilities and in their vision. They set out. Even if they don't reach the land of their original destination, they always discover something.

Learn to develop the faith of an explorer. Your anxiety is due to lack of faith in yourself and in the world. You lack faith in airplanes to stay in the air, in cars to stop at red lights, in your body to function properly, and in others to act reasonably.

If you have public speaking anxiety, for example, you may lack faith in the audience's ability to understand you or in your own ability to speak or to handle questions. You may have a general lack of faith in yourself and in your ability to face adversity ("What if someone disagrees with me and asks a pointed question?"). With self-faith, you overcome your fears, and this in turn communicates your authoritativeness to your audience.

When you lack faith in others, you feel compelled to take on responsibility for their actions and feelings. You lack faith in their abilities to take care of themselves ("My son hasn't called. I'm worried about him because he's a poor driver"). You also lack faith in others' ability to relate to you ("The audience will never understand my speech") or to do their jobs ("All airplane mechanics are careless"). When you learn to have faith in yourself, you begin to have faith in others.

Across the River, Beyond the Sun

You develop faith through knowing. The Chinese have a saying, "What is difficult is not known; what is known is not difficult." You might rephrase it: "What is fearful is not known; what is known is not fearful." When you get to know what frightens you—when you make friends with it—your fear, not your respect, disappears. When you know something, you no longer expect the worst.

You probably can think of many objects and events of which you think you *should* be frightened. If nothing else, you should be frightened of electricity and poisonous snakes, right? Yet, electricians, who work around electricity all the time, are not frightened by it. They respect it, but they do not fear it. Their secret: They know all about it. As for poisonous snakes, Gary's wife used to work in the Reptile House at the Philadelphia Zoo. She and her fellow zookeepers were not afraid of the poisonous snakes even though they worked around them every day. They knew what the dangers were, what their own capabilities were, and how to avoid a potentially fatal bite.

The Anxiety Formula   Anxiety is the degree of known multiplied by the importance of loss:

$$\text{Unknown} \times \text{Importance} = \text{Level of anxiety (0-100)}$$

If you were to be placed into the middle of a rattlesnake exhibit at a zoo, you would have every right to be frightened. The unknown factor in the situation would be enormous (remember the equation: Anxiety = Unknown × Importance of the situation). However, if a snake handler gave you a course on how to handle rattlesnakes—how to pick them up, how to stay out of striking range—you could walk into the exhibit and your anxiety, although not absent, would be manageable.

When you face a fearful situation, rate the unknown on a scale of 0–10. A rating of 0 means you know everything about the event. Also rate the importance of the situation on a scale of 0–10. A rating of 10 means the situation is vitally important to you. To compute your anxiety percentage, multiply the unknown times the importance.

Take the rattlesnake cage. You are in there, and you know nothing about rattlesnakes except that you shouldn't play with them. Rate the unknown a 9 (10 if you don't know whether or not rattlesnakes are dangerous) and rate the importance of the situation a 10 (definitely life-and-death). Your anxiety = 9 (Unknown) × 10 (Importance) or 90 percent. Now you take a course in how to handle rattlesnakes. You know everything about them you can possibly know—how close to you they must be to strike, how to pick them up, how to set them down again. Your Unknown rating goes down to 4. The Importance stays at 10 (still life-and-death). But your anxiety = 4 × 10 or 40 percent, which is definitely manageable.

1. Think of something that is worrying you.
2. Rate its degree of Known-ness and its Importance (0–10) to find your anxiety score.
3. Generate ideas that would help you lower the Unknown aspect of the event.
4. Generate ideas that would make the event less important to you. Then go back and redo Step Two.

Did your anxiety go down? If not, redo the exercise in several hours.

If you can reduce either factor in the equation, you can reduce your anxiety. Usually the two factors are inversely related. When one goes up, the other usually goes down. A high Importance score ("I'm afraid I have cancer") usually has a low Unknown score ("I can check it out with a doctor"). A high Unknown score ("I don't know if I'll stumble over a word in my presentation") usually has a low Importance score ("Stumbling over a word in my talk will make little difference in the total speech").

EXERCISE

You can also lower the Importance side of the equation by making up a scale from 0 to 100. As you go up the scale from 0, list bad things that could happen to you. For instance, 5 might be a flat tire in front of your house; 40 might be having an auto accident with legal problems; 60 might be having been badly hurt in the auto accident; 80 might be having your child seriously ill; and 100 might be seeing someone you love slowly tortured to death. Label this scale "Bad Things That Could Happen to Me" and save it in your notebook.

The next time you feel anxiety about an upcoming event, get out your scale. If you are going to a company picnic and are worried that you won't remember the names of your boss's children, see where forgetting their names fits on your scale. Comparing what you are anxious about to watching someone being slowly tortured to death helps you rate the importance of a feared event much more realistically.

Mastery: Making the Unknown Known

Nearly all positive experiences in life have some link to mastery. Longevity, for example, has been attributed to a sense of mastery. Mastery is something you develop, not a set of skills that you are born with. People have talents in different areas, but everyone can have mastery experiences. Mastery is how you develop faith, how you make the unknown known, how you disprove the idea that you are helpless, how you eliminate anxiety.

When you do something for the first time, you're usually scared. That makes sense. You lack mastery in that area. But to learn to deal with new challenges with a manageable amount of anxiety, you need to learn to trust that your action (deciding to do the new activity) will lead to self-confidence, which will lead to faith. If you stay in the water long enough, you will learn to swim. Your fear of water will vanish. But if you refuse to go into the water at all, your fear will not only remain but grow.

Roger, a young man just out of college, came to Gary for counseling because he was afraid of women. "I never learned to talk to girls, because I was self-conscious. I was afraid they would laugh at me," he said. He was unhappy because he wanted to be able to relate to women, to marry and raise a family. Gary set up exercises through which Roger would learn to become a master in the art of talking to women. The first few times he tried, he panicked; he forgot the conversation starters he had practiced. He repeated a phrase to himself, though. "Okay, ye of little faith, you learned to ride a bike and do calculus, and you can learn this, too." And he tried again. Even if he felt the conversation was a total flop, he gave himself credit for trying. "I skinned my knees a lot learning to ride my bike, too," he told Gary in the midst of his program. "I just keep reminding myself to get back on that bike."

Roger eventually overcame his fear of women, and he started dating regularly. He didn't turn into Don Juan, but he was no longer so afraid of women that he avoided them. He refused to let the skinned knees bother him. And he did the mastery exercises.

Building Mastery Learning self-faith is like constructing a building. Stone by stone, board by board, the building grows into a house, school, or cathedral. Mastery experiences are your building stones—the material with which you construct your self-faith. Here is how you can create mastery experiences:

Stretch your awareness of choices. Write down three areas (social, on the job, health) in which you experience anxiety. Next, list ways that you can increase your mastery in each area. For example, if you are a new teacher anxious about speaking before the class, you might list "take public speaking lessons, study acting, work with a videotape machine" as ways to increase your mastery.

Give yourself free rein. Brainstorm! Your purpose is to stretch your awareness of your choices. You can learn just about anything if you (a) make up your mind to it; (b) break the task into small steps—no step is too small; (c) master one step at a time; and (d) do what is necessary in the situation.

Own your past successes. You have been able to handle every moment of your life up to this moment, even if you feel you handled it poorly. Review your past successes to build your self-faith ("I learned to swim, I can learn this, too").

List success experiences that are similar to the present problem ("I handled my son's illness"; "I was able to go back to school"; "I was able to handle my new job"). Periodically review the list. Use your past successes as "cheerleaders" when you feel anxious.

Use past partial successes productively. Instead of berating yourself because you have not achieved full success, ask yourself how you would handle the situation if you were placed in it again. You probably would make wiser choices. The gap between what you did then and what you would do now is a measurement of progress to date.

Remember, there are no failures, only partial success. If you ask someone for a date and he or she says no, you did something, so you were partially successful. If you stay at a new job for only one day, you have been partially successful.

Keep accurate books. Make sure you give yourself full credit for all your mastery experiences. You can have mastery experiences and not develop self-faith if you fail to incorporate your successes into your self-image because of faulty bookkeeping.

When you use faulty bookkeeping, the 30 percent you get wrong on an exam overshadows the 70 percent you get right, the two years of college you didn't finish rate higher than the two years you did finish, or the people you didn't talk to at a party count more than the people you did talk to. You let nonevents greatly outweigh events that do occur. Because you inflate your losses and deflate your gains, you always end up in the hole.

Get rid of the loss side of the ledger. Keeping track of losses is senseless anyway, because you gain something from anything you do. If you get an *F* in an English class, give yourself credit for enrolling in the class, for the days you went, and for the work you did. *For any activity you do—even if you fall below your expectations—give yourself credit.* You can always get points for experience gained.

Remember your successes. If you forget your successes, you are "always a beginner." Your self-faith fails to grow because you fail to store your successes in your memory. You are, as a result, always a greenhorn, never a veteran. One way to remember your successes is to tell others about them.

Keep "proof" of your successes. Each time you have a mastery experience, write a description of it on a 3 × 5 card and put the card in a file box. Keep the cards in a conspicuous place; carry some with you when you go out. See each card as a building block. With every card you put in the file box, your self-faith "building" grows higher and higher. Once you have filled the box, you will probably find that your building—your self-faith—is on solid ground.

The process can also be done mentally. If you are unable to write about your mastery experience at the moment, imagine yourself writing your account on a card and dropping it into your box.

Make a list, each day, of ten successful experiences you had that day. A

success is anything you intended to do and did. If you have trouble finding ten successes, you probably are not used to giving yourself credit. Remember, successes can be anything from brushing your teeth to putting on your shoes to confronting your boss—something you intended to do and did. Whether the event is significant or insignificant is not important. For building confidence, a "What I have done" list is much better than a "What I need to do" list.

Focus on specific areas of mastery. As an alternative to keeping track of all your successes, keep track of those successes that lead you to mastery in targeted areas (feeling comfortable with people, going out alone, managing money).

Move your body. Jog. Work out. Take ballet classes. As you go through the exercise, think of what you've been resisting. Movement of any kind, even walking around the block, can help you build confidence. Experiment with exercises and sports that are slightly above your present abilities in order to make your body really stretch and work. You build confidence when you master new skills.

Do what needs to be done. Wash the car, clean out the garage, rearrange your closets, scrub the kitchen floor, pick up litter in your neighborhood. By getting actively involved in mastering a physical reality, you build your psychological confidence.

See yourself with the faith that others have in you. Write down the names of three people you know well. Then write down how they show faith in you. Imagine yourself in their shoes, looking at you with confidence. For example, you might write, "My neighbor shows faith in me because she trusts me to babysit her son; she sometimes asks me to deposit her paycheck; she enjoys talking to me on the phone; she asks me for advice; she goes shopping with me." Your sense of mastery will increase when you focus on the ways other people show confidence in you. When you are in an anxiety-producing situation, look at yourself as they would look at you. You'll feel much better about yourself very quickly.

Master a feat by taking the opposite approach. At critical moments, do the opposite of what you feel like doing. If you feel like fleeing, stay. If you feel like attacking, retreat. If you feel like defending yourself, admit your flaws. A helpful aphorism to remember is: To get back on track, take the opposite tack.

Be impulsive. Surprise yourself. Get up right now and do something you've been avoiding. Make a dental appointment; call the neighbor you've been avoiding; balance your checkbook. Taking risks increases faith.

Watch others. Modeling is a time-tested way to overcome fear. Watching people you admire or people similar to yourself do what you fear helps you disprove the idea that you need to be afraid.

When Gary was in Fiji, he saw men in a firewalking ceremony walk barefoot across hot coals. He talked to them and asked them how they did it. They said that there was no trick or hypnotic trance involved. It was pure modeling. The head priest walked safely across and they followed. Later Gary took a workshop in firewalking and experienced the same phenomenon. The leader of the workshop walked across the hot coals safely, so the rest of the group, including Gary, followed. Obviously humans can walk safely across hot surfaces if it is done fast enough. But it is the modeling that gives one the courage to take the first step.

Make a list of possible models; choose one you would like to emulate. Pinpoint specifically what it is that you admire about that person. When you get into tough situations, imagine that person climbing into your skin and facing the situation. Ask yourself such questions as, "Would she take this?" or "Would he approach this situation or run away?" At first you may have to fake (act *as if*) your self-confidence, but with practice your actions turn into real faith.

See life as an experiment. Structure your experiences as experiments and you can't lose. Even if your predictions are not borne out, you gain valuable information about yourself and the world. For example, if you are unsure about which car to buy, buy the one that you predict will be the best for you. View the experience as an experiment to see if your prediction is correct or not. Even if it isn't correct, even if you have bought the least desirable car, you've still learned something ("I didn't need a prestige car"; "A van is too cumbersome to park"; "A BMW's insurance premiums are too high").

The Samurai Spirit

Take the offensive when you face the unknown. Much of life involves confronting and conflicting with others. Your opponent may be an official of the bank that lost your check, a graduate school adviser blocking your path toward your degree, a boss who constantly criticizes, or a teenager who manipulates you. Once you accept the reality that you are in an advocacy situation—if not in an outright battle—your options become clear. You have to face the opponent.

When you take the offensive, you make the unknown more quickly known. What you know has no power over you. You can take the offensive in many ways: introduce yourself, make the first call, overwhelm the other person with kindness, expand out rather than constrict in.

Your anxiety wants to convince you of your helplessness in the face of imaginary danger. Don't let it. Letting go of your anxiety and creating self-faith is a skill like any other skill. It is something that you can do now, and with practice, you can master it.

8. Let Go of Anger and Create Cooperation

nger is a powerful, frightening emotion, but it needn't be. You can bring it *into* or *out of* your life. You bring anger into your life when you emotionally react to your need and inability to change things (your spouse's nagging, your secretary's dawdling, your neighbors' barking dog). You get rapid relief from anger by moving to the choice system (choosing to create the relationship you want, choosing to hold your secretary accountable by docking her pay, choosing to speak to your neighbors or to report them to the local animal control unit). This chapter covers eleven frequently asked questions about anger and will help you learn how you can let go of it.

"Can I Get Rid of Anger Right Now?"

Yes, you can eliminate anger immediately with the "No-Lose Method." Use these three steps:

1. Find the conflict.
2. Remove the conflict.
3. Create the experiences you want.

Find the Conflict

You'll find a conflict in every upsetting situation. It arises between what you want and what you think prevents you from getting what you want. You can always identify conflict by the word *but* ("I want to sleep late, *but* the kids next door are making too much noise"). You can also have more than one conflict or *but* in a situation ("I want to have a good vacation *but* the car is broken down, I'm out of money, and all the kids are complaining").

To make the conflict explicit, write it down and underline the *but*.

"I want to find a good job, *but* they are difficult to find."
"I want my husband to love me, *but* he doesn't."
"I want to become more peaceful, *but* I don't know how to do it."

Don't exaggerate the conflict. State it clearly and honestly. Be specific. Instead of saying, "I want to be successful, *but* I'm a complete failure," say, "I want to be successful, *but* I've failed on this project."

Remove the Conflict

To resolve the conflict, cross out the *but* and replace it with *and*.

> "I want to find a good job, *and* they are difficult to find."
> "I want my husband to love me, *and* he doesn't."
> "I want to become more peaceful, *and* I don't know how to do it."

And immediately removes the conflict, and you accept your current reality.

Create the Experiences You Want

Decide what psychological and physical experiences you do want. State both visions: "I want to feel financially comfortable [psychological] and make $50,000 a year [physical]"; "I want to feel good about myself and be in a great love relationship"; "I want to feel confident and to give a good speech." Finish the creative process by choosing to create your vision and taking action to bring it about by acting as if it's true. You can use the No-Lose Method:

1. *State the conflict* ("I want to have a good meeting, but I'm angry").
2. *Remove the conflict* ("I want to have a good meeting, and right now I'm feeling angry").
3. *Choose and visualize* (imagine yourself having a good meeting).
4. *Act as if what you choose is true* (act as if you're having a good meeting).
5. *Repeat the process whenever necessary.* Remember the ACT Formula:
   Accept where you are.
   Choose where you want to go.
   Take action.

"Where Does My Anger Come From?"

Anger is a physiological response to a threat to something you want. When you are faced with danger to your physical *or* psychological well-being, your autonomic nervous system sends you signals either to fight or to take flight to protect yourself. Anger is the signal to fight. When you perceive a threat, whether real or imaginary, your heart beats faster, your adrenaline pumps, and your mind narrows to focus on the danger.

You usually become angry at perceived psychological threats. Someone threatens your self-esteem, your reputation, your peace of mind, or your sense of well-being, and you explode in anger.

Your autonomic nervous system functions outside of your conscious control. When you perceive a danger (a coworker snubs you) you will get the signal from your autonomic nervous system to fight or to withdraw.

When you operate from the choice system you are able to eliminate anger when it arises for two reasons:

1. Because you know that you create your own psychological experiences: you don't perceive others' treatment of you as a threat or danger to what you want to create. It is simply the removal of one choice. When there is no threat, there is no signal from your autonomic nervous system.
2. If you do get angry, you can relieve it immediately by accepting current reality, choosing the experience you want, and taking action to get it.

    "*I accept* the fact that I'm angry about the way he treated me."

    "*I choose* to envision a good relationship with him."

    "*I will take action* by taking several slow breaths, by thinking of some good times we had in the past, by going over to his desk and asking if he will join me for a cup of coffee at break time so we can talk, and by honestly telling him how I didn't like what he did."

"Why Does My Anger Feel So Good at Times?"

Anger feels good for a number of reasons. When you believe others are responsible for your unhappiness, your anger feels right. If events go your way, you call it "fair"; if they go against you, you call it "unfair." When you think something or someone has been unfair to you, your anger feels well deserved. All anger feels like righteous anger. You think it will set the world right, and it feels justified.

Fairness is a mental concept—a psychological label you put on physical reality. *The label comes from you, not from something outside of you.* The physical universe is neither fair nor unfair. It simply is. And the same principles apply to everyone.

Anger often is a way of getting rid of anxiety, and the relief from anxiety makes you feel good. Anxiety is the most uncomfortable feeling, the one that people want to avoid the most. Inside the bully who uses anger to manipulate others is often a scared person.

Anger feels good because you feel powerful when you're angry. This power is an illusion, because when you're angry you're usually less effective in making things happen. Anger is usually a response to feeling powerless; the anger can generate a fleeting, false sense of power.

When you are angry you are acting out your contempt for others. By cutting off others (psychologically or physically), you feel superior and better.

Even though your anger feels good, the relief is only temporary, because you can't set reality right and you aren't moving toward what you want. You can only accept current reality and look for choices in it. But anger blocks your ability to do that and usually alienates you from others.

"Don't I Have a Right to Get Angry If People Treat Me Wrong?"

You continually have the choice or response ability to get angry if you want to. Right has nothing to do with it. How other people act is their responsibility. How you think, feel, and act is yours. *The question is, Does anger help or hinder you?* Anger is usually an attempt to change other people. You can influence other people, but if you try to change them you will experience emotional distress. People may "do you wrong," but if you keep your eye on your vision and take action to create it rather than try to change people so that they will "do you right," you will have a richer, happier life.

Wayne, one of Gary's clients, had trouble with anger and withdrawal. Wayne's marriage suffered under the strain of his violent bursts of anger and his long bouts of depression. "I want to feel like somebody when I'm with my wife, but when she nags me in front of others, I just have to get angry. I can't help it. She has no right to do that to me," he said in his first session. Gary told him there was nothing wrong with wanting to feel important when he was with his wife, but a more important choice was to want to create his own experiences.

Wayne agreed to try the ACT Formula during the week and to use the No-Lose Method if he became angry. The following week he reported that he chose to feel good and have a good time, "But when I was in public and my wife told belittling stories about me, I just got mad. I couldn't help it."

Senior Beliefs and Junior Beliefs

We all have the same senior belief: "I will get what I want." Each person has his or her own personalized junior beliefs that are tied to the senior belief. Some of Wayne's junior beliefs were: "I need to belong before I can get what I want"; "I need to feel worthwhile before I can get what I want"; "I need to be accepted by others before I can get what I want." When Wayne's wife threatened one of his junior beliefs ("I need to feel worthwhile in my wife's eyes before I can get what I want"), he simply trumped it with the senior belief ("I will get what I want").

"I was at a party," Wayne said, "and my wife was having her usual fun at my expense. I began to feel my blood boil, because I had wanted to have a good time and feel good about myself. Right away I brought in my senior belief and decided to create the experience I wanted. I said to the group that I would like to have the subject changed. There was a moment of deathly silence. Then someone asked what I thought about the football play-offs. Not only had my anger gone away, but I felt great."

Wayne's wife continued to demean him in public and nag him at home. Eventually he decided to get a divorce because his wife was unwilling to participate in any kind of marriage counseling to create a better relationship. In a recent phone call Wayne reported that he was dating a woman with whom he felt much more compatible and that he was continuing to use the choice principles to create the experiences he wanted.

"Won't Anger Get Me What I Want?"

Although anger may make you feel more powerful, it usually won't get you what you want in the long run. You can at times use anger to get what you want in the short run by intimidating others. However, anger is a failure force. Anger blurs your vision, misdirects your attention, depletes your psychic energy, breeds other painful emotions, and destroys cooperation.

Anger blurs your vision. When you are angry you focus on the emotion rather than on your vision. Your prime motivation becomes to get revenge, and you forget about what you really want. Because you don't focus solely on your vision (what you want), you don't see it as clearly.

Anger misdirects your attention. Instead of looking for choices that will get you want you want, you look for ways to get even. You ruminate about what made you angry and what you're going to do about it. Because your attention is focused on these details, you overlook the details that will take you where you originally wanted to go. You get so mad at the driver who cut in front of you that you miss your turnoff. (Many accidents occur after people get angry.)

Anger depletes your psychic energy. At any one time you have a limited amount of psychological energy or focus. You need psychological energy to create what you want to happen. Getting angry is like racing your engine—you make a lot of noise and burn up fuel, but you don't get anywhere.

Anger is a major energy burner. Afterward, when your energy (ability to focus clearly) is low, you are much more prone to other psychological problems, such as apathy and depression. You slip down the emotional ladder to the lower levels. The path of least resistance is for your focus to turn toward the negative.

Anger breeds other painful emotions. When you are angry, your emotional distress can include:

• Hurt—"Why did he have to say that to me? I thought he liked my work."
• Fear—"I want to ask her out, but she might say something that will set me off."

• Frustration—"I could kill the people who manufacture junk like this. I'm so sick and tired of buying cars that turn out to be lemons."
• Resentment—"If it weren't for her, I'd have been a success."
• Surface communications—"I'm afraid if I really say what I mean she'll get angry at me and we'll have a fight."
• Low self-esteem—"I'll do just what they want so no one will yell at me and make me lose my temper."

Anger destroys cooperation. If you are chronically angry, people will avoid you. No one wants to form a lasting collaboration with someone who is always angry. Problems with anger are a significant reason for inability to keep relationships going and a major reason many people are unsuccessful on their jobs and in their careers.

"Won't Anger Get Other People to Do What I Want?"

Getting angry is a manipulation tactic to change others. Manipulation occurs when you say or do something you believe will cause an emotional reaction in others—make them feel good or bad—and thereby prompt them to act as you want. Needing to change others naturally leads to manipulation. If you think others prevent you from getting what you want, you feel you must emotionally maneuver them into doing what you want. Anger is a common manipulation tactic because most people are easily manipulated by it ("If I don't have dinner ready at six sharp every night, my husband gets upset"). Use the following manipulation inventory to see how you manipulate others and how others manipulate you.

Manipulation Inventory

Answer the following questions using this scoring system:

0 = Almost never
1 = Seldom
2 = Often
3 = Most of the time
4 = Always

1. I imply that the other person is wrong ("How could you do something like that?").

            0   1   2   3   4   5

2. I imply that the other person is immature ("Don't you know anything?")

            0   1   2   3   4   5

3. I imply that others are stupid ("Everyone knows that").

            0   1   2   3   4   5

4. I imply that others are the cause of my problems ("How come you didn't remind me about the meeting?").

                0   1   2   3   4   5

5. I use praise ("No one can help me the way you can").

                0   1   2   3   4 · 5

6. I put people in double binds so that whatever they do is wrong (if they call: "Why did you call now?"; if they don't call: "Why didn't you call?").

                0   1   2   3   4   5

7. I use blackmail or threats ("You won't do that if you know what's good for you").

                0   1   2   3   4   5

8. I set others up to lie ("You would never do anything terrible like that, would you?") and then catch them in the lie.

                0   1   2   3   4   5

9. I act helpless ("I can't do it on my own").

                0   1   2   3   4   5

10. I cry ("I'll stop crying if you'll stay with me").

                0   1   2   3   4   5

11. I get angry ("It's not right!").

                0   1   2   3   4   5

12. I threaten suicide ("What's the use of living?").

                0   1   2   3   4   5

13. I say one thing ("I'll send it to you") and then do another ("Why should I do anything for him?").

                0   1   2   3   4   5

14. I act sick or I get sick ("I don't feel up to it").

                0   1   2   3   4   5

15. I make a mess ("Help me, I'm in a jam").

                0   1   2   3   4   5

16. I keep others waiting ("Just a few more days until I figure it out").

                0   1   2   3   4   5

17. I use my authority ("Because I'm your father/mother").

                0   1   2   3   4   5

18. I intimidate others ("I know what's right").

                0   1   2   3   4   5

19. I ridicule and shame others ("You're a wimp").

                0   1   2   3   4   5

20. I exaggerate my deficit ("Nothing I do works").

                0   1   2   3   4   5

21. I grandstand it ("Well, we'll just sell the house").

                0   1   2   3   4   5

22. I discount what others say ("You don't mean that").

                0   1   2   3   4   5

23. I get others to fight ("He really did you dirty, didn't he?").

0   1   2   3   4   5

24. I put others in the middle ("Your father is causing me trouble").

0   1   2   3   4   5

25. I keep repeating my point until I wear the other person down ("I understand what you're saying, but . . .").

0   1   2   3   4   5

26. I withhold crucial information ("You didn't ask me if it cost anything").

0   1   2   3   4   5

27. I escalate ordinary events into life-or-death situations ("This could ruin my life").

0   1   2   3   4   5

28. I always try to be one up on others ("Let me tell you what happened to *me*").

0   1   2   3   4   5

Add up your score:

0–10	=	Manipulation is not a problem.
11–20	=	Manipulation is a moderate problem.
21–30	=	Manipulation is a significant problem.
31 or above	=	Manipulation is a major problem.

Aggressive people use anger to manipulate others (make them scared); passive people use withdrawal to manipulate (make others feel sorry or guilty). Withdrawal is an attempt to get just far enough away from others to make them feel responsible for you. By assuming a forlorn look, you ignite others' rescue fantasies ("I can't let him feel so bad").

Tony, at fifteen, was an expert at manipulating adults. His parents brought him to Jim for therapy because they were concerned about his temper tantrums and poor grades. He adopted an "I couldn't care less" attitude around the house and projected an image of "nothing matters."

Tony and his parents were involved in sophisticated manipulations. Each tried to maintain power over the other by seeing who could make whom feel worse. The parents wanted Tony "to care," so that their anger and punishments would make him feel bad and act the way they wanted. When they took away privileges, such as the phone in his room, Tony would say, "Why not take the rest of the stuff while you're at it? Who needs it?" They were locked in a stalemate, each trying to change the other by anger and withdrawal.

Jim asked the parents if they thought their anger was achieving their vision of a cooperative family. They said they would be willing to try the choice system since their approach wasn't working. Tony also admitted that his methods of withdrawal and anger were not getting him what he wanted (to be more independent). In a joint therapy session, the three of them agreed to begin stating plainly to each other what they wanted.

When Tony and his parents stopped using anger to get what they wanted, they were able to cooperate with each other to create what they wanted—more quiet in the house, fewer restrictions on Tony's weekend time, more communication about family issues.

Tony's parents stated that they wanted their evenings to be free of the incessant rock music Tony played in his room. They told Tony they would help him buy a good set ot headphones in exchange for some yard work. Tony stated that he "just wanted to quit being treated like a baby." His parents agreed to later curfews on Friday and Saturday nights and also told him he was free to schedule his own weekend homework time. They wouldn't make going out contingent on whether or not his homework was done. They agreed to have a regular family meeting once a week. Any member of the group could bring up an issue by stating what he or she wanted. The others would then help that person find ways to achieve the result in a way that would please everyone. They agreed to help each other try to focus on actual choices. For example, in one of their first family meetings Tony said he wanted his father to let him practice driving on back roads. His father was unwilling to do this because it was against the law. But he agreed to begin teaching Tony about the car and letting Tony help when he worked on it. He also picked up a manual of traffic regulations and spent time each evening helping Tony study for his driver's test.

Anger is the change (blame) system in action. The *Los Angeles Times* recently had an article on boxer Bruce Curry:

> . . . Curry was arrested Thursday after he allegedly got into a fight with Reid [his manager] and then fired several shots at him. Reid was not hit by any of the shots. . . . Curry was allegedly angry with Reid over the title fight loss to Bill Costello and blamed Reid for his 10th-round knockout.

Although homicide is less common than suicide, it is another, final act in holding others responsible for your life. One of Jim's patients at a hospital where he works felt justified in trying to kill two recreational therapists. They had scheduled a meeting at the same time he wanted to work on his projects. "They" had prevented him from doing what he wanted, so "they" were responsible for his feelings.

Many explanations have been given for the high rate of violence in America, but the possibility that murderers kill because they blame others for their problems is often overlooked. A man who killed twenty-one people in a fast food restaurant was mad at the world. According to the *Los Angeles Times,* he "blamed such external forces as former President Jimmy Carter, the Trilateral Commission, high interest rates and the Federal Reserve Board for his career failures."

You usually start to manipulate others when you feel powerless to change a situation. It's a last ditch effort because you don't know what else to do. Your anger is an attempt to gather strength to overcome your adversaries. Anger is an admission that you lack other means for getting what you want.

Power plays are lose/lose situations ("I'll make him marry me by getting pregnant"). You may think you'll be top seal on the warm rock, but both of you end up in cold water.

Although you can isolate yourself to some degree from others, you still have to deal with people throughout your life. If you use cooperation rather than power to achieve your goals (and theirs), everyone wins.

"What If Someone Gets Angry?"

If you cave in to avoid someone's anger, you are allowing yourself to be manipulated. *You may even train other people how to manipulate you by telegraphing what makes you feel bad.* If you're sensitive to rejection, they'll use withdrawal; if you're sensitive to threats, they will use anger.

You can avoid being manipulated by others by refusing to allow them to make you feel bad. Be responsible for your feelings. Refuse to assign your bad feelings to others ("He made me feel awful when he yelled at me"). Use the ACT Formula and the No-Lose Method to stay on target:

1. "*I accept* the reality that my boss is yelling at me."
2. "*I choose* to feel good about myself and to enjoy my work."
3. "*I will take action* by asking the boss for specific ways I can be of benefit to the company and by asking him to notify me as soon as I don't meet his requirements rather than wait till he gets angry."

Anger has a tendency to breed anger. However, by responding in kind you put yourself in a weaker position. If you get angry at someone, that person is likely to become even more furious, and an argument can escalate into a war. If someone who is trying to manipulate you gets *any* emotional reaction out of you, you usually end up losing.

Take the initiative and set the emotional tone. If you have to deal with angry clients, customers, employees, or family members, your best bet is to see if you can raise the emotional tone of the interaction. Irritation, annoyance, boredom, and interest are the emotional states above anger.

The best way to raise the emotional tone is to ask the angry person questions in a calm manner. A good question is, "Is there anything else bothering you?"

After repeatedly stating what is making them angry, people generally lose steam; their anger turns to irritation, and they eventually get bored with what originally made them angry. At this point, they often become interested in solving the problem.

Anger with the threat of violence is usually used to maintain a power position. Angry people often strike out and can physically hurt you; their manipulation thus becomes physical. They try to make you fear their anger. Others may also try to use power over you ("If you don't do what I want, you'll be sorry"), but you always have the choice not to go along. Accept your reality and look within it for choices. Gather facts that can help you. Are there shelters for battered women near you? What are their phone numbers? If you call the police, how quickly will they arrive? Can you afford to move away from abusive neighbors? Would marriage counseling help resolve the continuous bickering between you and your spouse?

Don't be helpless. The area where you feel the most powerless is often precisely the area where you have more ability than anyone else to get what you want. A woman terrorized by her thirty-year-old alcoholic son at first felt powerless to protect herself. She then saw that in reality she had the ability to prevent both his psychological and physical abuse. She got a police restraining order and called the police to come and intervene whenever her son came around drunk.

You can choose what you want in life and create it. Make the choices that will take you there, even if you need to make such major choices as divorce or relocation.

"Isn't Anger at Myself a Good Way to Get Motivated?"

Anger can be a strong motivator, but the costs are high. Using emotions to manipulate yourself has some serious drawbacks:

• You turn your life over to your feelings instead of to your creative ability to choose what you want to happen. You let your feelings "wag the dog."
• You have to keep the strong negative emotions at high intensity lest you lose your motivation once the emotions drop.
• You make yourself more vulnerable to being manipulated by others.
• You undermine your self-esteem, waste your energy, and give your mind conflicting messages ("I'm a terrible person for doing that, but I'm also a good person who will never do it again").

Anger is unnecessary. You can set limits with others ("If you don't do your job, I'll let you go"; "If you go out with others, I will no longer go out with you") without having to get angry. You can be honest without having to use anger to override your inhibitions. You can motivate yourself with the vision of what you want to do rather than with anger at what you didn't want to do.

"Isn't It a Good Idea to Express Anger to People Who Make Us Mad?"

Although a whole school of thought suggests that you are better off when you tell others off, a great deal of recent research has found the opposite to be the case. Social psychologists have been studying what is called "expressed emotionality"—this is where people "let it all hang out" and verbally express their hostility. In recent studies researchers have found that mental patients who return to homes with highly expressed emotionality are much more likely to have relapses than those who return to homes with low expressed emotionality. Recent research has also shown that this detrimental effect similarly affects depressed people and people trying to lose weight. When others try to nag the depressed person into being happy or the obese person into losing weight, the problem generally gets worse, not better.

If you are in the position of having someone use anger or some other expressed emotion to change you, be aware that you will have an inclination to do the opposite of what they want. You can end up in a no-win situation if it's a matter of problem behavior you're trying to deal with— either you do what they want and you lose, or you continue with the problem behavior and you lose. The way out is to *do what's in your best interest* in spite of what they are doing ("I'm going to lose weight even if you are nagging me to lose weight"; "I'm going to get up and get active despite the fact that you're angry at me for staying in bed").

Other researchers have found that freely venting your anger corrodes relationships and breeds more anger, not less. Psychologists Jeanette and Robert Laver studied what makes a happy marriage. Only one out of 300 happily married couples reported that they yell at each other.

The happy couples in the study emphasized the importance of restraint in expressing emotions. A salesman with a thirty-six-year happy marriage gave a typical response: "Discuss your problems in a normal voice. If a voice is raised, stop. Return after a short period of time. Start again. After a period of time both parties will be able to deal with their problems and not say things they will be sorry about later."

"How Can I Prevent Anger?"

There are five constructive ways you can prevent anger in yourself:

1. Let go of expectations.
2. Be accountable.
3. Make a decision.
4. Be honest.
5. Create cooperation.

Let Go of Expectations

Negative and positive expectations blind you to the real opportunities for happiness and achievement that exist in current ability. They undermine your vision. When you expect the specific means to something ("Bill is the only one I could be happily married to"), you overlook your choice of means. If that particular "how" doesn't happen and you get angry, you blind yourself to the other "hows" that may get you what you want (other people with whom you could have a satisfying relationship). If what you want doesn't happen the way you expect it to, you believe that it will never happen.

Expectations are different from your visions. Expectations often lead to failure. Expectations usually revolve around one of your habitual side issues (worth, control, trust, perfection, belonging, achievement). You start to expect you'll get (or won't get) some psychological commodity you believe you need.

The way out of the expectation trap is to focus on the vision you want to create ("I want to feel good about myself at the party"), not on "how" or "if" it will happen. Expect the unexpected and focus on your vision. Separate your expectations (what you think should happen) from what you want to create.

For example, let go of the expectation that your vacation will be perfect (no car trouble, clean hotels, good weather), and hold the vision that you will find ways to enjoy yourself no matter what happens on your vacation. Let go of the expectation that everyone will laugh at you if you ask a stupid question in class, and hold the vision that you will seek and gain knowledge from the class. Let go of the expectation that someone will ask you out on Friday night, and hold the vision that you will enjoy yourself Friday night whether you are asked out or not. Life is full of surprises. The best overall stance is to *expect nothing and get ready for everything.*

Be Accountable

You did something directly or indirectly to bring about the situation that triggers your anger. Maybe you failed to look at all the possibilities before you jumped into a project. Because you didn't look at the possibilities (the project could last a full year; the project could involve financial sacrifice; it could involve significant time away from home) you are caught off guard. You get angry at the project leader or at your coworkers, who don't seem to be pulling their share of the load, or at your family, who can't understand your absences. If you look objectively at the situation, you can see the role you played ("I didn't pay attention to all the ramifications of getting involved in the project").

When you hold yourself accountable, you can more clearly see what to do about the situation ("I can resign from the project") and assess the price you may have to pay (misunderstanding by coworkers, hard feelings on the part of the leader). If you are willing to pay the price (relocate, look for a new job, leave your marriage, refuse to give your daughter money if she doesn't get a job), you can always do something about your situation once you learn to recognize the role you played in causing it.

One of Gary's clients, Lew, was angry because his twenty-three-year-old son lived at home, had no job, and no intentions of looking for one. Lew could have kicked him out of the house but was afraid his son would have to live on the streets and then their friends would think he and his wife were bad parents if they pressured their son to leave. Lew didn't like the alternatives, so his son stayed home and Lew stayed angry.

"Now I realize," Lew said, "that I wasn't stuck. I did have a choice, even if I didn't like it. I knew it was the choice I had to make to get my independence back. I had been fueling his dependence by my fears for him. If he wants to live on the streets, that's his choice."

He gave his son a week's notice, and although the son tried to make his father feel guilty, Lew stuck by his ultimatum. At the end of the week the son moved in with friends and took a part-time job with a gardener.

When you get angry get out your notebook and make a list of all the ways in which you are accountable for bringing the situation about. Then become choice-oriented and focus on what you can do right now to bring about what you want.

In the psychological world you can nearly always create the experience you want. In the physical world what looks like someone blocking your way is merely the removal of one choice. You may not see the choice you want, but that doesn't mean it's absent. Hold the tension between where you are and what you want, and your choices will appear.

For example, you might say, "I am stuck in this job, and I don't like it because the manager constantly checks on me. I accept this situation and hold the vision of what I want—to be in an interesting job where I am trusted." Any number of choices may appear: speaking with the manager about how to gain his or her trust, going to night school to broaden your skills, speaking with a coworker about whether or not you provide reason to be mistrusted, using a vacation day to apply for other jobs.

Or you might say, "I accept the fact that right now my marriage isn't sexually satisfying, and sex is important to me. I hold the vision of a warm physical relationship with my husband." Choices will appear according to your situation: having an honest talk with your husband, going to marriage counseling, consulting sex manuals for ways to spice up your side of it, confiding in a doctor. You may find that you need to correct your vision to "having a warm physical relationship with *someone*" if your husband is totally unresponsive to your requests to work the situation out or to your physical advances. Then your choices may involve separation, divorce, and finding ways to meet new people.

Make a Decision

Anger comes from an unwillingness to make a decision, usually because you try to avoid being accountable for your actions. When you're angry about something, you don't like the alternatives. You have choices, but because you dislike them, you pretend that you don't have any at all.

You don't have to act to get your anger to go away. Merely *deciding* on a course of action usually dispels the anger.

EXERCISE

Think back to a past episode when you were angry. Were you able to get rid of the anger? Was there some decision you made that enabled you to get rid of it? Jot down in your notebook any methods you used.

You probably can recall how your anger disappeared once you decided what you were going to do. You anger evaporates whether or not you act on your decision, because decision, not action, alleviates anger.

Many angry people decide to sue someone. Making the decision to go into court reduces the anger, even though in most cases the person does not follow through with the lawsuit. After you make a decision and your anger has subsided, you can see whether the decision is really in your best interest. Your first decision is usually reactive and self-defeating. It doesn't serve the result you want, but you can get major reductions in anger with almost any decision.

Be Honest

You may be afraid to express directly what you want because of possible repercussions. But when people have to guess what you want, they may guess the wrong way. Then you get angry or you build up resentment. Say directly what you want ("If you borrow the car, fill it with gas before you return it"; "If you agree to pick me up for the meeting, I would like you to be on time"; "I would like to volunteer for the project, but I am not willing to work on weekends"), and you will stop the misunderstandings that can lead to anger.

Create Cooperation

Because you live in a world in which you must interact with other people, the best way to eliminate anger from your life is to create cooperation. Cooperation is usually needed to fully create what you want in your life.

"How Can I Develop Cooperation . . . If Cooperation Is the Opposite of Anger?"

You first need to know that cooperation is:

• Accepting—"I can accept them as they are despite what they did."
• Active—"I may make a mistake, but we'll both benefit if I get started with the project."

• Aware—"I'll be aware of her feelings and mine to help me see the choices that can help us both."
• Resourceful—"Let's see what we can each give to the project. I can help you and you can help me."
• Self-elevating—"I may make mistakes, but I can be honest about them and confident about my ability to cooperate with you."
• Honest—"I can directly say what I did to bring about the situation, and so can you, because we aren't afraid of each other."
• Independent—"Because I'm not afraid of you, I can take action."
• Kind—"Because I'm not trying to change you, I don't have to focus on your weaknesses."

To get cooperation you need to ask for it. Would you help me solve this problem?" "Can we work this conflict out together?" The simple act of asking for cooperation can create it. If you get a negative response, hold your vision of cooperation. You might ask for cooperation later, when the other person has cooled off or has had a good night's sleep. You might think up a specific act of cooperation and ask for that:

"We seem to have trouble communicating about money. Do you think we could both agree not to discuss money over dinner?"
"We're both angry over the shift in responsibilities here in the department. Could we agree to take one coffee break together next week?"

Develop a shared vision. If you have a relationship in which there is a sore spot ("We always fight over money"), develop a common vision ("All bills paid off, a savings account, cash in our wallets every Friday for the weekend"). Whenever you find a situation in which anger erupts, look for a common vision that you can create together.

Acknowledge others. Give others their due. If someone does something, acknowledge it. Let people know you appreciate them for who they are and for what they do. Listen to people when they talk to you. Let them have their say without interruption. Look them in the eye when they are talking.

Look for win/win situations. When you negotiate, set up win/win situations. Always aim for both sides to get what they want:

"You want to go away for the weekend and I want to stay home and work, so you can go by yourself and I can stay home."
"You and I both want to chair the committee. Can we work out a way to divide the job so that the experience is fulfilling to both of us? I enjoy public relations work and would be willing to support you for chairperson of the committee if you would appoint me head of the public relations subcommittee."
"I know you have trouble getting to work on time because of your mother's health. I'll be happy to cover your desk first thing in the morning in exchange for an afternoon off once a month."

You will find the cooperation that is developed more than compensates for the time you need to create a win/win situation. In the long run what you gain (good feelings, friendship, respect, loyalty of others) will accelerate your progress toward your vision.

Avoid blame. Be aware of those times when you have switched onto the blame track. Switch immediately to the responsibility track. Blame is useless. It gets you nowhere.

Keep agreements. When you commit to something, do it. If you don't think you can keep an agreement, don't commit to it. When you come through for others, they will usually follow through for you.

Reward others. When someone has done something for you, tell them but also reward them. Give them a smile or a pat on the back. Take them to dinner or buy them flowers. People like to be rewarded. If their efforts toward cooperation with you are met with indifference, they will have a tendency not to make the effort to cooperate in the future. Reward your own efforts, too. Tell yourself, "Good job," or "Way to go." Buy yourself a new book, a new outfit, or a bouquet of flowers for your desk.

Be open to all. Include rather than exclude. You nearly always win when you include people. All people won't be your closest friends or your wisest advisers, but you gain when you are open to the "otherness" of all people.

The man at the desk next to yours may be quiet and hard to get to know, but if you remember to greet him, invite him to join the crowd for lunch occasionally, and are open to his attempts (however subtle) to be friendly, you will find you've gained an acquaintance, maybe a friend.

Perhaps you volunteer at a school lunchroom and work with a woman who speaks little English. If you are open to her differences ("How do you say *eggs* in your language?") and find points of common interest ("Aren't the children noisy today!" "These cookies look delicious, don't they?") you will have created a relationship that is pleasant. Your experience in the lunchroom will be positive instead of negative ("I feel so uncomfortable around her").

Look for the good. In every situation, look for the good that has occurred rather than focus on the bad. People like to associate with positive people. They feel better about themselves and about their lives. The more positive you are, the more people will want to cooperate with you.

Avoid contempt. Contemptuousness ("Isn't her hair a rat's nest?") breeds separation, distrust, and resentment. People who constantly put someone down are assumed to be the types who put everyone down ("If she talks that way about her, I wonder what she says about me when I'm not around"). People avoid people who are contemptuous.

Be empathic. Be sensitive to the feelings of others. You don't cause the feelings of others and they don't cause yours, but you can acknowledge their feelings and offer support. Each person can create his or her own life, but when you connect your psychological world to that of others, you see the great possibilities that are within each human being.

Love. Love breeds cooperation. It is the consummate expression of the choice system. You accept people for who they are without trying to change them. You love them unconditionally and focus on the potential within them.

9. Let Go of Loneliness and Create Intimacy

Loneliness is a common painful experience. All of us feel it at one time or another. You feel lonely when you fail to connect with others on a psychological level. Even if your physical world coexists with another's, your psychological worlds are separate and disjointed. Alone or with other people, you feel lonely, isolated, and vulnerable.

When you're experiencing loneliness, you feel separated and cut off from others. Your acceptor is blocked—you're not accepting yourself or others. You're not in the flow.

Intimacy is the opposite of loneliness. Intimacy flows two ways. You accept other people for exactly who they are—whatever they say and whatever they do—and you act *as if* others accept you. You are more natural, more yourself. When you act as if the other person accepts you, you have the confidence to speak or to act because you don't assume you'll be rejected.

When you feel intimate with others, you are allowing yourself to know and be known. Knowing is how you connect with others and the world. Poet and philosopher Eli Siegel said that we get to know and like the world (and ourselves) on an honest basis by getting to know another person.

You develop intimacy by seeing how others are the same and different from you. People bothered by loneliness often say, "That person is just like me, so why bother?" or "We have nothing in common, so why bother?" Intimacy is getting to know how you are *similar and different* from others. Rather than trying to know others so you can change them, you get to know them so you can accept them, accept yourself, and accept the world.

Loneliness is caused by confusion over your degree of responsibility. You are only responsible for what you can think, feel, and act. You don't have the ability to respond for others (make them call you for a date), and they don't have the ability to respond for you (make you get out of the house and get involved with other people). If you are lonely, you are usually trying to change others (get them to ask you out, get them to involve you in activities) or hoping you'll change (get up the nerve to go to the club meeting).

To create intimacy, you first have to stop creating loneliness. In other words, stop holding others accountable for your experiences and trying to change them.

Isolation Communication: Backing Away from Others

When you think you have to change others or the world to achieve intimacy, your communication is (1) shallow, because you are afraid to say what you mean and to hear what the other person means, and (2) manipulative, because you choose words and actions to change others and yourself. Surface communication and manipulative communication create isolation and loneliness. The following symptoms of isolation communication will help you catch yourself when you start to move into the change system.

Surface Communication

Selective, Secretive Communication   Blame and fear of blame strangles a relationship. You may be so used to not saying what you really mean that you don't say anything even if it's pleasant. The other person cannot read your mind and may interpret your thoughts with total inaccuracy.

WIFE: "What are you thinking?"
HUSBAND: "Oh, nothing." (*Thinking:* "Where would be a nice place to take her tonight?")
WIFE (*snaps*): "I know better." (*Thinking:* "He is thinking about wanting to be with his friends and has forgotten all about saying we would go out tonight.")
HUSBAND: "No, really." (*Thinking:* "The hell with her, I'll go out with my friends.")
WIFE: "You're impossible."
HUSBAND: "You're always complaining." (*Thinking:* "Why is she attacking me? I don't deserve it.")
WIFE: "Well, if you would talk to me once in a while, it wouldn't be so boring around here."
HUSBAND (*getting angry*): "So you think it's boring here, do you? Well, why don't you go back and live with your mother if you want to be around someone really exciting?"
WIFE (*feeling rejected*): "You're always trying to get rid of me! You don't care about me at all."
HUSBAND (*in reaction*): "Well, if you don't think I care, why don't you get out?"
WIFE (*angrily*): "Well, maybe I will do just that." (*She storms out.*)

Later in this chapter we'll explain how to communicate in a way that connects you to the other person and avoids the kind of misunderstanding that occurred between this husband and wife.

Taboo-Loaded Communication   In the change system, you cry for the person to talk to you, and when the other person does, you cry again. You train the other person to keep it superficial by reacting emotionally with anger, tears, or withdrawal. The only topic you can discuss is the weather.

One of Gary's clients, Karen, flared up when her husband, Steve, talked to her about spending money (buying a new car; playing the stock market). He began to keep quiet about how he spent money, but his deceptions made Karen even more angry; she retaliated by keeping Steve in the dark about her life.

Taboos encourage deception, and deception feeds back into the negative emotionality of the situation. You refrain from saying something because the topic causes the other person to get angry; then they get angry because you didn't say anything—and vice versa. But you don't talk about your deteriorating relationship, so the relationship continues to go downhill.

Talking for the Other   Steve and Karen stepped on each other's lines and constantly talked for each other ("What Karen is trying to say is"; "What Steve really means is"; "What she really thinks is"; "What Steve is trying to get at is").

Gary asked them to begin speaking only from the first person ("*I* think that . . ."; "*I* feel that . . ."). Karen found it hard to do at first but was willing to try. "At one point I was starting to interpret Steve's sentence when I realized that I wasn't speaking from the first person. I kept quiet and was surprised, as I listened to Steve finish his sentence, that what I had thought Steve was going to say wasn't what he said at all." Steve said he felt liberated from having to rescue Karen from appearing foolish. When he didn't try to rescue her by speaking for her, he realized that what she was saying wasn't foolish at all.

When Steve and Karen stopped trying to say what the other was thinking or feeling, they began to communicate. They were able to talk *to* each other rather than *at, for, up to, down to,* and *around* each other. They chose to respond not for the other person, but for themselves. It was the beginning of their "relationship" relief.

Talking Through a Middleman   When you are afraid to be direct and honest in your communication, you often elicit the help of a middleman ("You tell him for me"). You ask others to rescue you ("Would you tell the mechanic this is shoddy work?") and to run offense for you ("By the way, if she calls, tell her I won't go because she snubbed my mother").

Once direct communication goes, you have to rely on manipulation—anger, silence, or withdrawal—to get your point across. The relationship deteriorates even further and you psychologically back away from each other. A wall goes up.

Lying Dishonesty by omission (withholding the truth) or commission (telling an untruth) is a byproduct of the change system. You don't tell the truth because you want to control the outcome. Adrienne Rich, in her book *On Lies, Secrets and Silence,* says, "The liar lives in fear of losing control. She cannot even desire a relationship without manipulation, since to be vulnerable to another person means for her the loss of control. The liar has many friends, and leads an existence of great loneliness."

If others' displeasure can make you feel bad, you feel that you have to tell them what they want to hear. Lying becomes the only option to feeling bad. When you fail to tell the truth, minor issues escalate into major ones.

You reserve honesty as a last ditch defensive weapon. You use it to hurt others and to get the upper hand ("Someone like you who would cheat on his business partner has no business trying to talk me into investing"). The solution is always to say what you want and let the chips fall where they will.

Fast Talk—Being a Con Artist If you are highly verbal, you can use fast talk to manipulate others.

WIFE: "I want you to help out more with the yard work."
HUSBAND: "I want to help you, but we both know you lack self-esteem. And the only way you'll ever get any respect for yourself is by taking on and carrying out duties. If I were to start doing more of your jobs, I would be robbing you of your chance to develop self-esteem. I love you too much to let that happen."

Tuning Out When you are scared to rock the boat or to make waves ("One false move and I'll tip over and drown"), you avoid making waves at all and become watchful of what you say. Your messages become weak, complex, and peripheral.

You tune others out because it's the only way you can get them to change. By refusing to listen to the other person, you force your way on them. If that maneuver fails, you withdraw until you get your way.

Explosive Words Tuning out is a natural defense against the belief that words can hurt you. If you think they can hurt you, you think they can hurt others, so you use words hurtfully ("You're just like your mother"). Explosive words lead to big blowups. You will find it helpful to make a list of explosive words so that you can learn to avoid them.

Argument Arguments are staples in the change system. You take the offensive to change others and the defensive to resist being changed. If you are afraid of getting close to others, this is a way to stay connected but distant at the same time. Rather than accepting differences, you try to mold others into your image.

Side Effects of Isolation Communication

Loss of Spontaneity When communication breaks down, spontaneity goes. You begin to rehearse what you're going to say ("If he says _____, I'll say _____"; "When she says good morning, I'm going to say _____"), and you become overconcerned with saying things perfectly so that you can make an impression, get revenge, or appear brilliant. Being obsessed with what you are going to say hinders communication because you stop listening and responding to what you hear. You speak from a script that you've written in advance.

Affairs The probability of extramarital affairs increases as communication decreases. People usually have affairs to avoid the painful interactions in their marriage and to make the contact with something that they feel is missing in their marriage.

At the beginning of an affair, you do not feel responsible for the other's feelings, so you're not trying to change the person. You feel free to be yourself and can spontaneously express what you're thinking and what you're feeling. You have no strings attached. Your honesty feels great, but it's usually short-lived. Most often you soon start taking responsibility for the other person, and once you do that, you're back in the hurt/loneliness cycle.

How Do You Communicate?

Use the following checklist to see where your communication breaks down. Ask your partner or a friend also to assess you on each item.

Loneliness or emotional isolation, is the natural result of distancing from others. It is a protective mechanism: Distancing represents a logical step in the unrewarding change system. You create what you expect ("Others hurt me, so I have to move away"). If others are responsible for your pain, you have to attack them or distance yourself.

	Self	*Other*
1. I keep secrets.	☐	☐
2. I lie.	☐	☐
3. I get angry.	☐	☐
4. I make faces (grimace).	☐	☐

	Self	Other

5. I say one thing and mean another. ☐ ☐
6. I tune others out. ☐ ☐
7. I censor what I say. ☐ ☐
8. I protect others' feelings. ☐ ☐
9. I use a middleman. ☐ ☐
10. I'm indirect. ☐ ☐
11. I tiptoe around sensitive issues. ☐ ☐
12. I am defensive. ☐ ☐
13. I say what others want to hear. ☐ ☐
14. I use diversion. ☐ ☐
15. I try to phrase everything in the perfect way. ☐ ☐
16. I rehearse what I'm going to say. ☐ ☐
17. I blame. ☐ ☐
18. I say I agree even if I disagree. ☐ ☐
19. I use the truth to hurt. ☐ ☐
20. I pick poor times for serious discussions. ☐ ☐
21. I hang the phone up on others. ☐ ☐
22. I pout. ☐ ☐
23. I clam up. ☐ ☐
24. I rant. ☐ ☐
25. I grandstand ("Okay, then we won't go!"). ☐ ☐
26. I obscure points. ☐ ☐
27. I cry. ☐ ☐
28. I attack. ☐ ☐
29. I use guilt. ☐ ☐
30. I use shame. ☐ ☐
31. I talk down. ☐ ☐
32. I scold (shake my finger). ☐ ☐
33. I belittle. ☐ ☐
34. I'm sarcastic. ☐ ☐
35. I hit sensitive spots. ☐ ☐
36. I play dumb. ☐ ☐
37. I mind read. ☐ ☐
38. I exaggerate. ☐ ☐
39. I say, "In other words . . ." (rephrase to my benefit). ☐ ☐
40. I cover up. ☐ ☐
41. I play wise (fake what I know). ☐ ☐
42. I talk for others. ☐ ☐
43. I sigh a lot. ☐ ☐
44. I roll my eyes. ☐ ☐
45. I'm pathologically honest. ☐ ☐
46. I'm evasive. ☐ ☐
47. I mince words. ☐ ☐

	Self	*Other*
48. I use explosive words.	☐	☐
49. I psychoanalyze.	☐	☐
50. I dig at others.	☐	☐
51. I'm relentless at getting my way	☐	☐
52. I'm ambivalent ("Yes and no").	☐	☐
53. I answer a question with a question.	☐	☐
54. I always get the last word.	☐	☐
55. I use double-talk.	☐	☐
56. I throw tantrums.	☐	☐
57. I invalidate ("You don't really mean that").	☐	☐
58. I click my tongue.	☐	☐
59. I talk under my breath.	☐	☐
60. I act victimized.	☐	☐
61. I act cute.	☐	☐
62. I get up and leave.	☐	☐

EXERCISE

Get out your list of three disappointments. See how distancing communication played a role at bringing the events about. Now look at the event and see how accountability would have enhanced your communication and prevented the problem from arising.

How to Develop Laser Communication

Communication is connecting, the way to develop intimacy. It is the bridge (of words, gestures, facial expressions, touch) by which you reach another person. When you use choice to create what you want, you communicate with synchronization, purity, and directness, like the laser. Laser communication is:

- Honest—*how* you communicate
- Timely—*where* and *when* you communicate
- Accurate—*what* you communicate
- Unifying—*why* you communicate

Use the following steps to develop laser communication in these four areas.

How to Achieve Honesty

Be specific. Stay at the concrete level ("When you borrow my sweater, please have it cleaned before you bring it back") and avoid the abstract ("These situations always turn out like this"). Stick to the present ("This is how I feel right now"); avoid dragging up the abstract past or future ("You've never treated me right from the day we met").

Be direct. Say what you mean and mean what you say ("I love you and I want to make the relationship work"). Hinting or expecting the other person to play Twenty Questions with you diffuses and confuses what you want to say. The more direct you are, the better.

Ask for what you want. Free yourself of your bias against asking. People are not mind readers, and if you expect the other person to guess what you want, very likely you won't get it.

Be straight. Make your thoughts, feelings, and actions move together. Get rid of double messages ("I'm not questioning your decision; I just want to know why you made it"). Be aware that ambivalence ("I want to do it . . . but I don't") is an attempt to avoid accountability.

Be clear. First think about what you want to tell the other person, then tell them in the straightest and simplest way you can ("I would like to have this job"). Although *too much* planning can hamper communication (as when you rehearse what you are going to say), *some* planning can help you. Too much planning is trying to control how the conversation will go despite what the other person may or may not say. "Just enough planning" is having your facts (current reality) and knowing the ideas you want to get across (your vision). It also involves taking the other person into account (for example, considering if your boss is more open to discussion before or after lunch). You usually have to create and adjust the conversation to get the result you want.

Create a climate for honesty. Encourage honesty in the other person. Instead of casting your eyes heavenward and muttering under your breath when someone says something you dislike, reinforce the person for being open ("I don't like hearing it, but I'm glad you brought it up").

Tell the truth early. Even if the other person becomes angry, tell the truth. Refuse to let the other person's attempt at manipulation or denial take away your choice to be honest. Don't lie, even if you think it's going to get you what you want. It won't.

Tell the appropriate truth. To see whether or not the truth is appropriate in a situation, ask yourself three questions: (1) Does the person need to know the truth? (2) Am I giving them a fair representation of the whole truth? (3) Can I tell the truth in a kind way? If the answer is yes to the three questions, then tell the truth.

Timeliness—Know When to Raise the Issue, and When Not To

Use common sense. Be sensitive to time and place. If you need to resolve a matter of any complexity, be aware that it will take at least an hour. Don't try to resolve a conflict as you walk up the porch steps to a dinner party. If your partner has only ten minutes to catch a plane, wait until a more appropriate time to bring up a complex issue.

Communicate to the other person when you are ready to move on. If you just want to get back at someone, wait. Many times the mere passage of time aids resolution.

Stick to one topic. Topic jumping diffuses energy and confuses the issues. Be aware of what you are talking about and stick to it ("Okay, we can deal with that in a moment, but let's finish this first").

Be Accurate

Clarify. If you are unsure of what is being said, ask for clarification ("Please elaborate on what you mean by that"). Avoid inference, assumptions, and jumping to conclusions ("I'm not really sure what he said, but he must have been criticizing my work because that's the kind of boss he is"). Develop a mental picture of what the other person is saying. If the picture is fuzzy or unclear, ask the person to clarify it.

Go to the source. If you hear a rumor or remark that affects you, check it out with the primary person ("I heard you have a problem with my work. Is this true?"). Secondary sources have only secondary reliability.

Avoid the words *always* and *never.* They are red flag words and are rarely accurate: "You *never* do the dishes!" "Yes, I do. I did them last week." Already the discussion is off-center. A more accurate statement is: "I'd like to discuss the housework and tell you what I would like to see happen."

Speak from the first person. Because you can only think, feel, and act for yourself, speaking from the first person is more accurate than from the second person. "You ignore me" may seem accurate to you, but to your partner it may not be because he thinks he is just reading the newspaper. A more accurate statement would be, "I would like you to talk with me when I get home from work, rather than read the paper. What can we do about it?"

Err on the side of inclusion. Decide to include information, even if you don't need it all, rather than to exclude it for fear of appearing foolish. If you're unsure about what is being said, say so. If you're not sure the other person understands you, repeat what you said. It is far better to appear foolish than to miss important information ("I know this is the third time I've asked, but I don't understand what you're saying").

How to Achieve Unification

Listen. Tune in to what the other person is saying even if what you hear is painful. When you connect through listening, you create a climate in which the other person can be more honest, accurate, and timely with you. When you really listen, you can look within the relationship for what you need to improve the relationship.

Keep in touch. Absence does not always make the heart grow fonder.

Look directly at the other person. Use touch if you can. If the other person is at some distance, use frequent phone calls and letters to keep the bond between you strong.

Collaborate. Avoid secrets or hidden agendas. Refuse to keep information from someone to whom you're close. Collaborate ("How can we handle your mother's drinking?") with others rather than sabotage them ("He wants me to be nice to his mother, but if she takes a drink I'm going to be cold to her").

Be creative. Brainstorm ways to communicate. If you have trouble talking to someone in the morning, leave notes. Switch roles in order to understand the other side. Try solving a problem nonverbally.

Draw pictures of how you feel, then draw pictures of what you would like to see happen. Play music with lyrics that express what you want. Play a game of charades, acting out what you feel, what you think the other person feels, what you want, how you could solve the problem together. Do an "interpretive dance" together and try to reach a resolution by the end of the dance.

Let others be right. You can eliminate more than half of your communication difficulties by telling the other person "You may be right." You are verbally giving them the right to their own choices, the right to see the world as they see fit (which is theirs anyway). You aren't caving in, because you still have the right to your choices and the way you see the world ("You are right, but this is how I see it"; "You are right, but this is how I am going to do it"). Letting the other person be right sets the stage for cooperation.

Use after-action talk. After heated discussions, talk about how you communicated ("We both seemed to get defensive about the custody issue, didn't we?" "Did my comparing you to your brother help you or make you angry?" "I felt defensive when you kept answering my questions with a question"). Get feedback from the other person. Welcome it and learn from it. After-action talks can normalize confrontations and iron out communication problems.

Give concrete feedback. Use no-fault criticism. Ask if the person wants your input. If they say yes, stick to the facts on the concrete level without blaming ("I've noticed that when you are with your mother, you . . .").

Choose to accept criticism openly from others. Listen and be aware of how you can gain from others' feedback. No matter how unfair, exaggerated, and manipulative someone's remarks might be to you, you can nearly always learn something from it. When your feelings are hurt, you often have a chance to accept some useful truth about yourself. If you operate from the choice system, you can ask yourself, "What is true here?" Others may want to throw blame at you, but you can always find some helpful information from feedback.

Let go of the past. Let go of past hurts so that you can start anew.

Become aware of the feelings about past hurts that might be clouding a present issue. Decide to act concretely in the present to create a common future:

"What do we both want in the future? What is our shared vision and common ground?"

"I was hurt when he was unfaithful to me, and I guess I'm transferring that to you. I'd like to accept that, and I would like to start fresh from right now."

"I've learned a lesson from her gossip, but I don't need to make my day miserable by harping on it, because I do have to continue working with her. I'll be pleasant to her but I'll be careful not to confide my private life to her anymore."

How to Create Good Relationships

Honesty sets the stage for a healthy relationship. Whoever you are, when you are truly yourself, you are more confident and more attractive. When you choose to create your own life, you become yourself.

EXERCISE

Imagine you are at a party and introduce yourself by saying, "Hi, I'm extremely dependent. I'm looking for someone to make me happy and to shore me up emotionally." What do you imagine would happen? Now ask yourself how you might be saying this nonverbally (not listening, keeping to yourself, not looking someone in the eye, sighing). Look at the situation objectively and decide if people would be attracted to you.

Except for rescuers, most people would move away from you. Social psychologists have found that people like emotionally independent people and dislike overly dependent people. The more self-confident and emotionally self-reliant you are, the more people will be attracted to you.

Look at the film stars who attract a solid following: Katharine Hepburn, Robert Redford, Paul Newman, Jane Fonda, Clint Eastwood. Each has an image of emotional self-reliance. Researchers at the University of Utah found that marriages based on independence, as opposed to dependence, lasted longer and were of higher quality.

The issue is not dependency versus independency but change versus choice. *Change dependence* is based on a need for others to make you happy. This tends to drive others away, and you end up lonelier than ever. *Change independence* is a need to move away from others because you believe they can hurt or control you. Your independence (self-absorption) and compulsive self-reliance are a strategy to protect yourself—you're afraid others will take over if you invite them to help you.

Choice dependency is healthy cooperation. To create anything of note and to be able to form a relationship with others, you need healthy dependence. Because you are accountable for your own feelings, others feel comfortable with you and are willing to cooperate. They move toward you. *Choice independence* is simply your awareness that you create your own experiences. You are the author of your own life and don't need others to plot it out for you.

To create a relationship, you can use the principles of acceptance, vision, and choice. You tap into your intuition for the type of relationship you want. You hold that vision, and then you make the choice to have it and follow your hunches to make it happen. Once you start to meet people, you need to focus on knowing them.

How to Build to Intimacy

Use the following eleven techniques to enhance the type of knowing that leads to intimacy.

Decide to know the other people in your life instead of taking them for granted. When you meet other people or go on dates, rather than trying to impress or possess them, ask yourself how you could get to know them better, then make that your aim. When you want to get to know people, listen to them. They, in turn, will usually want to know more about you. They will begin to listen to you, and true communication will be established.

Interview people. Become a focused listener. You can practice on strangers you meet or people you see every day. Interview others with goodwill—use what they say as a way to get to know them, not as a way to put them down.

> "You seem to enjoy meeting the people who come through your line. How long have you been a cashier?"
> "You seem tired today. Did you have a hard day?"
> "That's a lovely sweater. Are you interested in knitting?"
> "I saw your wife at the store with your grandson. Is he with you for the summer?"

Let go of your need to possess or own the other person. See how getting to know the other person can help you connect with others rather than use the other person to help you put up a wall between you and the world ("It's us against the world").

Consider how you can earn others' goodwill. Rather than looking to see how others are taking advantage of you, ask yourself what you can do for them.

Accept your insecurity with others. In all relationships there is a degree of insecurity ("Will they like me? Will I continue to like them?"). You have to be willing to accept this insecurity to get to know the person more fully.

See knowing as a process. Rather than having to know a person all at once, let the relationship develop naturally on all levels.

Be there fully. Allow yourself to be 100 percent with the other person. Don't hold back physically or be somewhere else psychologically. Look the person fully in the face and put your focus on that other person.

Be consistent. If you can't be consistent, explain why you are acting and feeling differently ("I'm in a bad mood"; "I'm feeling under the weather").

Be a true friend. A true friendship is the best basis for a love relationship. Treat a friend with honesty, appreciation, consideration, and acceptance. After a breakup people often say, "Can we remain friends?" But had they been friends to start with, they probably would not be breaking up. You create freedom by cutting the strings you put on yourself ("I should be cool"; "I have to appear noble"; "I have to be smart"; "I have to always . . ."). Imagine cutting these strings with a pair of scissors whenever you recognize you are attaching strings to yourself.

Be willing to tell the truth. Learning to tell the truth to yourself and others is necessary to create the experiences you want. To connect with others you have to tell the truth.

Not telling yourself the truth is like driving with your eyes closed. And not telling others the truth is letting them drive with their eyes closed.

Most people dislike hearing the truth—especially around sensitive areas. But most people are ultimately glad they are told the truth. At times people will react to the truth by getting angry at you or by withdrawing from you. Many clients, for example, come to therapy to hear the truth, yet take steps to see that this doesn't happen.

For example, clients train their therapists to lie to them, just as they have trained others to lie to them, by getting angry at the therapist or by having their feelings hurt. If the therapist continues to tell the truth, the client often will fire the therapist.

Many people say, "I'm successful in life because I always tell the truth," and many other people say, "The reason I fail so often is because I always tell the truth." The following are some guidelines for telling the truth in a constructive way.

• Am I telling my truth or The Truth? You get in trouble when you start to believe that you have absolute truth instead of personal opinions about what is the truth. Your best bet is to start by being humble about your ability to see the truth.
• Am I being asked to tell the truth? You are on safer ground if you have been asked to tell the truth or if your job is to tell the truth. Many people create difficulty for themselves by injecting their opinions into areas where they have not been invited. One accountant, for example, made a point of telling people in the creative department how "lousy" their work was. He couldn't understand why they disliked him since he was being so honest and open with them.

Often "telling others the truth" is just a camouflage for putting others down in order to make yourself feel better or superior.

• Are you telling the truth in a way that others can hear? You can tell the truth in an insulting way or in a helpful, matter-of-fact way. Will Rogers was liked by nearly everybody because he told the truth in a way that people could comfortably hear.

• Are you telling the whole truth? Don't slant the truth to make a point. Tell the truth as you would report the news—tell the good as well as the bad.

• Are you underestimating others? Most people discount people's ability to take in the truth. In the last few years the shift in medicine has been toward telling patients the truth. Medical professionals have found that people are much better at handling the truth than they earlier thought and that the patients function much better once they have the truth. When you tell people the truth, you are showing them that you believe they are capable of dealing with current reality as it is.

• Are you erring on the side of telling the truth? If there is a question of whether or not to tell the truth, tell the truth. Over the long run, honesty is the best policy.

• Do you want to stay in a situation where you are consistently punished for telling the truth? You may find yourself in a situation or relationship where you are penalized for telling the truth. At times you may decide not to tell the truth. You may for practical reasons want to keep a job from which you would be fired if you told the truth. Keep in mind you do pay a price for not telling the truth. Humans function better when they feel free to tell the truth. If you continue to lie, you will feel bad and may become physically sick.

Civilization has evolved because of our ability to recognize and tell the truth. If someone didn't say the emperor had no clothes, we would still be living in caves.

Feel free to be yourself. You have to be willing to be yourself. The sense of freedom can only come from you.

Love in the Change System

Everyone uses the word *love*. It can mean the best of life or the worst of life, depending upon which system you are in. If you are trying to get others to love you, your desire for a relationship is based on need ("I need you to love me"). This creates pain, not happiness. When you are half a person, looking for another half person to make you whole (and happy) you experience the following:

• Pain—"Why did she have to do that to me?"
• Frustration—"I can't get over this broken heart until I find someone new."
• Dissatisfaction—"You have to change before I can love you."
• Discontent—"I'll give to you but you owe me."

• Guilt—"I have to do this for you or else I'll feel terrible."
• Resentment—"You made me love you."
• Desperation—"What can I do to make you love me?"
• Low self-esteem—"You have to do this for me to prove that you love me."
• Fear—"I have to give this to you, or you'll be angry at me."
• Bitterness—"I've invested a lot in this relationship and get nothing back."

Love in the Choice System

When you *choose* to love, you accept others as they are. You appreciate the ways in which they are the same as you and yet different. You connect with the sameness and appreciate the differences.

You get immediate enjoyment from the love you give and receive. If you give love, no one owes you, and if you receive love, you do not owe anyone.

Love by choice is mature, sustaining, and transcends infatuation and physical attractions. Because it comes from within you, this love can be fostered and expanded. This is a love *you* can create; you don't have to fall into it. Use the steps in the ACT Formula:

1. *Accept* the other person.
2. *Choose* love.
3. *Take action* to bring that love about.

Acceptance is a large part of loving others. Accept them as they are at the moment, and accept the idea that they have the responsibility for their own experiences.

Gary's marriage to Pat improved drastically several years after they were married. Looking back on it some nineteen years later, Gary realizes that the shift was due to his accepting her as she was. When Gary first met Pat, he believed that he would be able to change her. Now he has a difficult time remembering what he wanted to change. Gary recently completed an exercise where you list twenty traits you want in a partner and then rate a possible partner on each trait on a scale of 0 to 5. The highest possible score is 100. The author of the exercise suggests that if you rate the person over 80 you should marry the person. Gary rated Pat as a 98. Once you stop trying to change someone, you start experiencing that person as nearly perfect.

Researchers have found that good marriages result from a combination of commitment and friendship. The crucial success force in a good relationship is commitment: valuing the vision of love enough to make it happen. If you devalue the other person or the relationship, you kill the commitment. If you make the choice to value yourself, the other person, and the relationship, you have committed to the vision. That commitment sets the creation of love in motion. You are already more than halfway there.

When you choose to love someone or something, you will automatically start to move up the emotional scale. Think about what you can choose to love about something you're resisting. An attitude of love will help you move closer to your vision. When you give love, you will automatically get it back.

To go the rest of the way to your vision, act *as if* you do love the person. *This is one of the most important principles in the psychological world: You can create feelings by your actions.* If you want to care for your car, your dog, your child, your wife, or your husband, then take care of them. *You care about what you take care of.* To be interested, act interested. To be enthusiastic, act enthusiastic. To create love, treat the other person in a loving way. Here are some "action" suggestions to get you started. Invent your own ways as you tune in to the current reality of your partner.

• Put your partner's welfare before your own. For example, learn to stop what you are doing when your partner asks you something. Instead of saying, "Wait a minute," do what he or she asks you to do.
• Go out for your partner's favorite food instead of insisting on having your own way when selecting a restaurant.
• See your partner's favorite movie.
• Be gracious with your partner's friends.
• Let go of your partner's weaknesses rather than hold onto them.
• Model the behavior you prefer.
• Be neither teacher nor therapist.
• Ask if your partner wants your feedback—but ask at the right time.
• Give your partner time ("I'll be glad to talk about this whenever you're ready").
• Ask yourself how you can increase your partner's range of choices ("You can come with me or not; either one is fine with me").
• If your partner closes down *your* options, *increase your own* rather than close down your partner's options.
• Seek to reconcile your differences. Attempt to see your partner's point of view and then see how you both can win.
• Seek to reconcile differences as quickly as possible. You can rapidly resolve arguments by using the ACT Formula. Ask yourself what you can do to improve the relationship through direct or indirect ways.
• Sit down with a spirit of love and calmly seek a common vision—accept your differences, choose a shared vision, and work out the details.
• See the truth in your partner's truth.
• Let your partner have the truth ("You're right from your point of view").
• Use your notebook to keep a journal of all the ways *you* subtract from the relationship: greed, fear, anger, impatience, immaturity, lack of sincerity, demands, willfulness, putting yourself first, complaining to others,

intolerance, discouragement, ignoring, taking for granted, jealousy, put-downs (for example, reading a book or watching the ball game on TV while at the dinner table), comparing to others.

• Observe yourself without judgment. Objectively ask yourself how you might cause the other person trouble.

• Be honest and assertive. Tell what you think, feel, and act. Emphasize self-honesty, not your partner's flaws ("I'm feeling ignored" rather than "You're ignoring me"). An honest blame is just about as bad as a dishonest blame.

• Appreciate your partner. Tell your partner what you like about him or her as often as possible. Place emphasis on the small things ("I appreciate your putting gas in the car").

• Be affectionate, especially when your partner is feeling down.

• Show affection and appreciation even when your partner is in a bad mood.

• Be affectionate in word *and* deed.

• Do something for your partner at every opportunity: Bring a gift, give a loving word.

• Do some secret service for your partner. *This is one of the most important suggestions of all for creating loving feelings via your actions.*

For example, do one of the other person's usual jobs (feed the dog, fill the car with gas, put his or her clothes away). Solve a problem for your partner without the person asking you to (replace a light bulb, fix a broken door, return some unwanted merchandise). Try to do one secret service each day.

Doing good for others is love in action. You can create love by doing good. John Wesley, the eighteenth-century clergyman, captured this idea in a poem:

> Do all the good you can
> In all the ways you can
> In all the places you can
> At all the times you can
> To all the people you can
> As long as ever you can.

A good relationship has a certain easiness to it. When you are in the choice system, you don't have to work at intimacy (connecting with another's psychological world). It is there for you naturally when you choose to let go of loneliness and create connections between you and others.

10. Let Go of Depression and Create Self-Esteem

I f you are depressed, you may feel that you're incapable of getting undepressed, let alone of accepting yourself. You may feel that you can't even get out of bed. Depression can be a frightening emotion because you feel so cut off from the world, as if a layer of cotton surrounds you. Depression is an overwhelming feeling—but *remember: It is just a feeling, something you can affect by how you think and act.*

Why Do We Feel Depression?

When you are happy, you focus on gain and ignore loss ("It's true I don't want to be transferred, but I'll be closer to the mountains and can ski more often"). The reverse is true when you are depressed: You focus on loss and ignore gains ("If I'm transferred, I'll lose the best view in the building"). When you are depressed, you focus on the negative and create sadness. The sadness motivates you to focus on the loss so that you will eventually accept it and get on with your life.

Depression is usually preceded by a period of demoralization, an extension of helplessness ("I can't change reality") and hopelessness ("Nothing will change it").

Demoralization and depression are malignant end products of trying to change yourself and others. It is the final resignation—something is a particular way and there is no hope that it will change. Because you need it to change, the only alternative is to give up.

You see yourself as a loser after repeated failure at trying to change and control others and the world. You lose respect for yourself and become depressed. Your need for reality to be different creates the pain of depression.

Depression is another name for low self-esteem or low self-respect. Once you regain your self-esteem, you are no longer depressed.

Rating Your Self-Esteem

Most people have trouble with self-esteem because they tie it to external events. The following are the common believed requirements for self-esteem or happiness. Rate from 1 to 10 how much of each requirement you need to be happy: "I need perfect health (10)" or "I need average good health (5)." In the next column, rate how much of each you have in your life. For your happiness score, subtract the "have" from the "need" score.

		Need	*Have*
H	health	Need _____	Have _____
A	appearance	Need _____	Have _____
P	personality	Need _____	Have _____
P	pleasure in life	Need _____	Have _____
I	in love	Need _____	Have _____
N	novelty	Need _____	Have _____
E	economic security	Need _____	Have _____
S	self-expression	Need _____	Have _____
S	status	Need _____	Have _____
		Total _____	Total _____

Score:

5 or below	=	You have high self-esteem.
6–15	=	You have moderate self-esteem.
15–30	=	You have low self-esteem.
30 or above	=	You have very low self-esteem.

To make yourself depressed, just raise the requirements for self-esteem. Keep upping the ante until self-esteem is out of reach. You might think, "I make $25,000 a year, but I need $40,000 to be happy." Then if you do make $40,000, you say, "I need $60,000."

Your desire to change things comes from cementing your self-esteem to some requirement or need. You believe you need more love, more money, more success, or more status to gain your own respect. The solution is to uncouple your psychological world of self-esteem from your stature in the physical world.

Depressed? Get Active to Get Relief

Paradoxically, the way to separate yourself from the physical world is to get more active in it. Depression is maintained by overthinking and under-acting—you have difficulty focusing on anything but the negative. When you approach the physical world (get more active), you feel more connected to the world. Your focus shifts away from your negative view of yourself and toward what you want to create. Your action activates positive memories and disproves your negative thoughts that you can't do anything. Depression is at the bottom of the emotional scale—as you get more involved in physical reality, your emotional tone can only go up.

Depression is the result of trying to escape from reality. You become self-absorbed in your thoughts and feelings. Getting active counteracts your attempts to escape. It enables you to accept and assimilate current reality.

The first step in letting go of your depression is to accept the fact that you are depressed and do what needs to be done anyway. To create more purposeful activity in your life, schedule your day. When you become depressed, your normal range of activities is disrupted. Isabel, a fifty-six-year-old woman Gary saw in therapy, was so depressed after her husband died that she had problems attending to even the most ordinary daily activities. She spent days in bed, apathetic, listless, and depressed. She saw herself as a complete loser. She filtered out anything positive ("People only say they like me because they feel sorry for me"). All she could see were the flaws and her defeats. This outlook led to the symptoms of depression (sadness, withdrawal, loss of memory, lack of concentration, physical aches and pains).

Isabel finally began to get relief when she made out and followed a daily activity schedule to create the days she wanted. She even scheduled routine activities such as brushing her teeth and combing her hair. "I may not be able to face my entire day alone, with having to learn to drive, or go out alone at night, but I can at least get through the next step on my schedule," she said at one of our sessions.

By sticking to her daily schedule, Isabel regained her confidence. She began to develop confidence in herself and in her abilities to exist alone in what to her had been a frightening world.

You can benefit from planning your daily activities in detail if you are often depressed or if you are deeply depressed. It is one way to create the life you want. The schedule gives you a sense of direction and mastery as you focus on planned activities. Don't undertake an activity just for the sake of activity. Have some result or destination in mind before you start the activity. Walk to the beach to see the sunset, not just to be walking.

Guidelines for a Daily Antidepression Schedule

• Schedule one day at a time.
• Do one task at a time. Don't worry about future tasks. If you finish one task early, engage in a pleasurable activity between tasks, such as reading or taking a walk.
• *The idea is to engage in activities, not to perform them perfectly. The benefit comes from the actual doing.*
• Plan with flexibility. If an unexpected event occurs, you may switch your plans. For example, if a friend unexpectedly calls, adjust your schedule accordingly.
• Activities that absorb your interest and concentration are best—cooking

meals, cleaning the house, taking walks, filing, making phone calls, writing letters and memos.
• If the task seems too complicated, break it down into smaller steps ("Finish annual report: (1) get out paper, pencils, and calculator; (2) complete statistical work; (3) finish introduction; (4) finish next two sections; (5) finish conclusion").
• If the task seems too overwhelming, go to more simple tasks. No step is too small. You may feel too overwhelmed even to begin the annual report. If so, write a letter, clean your desk, make the coffee, or do some filing.
• Your activity scehdule should be related to your normal activities—getting up in the morning, making breakfast, exercising, taking a walk, talking with someone, answering mail, checking the answering machine, punching your time card.
• The planned activity should not be too specific or too general. Shoot for something in between ("I'll read the paper for thirty minutes" instead of "I'll do some reading").
• The last activity you schedule for the day should be sitting down to schedule the next day's activities. Developing activity schedules may take some time. You may have to spend thirty minutes to schedule just one day.

Choose Ten Daily Depression Fighters

Another good strategy for letting go of depression is to choose ten activities that you want to accomplish every day. With this strategy you don't have to construct a schedule for each day. Look for activities you would like to do *each* day. For example, one depressed client selected the following ten activities that she wanted to accomplish daily and listed them in her notebook, where she could refer to them daily:

1. Get out of bed by 8:30 each morning.
2. Prepare breakfast.
3. Talk with someone in person or by phone.
4. Walk the dog.
5. Read the newspaper.
6. Do some yard work.
7. Make a good dinner.
8. Do something with my son.
9. Ride my exercise bike for ten minutes.
10. Go to bed.

Another client selected these ten activities:

1. Get out of bed by 7:00 A.M.
2. Ride exercise bike for fifteen minutes.
3. Prepare breakfast.
4. Get to work by 8:55.

5. Complete phone calls.
6. Walk for fifteen minutes during lunch.
7. Keep filing current.
8. Finish correspondence.
9. Watch something I like on TV.
10. Read.

When you do these activities, do them in a way that allows you to merge and connect with your physical reality.

Choose to do it. You always have the choice to act in some way. You may feel you can't get out of bed, but you can always hang your feet over the bed and dangle them.

Pay attention. When you get out of bed, get out of bed. Focus on which foot hits the floor first.

Do it with style. See if you can make an art form out of getting up as quickly as you can. Put devotion into it.

Make the activity the sole purpose of your life. Get out of bed as if it were what you were born to do.

Accept your feelings. David Reynolds, in his book *Playing Ball on Running Water*, suggests that you accept your depression and do what is necessary (get out of bed) to get what you want (feeling good again). Don't be at the mercy of your feelings ("I can't get out of bed because I'm depressed, and I'm depressed because I don't get out of bed"). When you're trying to change your depression, you blame your depression for your lack of action and blame yourself for being depressed. Rather than try to change your depression, accept it; choose to do an activity, then do it.

Get interested. As you do your daily activities, look for what is interesting in them. Once you are interested in the world (focus on it), you will come to know it; once you know the world, you can like it; once you like it, you will like yourself.

Switch topics. You will get immediate relief by focusing on the world instead of yourself. One of your response abilities is to put your focus outside of you, even if only for a second. If you are ruminating about yourself, switch to a new topic—what your child did in school, what the news anchor is saying, how the sky looks.

Accepting Losses

When you are depressed you often have some major losses you need to accept. If you have not clearly defined the loss, your depression may seem overwhelming ("I'm a loser") rather than specific ("I've lost my job"). A helpful strategy is to label or name what you need to accept. Ask yourself what it is you have lost and try to answer *specifically* ("my reputation," "my promotion," "my sense of worth," instead of "everything," "all hope of happiness," "all chance of ever getting married"). Labeling allows you to specify the loss so that you can deal with it. Once you put a name on it, you'll find it easier to digest.

Another obstacle may be that the type of label you put on the loss or setback prevents acceptance. You add symbolic meaning by incorrect labeling, and that surplus meaning makes the loss too big to accept. A first step, then, is to knock off the gingerbread meaning by relabeling the loss. A number of examples of labeling and relabeling are given throughout this chapter.

You create your own psychological experiences by the way you label your current reality, whether you are talking about the weather or life in general. If you label reality negatively, you generate misery.

Gary once worked with an administrator who was so chronically depressed that even the days of the week became cues for him to be sad. If you asked him how he was, he would say, "Oh, another depressing Tuesday. I hate to come back to work after a three-day weekend," or "Oh, another depressing Friday afternoon, I hate it when there's nothing happening around here." Interestingly, many people agreed with his labels.

People in power often relabel reality for those under them. An employee says, "We have a problem with the Smith account," and the manager relabels it: "No, it's not a problem—this is what we'll do." Many problems in life are solved by someone in power relabeling them ("Your son isn't a delinquent, he's just developing healthy independence"). Government does a lot of relabeling, too. An "unacceptable" level of unemployment or rate of inflation becomes acceptable with the change of administration. Each administration labels reality to serve its interest.

You can buy the labels others give or make up your own. That's your choice.

Life and Labels: The Three Umpires

In life, events are only events until you label them. You step out of your door and someone says "Nice day" to you. That event is neither good nor bad until you label it ("Nice of him to say that" versus "I hate it when people say that"). You experience the event according to the label you place on it.

Consider the story of the three umpires discussing how they call balls and strikes. The first says, "I call them as I see them." The second says, "I call them as they are." The third says, "They aren't anything until I call them."

The first umpire acknowledges that his calls are related to how he sees the pitch. He knows that the way he *perceives* events is related to the way he calls them, and so he is able to alter his thinking.

The second umpire believes that his calls *always* reflect the reality of the pitch. He is convinced that what he labels a pitch is what the pitch really was.

The third umpire realizes that his labeling is something that he is *adding on* to what is happening; he realizes that the ability to create psychological reality lies in the person who does the labeling. The perspective taken by each umpire parallels a way you can look at the world.

Call Your Own Game

Whether you realize it or not, you do call your own game. How you call your game depends on what kind of an umpire you are.

First Umpire Characteristics   You realize that events might differ from the way you see them, but in general, you rely on your perceptions. You see what you believe and believe what you see. You alter your perception if the evidence is strong enough; you don't think your beliefs are chiseled into concrete.

Second Umpire Characteristics   You are zealous about your opinions. No argument is sufficient; no proof is adequate to budge you from your position. You are frequently in error but never in doubt (at least never outwardly). You talk *at* others and give them little opportunity to talk with you; your conversations generally turn into indoctrination seminars or brain-washing ceremonies.

You use indignation to put others "in their proper place." You know what is right for everybody. The second umpire has many faces—the religious zealot, the censor, the revenger, the know-it-all.

A major second umpire characteristic is that you don't think. On any issue your motto is, "I don't think, I know." Ironically, the more sure you are ("I know I can't do that"; "I know he would never do that to me"; "I know that I'll make a lot of money on this project"), the more likely you are to be in error.

Third Umpire Characteristics   You know your experience is directly related to the way you label a situation. Kids can play ball all day long without anyone calling balls or strikes. A pitch is a pitch. Each is an opportunity. An event is simply an event until you label it, and you can choose your own labels. You can decide how you want to call your game.

When the second umpire says, "I call them as they are," he is confusing a higher level of abstraction (his label about the pitch) with a real event (the pitch itself). The third umpire's perspective ("They aren't anything until I call them") is helpful because here you *know* you are adding a label (psychological world) onto what is happening (physical world). When you create your life by choices, you can use labels that are helpful to you.

Instead of focusing on what might be the "right" label, *you use labels that will help you create your vision.*

A relabel is not a euphemism. Euphemisms are used to cover up current reality. Relabeling helps you see more of reality, not less. Once you see more of reality you are in a better position to create what you want.

One of Gary's clients told him about his use of relabeling. "I was in a traffic jam on the freeway, and I found myself thinking 'another damn delay.' Immediately I decided to relabel it 'another chance to listen to my tape deck.' When I got home I felt relaxed instead of stressed."

Another client lost a lot of money in a business deal. He labeled the loss "a sign that I'm basically a loser" and stayed depressed for a year. Despite the evidence that this label didn't work for him, he refused to give it up. "It's the truth," he insisted time and again, using second umpire thinking.

Once you start to think in terms of choice instead of change, you discover that you can label current reality to your advantage. You can immediately create a different psychological experience without immediately changing the physical world.

Evaluate your labels by their results. You may find that a particular label will be helpful at one time and unhelpful at another. Ask yourself, Does this label serve my vision of what I want to have happen in my life or not?

You can easily move beyond obstacles by relabeling because most obstacles are caused by labeling. Use the following guidelines to help you learn to call your own game by choosing your own labels:

Guidelines for Relabeling

Look for the opportunity in the problem, then relabel it in a positive way. Postive labeling leads to greater acceptance. "A dull evening with my in-laws" becomes "a chance to learn to raise my emotional tone." See the problem as a gift.

Use bird's eye view labels. Take a step back from the problem and gain perspective before relabeling it. One man felt shame and guilt for owing back taxes. The big picture was that holding on to the money did help him start his business, so he relabeled his back taxes as "an unauthorized but well-deserved small business loan from the government." A woman client relabeled her lingering illness as "an opportunity to let my children learn to be more self-reliant."

Give the problem a more friendly name. Psychologist John Enright has written about relabeling and gives some examples: "Temper outburst against my children" for one person was renamed "dynamic limit setting." "Procrastination" was renamed "willingness to find out by inaction what really needs to be done."

Make the label personal. In each situation, look for a label that has special meaning to you. Enright reports that for one person, "lazy" was renamed "finding out through inaction what needs to be done" and for another person with a more mystical frame of mind, "surrendering to the Tao."

Try many different labels for each situation, then use the one that means the most to you. You could, for example, rename a painful experience (being fired) as "a way to learn humility," "being in the here-and-now," "testing social limits," "creative social engineering," or "expanding my social image."

Look at the situation objectively and positively. Describe it to yourself. Find the positive function it can have in your life. If you have a trait others call "being a miser," you might rename it "financial responsibility."

Many people suffer from what psychologist Dan Dunne calls "AA," or adjective addiction. Your favorite adjectives are chock-full of negative meanings ("I'm flaky," "I'm lazy," "I'm ugly"). Your addiction to negative adjectives keeps you depressed. A helpful technique is to review a negative experience, such as failing an exam, in an objective and positive way. Do this in the third person ("Bill is someone who wants to get ahead; he's sincere about his career; he has a desire to be excellent; he is willing to face current reality").

Go back to the time in the past when you first developed the problem and find the initial positive role it played in your life. Smoking may first have served as a way to express your independence, drinking alcohol as a way to enjoy the ambience of a party. You may want to quit smoking and drinking, but you do not need to hate yourself because you smoke and drink.

Relabel the problem in terms of the balance it plays in your life. Nearly all problems balance out other potential problems. Failure balances out narcissism, anger balances out fear, and shame balances out pride. You rarely want to get rid of your problem altogether; it usually plays some important role in your life.

One person, for example, failed his doctoral exams. He admitted that he had been an intellectual snob. He relabeled his failure "a way to temper my intellectual arrogance." Another client who was excessively dependent relabeled her divorce "a chance to develop my independence."

Look for ways in which the experience expands your awareness. You can come out of any adversity somehow much better for the experience. You might feel more empathic to others or more aware of your own humanity.

Find some other use for the experience. An advantage to being a therapist or a writer is that all experiences, negative or positive, can be used in work. Most people can use most of their experiences in some way as well. It makes a good story, if nothing else.

See how the experience could help others. You can use your experience to show others how to avoid the problem or how to cope with it if it should happen to them. Theresa Saldana has turned her painful experience as the victim of an attempted murder into a force to help others by founding Victims for Victims, an organization that helps victims of crime.

Relabel the problem as a "learning experience." To learn from a problem, look blamelessly at what you may have done to bring the situation about. The lesson you learn from adversity helps you to prevent its happening again. The lesson is usually something crucial to your development. If you don't learn it now, the problem will reappear until you learn what you need to know. Suppose you have a heart attack brought on by stress, poor appetite, and lack of exercise. What have you learned? Your suffering now can help you learn to avoid more suffering later. In order to avoid a repetition of the attack, you will inform yourself about nutrition, exercise, and stress reduction and create a new life-style accordingly.

Question the usefulness of your labels. Your beliefs generate your labels. Keep in mind that the beliefs that lead to depressive labels are formed when you are trying to change others so that they'll make you happy. Change system labels ("I need to have approval at all times from all people") are useless, whereas choice system labels ("While I can enjoy others' approval, I don't need it") work for you and for what you want in life.

Relabel others. That which rubs you wrong in others is usually a reflection of yourself. If you're overly critical, you'll be bothered by people who are critical. To become more accepting of yourself, accept others by relabeling the other person's problem. One client relabeled her husband's criticism as "quality assessment." Another client relabeled her secretary's refusal to make coffee as "concentration on important office tasks." This client also found it helpful to relabel one of her troublesome accounts as "a teacher of patience." Redeeming qualities in the label make the problem more acceptable. As a result, you accept that quality in yourself as well.

How to Create Self-Esteem

Self-esteem is self-acceptance. You project onto others what you cannot accept in yourself. One way to get self-esteem is to build up yourself and your achievement to match your idea of what you should be (change yourself). A more effective and lasting method is to *accept yourself as you are right now and hold the vision of what you want.* You accept what you have created in the past. The past is a closed issue; what you can create in the future is wide open.

When your self-esteem is high, you forget about yourself, the world, and the future; you're in the flow. What you do has its own intrinsic rewards, and you're doing it because you choose to do it, not to make you a "worthy" person. You are too busy creating and savoring a good life to ruminate about whether you are a wonderful person or not.

You will develop a greater sense of self as you use the choice principles. Use the following inventory to help you become aware of your sense of self. Rate from 0 to 5 what you're doing now and then review it later.

Self-Esteem Inventory

1. I am not overconcerned with what others think of me.
   0 1 2 3 4 5

2. I'm appropriately honest with others (not compelled to tell the truth or to lie).
   0 1 2 3 4 5

3. I'm not overconcerned with appearance (clothes, house, car).
   0 1 2 3 4 5

4. I feel free to approach people who might dislike me.
   0 1 2 3 4 5

5. I feel comfortable when people act negatively toward me.
   0 1 2 3 4 5

6. I feel comfortable when people act positively toward me.
   0 1 2 3 4 5

7. I'm able to see my strengths as well as weaknesses.
   0 1 2 3 4 5

8. I don't let flattery and praise keep me from being true to myself.
   0 1 2 3 4 5

9. I'm open to others' opinions, but in the final analysis I rely on my own best judgments.
   0 1 2 3 4 5

10. I seldom feel self-conscious.
    0 1 2 3 4 5

11. I'm influenced by the content of what people say, not by their charisma.
    0 1 2 3 4 5

12. I seldom repeat the same mistakes.
    0 1 2 3 4 5

13. I can easily tolerate uncertainty.
    0 1 2 3 4 5

14. I have purpose and direction in my life.
    0 1 2 3 4 5

15. I feel complete as a person.
    0 1 2 3 4 5

16. I focus on what I want, not on what others want me to do.
    0 1 2 3 4 5

17. I can feel happy and content even when those around me are unhappy.
    0 1 2 3 4 5

18. I nearly always feel authentic and real.
    0 1 2 3 4 5

19. I'm able to create what I want in my life.
    0 1 2 3 4 5

20. I can accept reality as it is.
    0 1 2 3 4 5

Results:

90–100 = You have a strong sense of self.
80–89   = You are moving toward a sense of self.
70–79   = You are often in the choice system but need to focus more
            on what you want.
60–69   = You can benefit by putting the choice principles into force.
Below 60= You can benefit the most by practicing the choice princi-
            ples.

You will also help your self-acceptance by acknowledging and accepting certain "resistance traits" and moving beyond them. Ask yourself the following questions, and if you answer yes, ask yourself if you can let go of the trait and focus on something higher.

• *Am I a perfectionist?* (You are rarely satisfied and may rationalize your dissatisfaction.)
• *Do I nag?* (You continually reprimand and criticize others. You need others to do what you want them to do so that you'll feel better.)
• *Am I rude?* (You interrupt people and are openly impatient with how they express themselves; you reject them as they are and need them to act in a certain way for your sake.)
• *Am I am bigot?* (You judge people according to race, religion, sex, age, social class, and other differences; you need people to be just like you to feel good about yourself.)
• *Am I anxious?* (You worry about what might happen. You refuse to accept that the future is unknown and uncertain, and you don't trust your ability to deal with the unknown.)
• *Do I always wait for things to happen?* (You wait for someone to write, visit, or call because you don't feel capable of doing it yourself.)
• *Do I obsess?* (You ruminate about past wrongs because you believe that they cause your present depression.)
• *Am I overinvolved?* (You meddle in others' lives. You try to change others for the better and reject them as they are.)
• *Am I a hypocrite?* (You pretend you are something you're not because you don't like what you are.)
• *Do I overmonitor?* (You watch other people's every move like a hawk and refuse to accept their actions for fear you may be "done wrong.")
• *Do I check and recheck?* (You continually double-check your thoughts, feelings, and actions to try to avoid blame.)

If you recognize any one of these traits in yourself, let go of it by accepting it, by choosing to envision the result you want, and by taking action to create it. Don't worry too much about resolving problems, just move on to something better.

Ten Reasons to Accept Self-Acceptance

Self-Acceptance Gives You Choices

Self-acceptance ("I'll accept myself even though I've lost my job") plus accepting available choices ("One of my choices isn't having that job") equals increased choices ("What job options do I have?"). You begin to see new choices all around you as soon as you stop fighting the loss.

One of your choices is to state what you want ("By the first of next month, I want a job that I enjoy, pays $25,000 a year, and has good benefits"). When you accept yourself, you are free to take the offensive. Because you don't ruminate on being a loser, you can move toward your vision ("I lost the job, but I'm still me and I accept myself").

Self-Acceptance Aligns You with Reality

Your success (getting what you want) depends on how good you are at self-acceptance. To create your own life, you have to take yourself as you are and stop demanding exchanges and refunds ("I'll be happy if I can just lose weight"). Self-acceptance aligns you with reality and with who you really are ("My vision is to be thin, but I can be happy even with the extra weight"). You start flowing with Mother Nature rather than swimming against the current. When you go with the flow, you can maneuver yourself to where you want to go.

Self-Acceptance Is Taking In Information

Self-acceptance is mentally taking in information ("I made a mistake") so that you can use the information to get what you want. You can use the information as a current building block, or you can put it in your memory for later use.

Acceptance happens at a concrete, mechanical level. You become wiser. Often all you have to do to overcome the obstacle is to take in (accept) the information. For example, accepting that you have a headache often cures it.

The more you know about something, the easier it is to deal with. Fighting the symbolic implication of the information ("This means no one likes me—how could they?") stops you from taking in the information. This is why getting the facts is helpful.

By taking in (accepting) information about yourself, you are adjusting your view of reality. You end up having a clearer picture. Even if you dislike the information you receive, you are still in a better position to get what you want. Clarity equals creative ability.

When you create your life by choice, you focus on what exists for you. You agree that it exists even if you disagree with it. What you accept is your reality—*what you perceive* ("I am overweight"), *what you use* ("This is my job"), *and what you act upon* ("This is what I did"). Anything that influences you and anything that you influence is part of your reality— your thoughts and feelings are reality.

You can go in two directions—toward reality or away from reality. The further you move away from *what is* ("I can't stand this"), the more powerless and distressed you are.

Self-Acceptance Opens New Avenues

When you stop trying to fight or right yourself, new doorways open. The father of one of Jim's colleagues was diagnosed as having inoperative metastatic cancer. The family was concerned about telling him this news, but when he was given the information, his response was, "Okay, what can we do about it?" Three months later, following a new experimental therapy that he was given, he was free of cancer and doing fine—perhaps in part because of his attitude (his acceptance helped open the door to treatment).

We have often seen that once a client accepts reality, new avenues begin to appear as if out of the blue. The woman who accepts the possiblity that she may never get married unexpectedly meets her future husband. The man who accepts losing a job finds a better one. They become more open to the opportunities that are always there.

Self-Acceptance Is Enlightening

With self-acceptance, you don't blame yourself or judge yourself morally. Your evaluations of your experiences are simply descriptive of current reality. You are free to say what you like and don't like, but you don't engage in contempt or moral judgments.

Acceptance is illuminating—a cognitive enlightenment. You see the light. Psychologist Abraham Maslow found in his well-known studies that mentally healthy people have an absence of moral judging. He described them as "noncomparative" and "nonjudgmental." The more mature a person, the more accepting.

Moral judgments foster resentment. The harsher your moral judgments ("I'm stupid"; "I'm to blame"; "I acted like a fool"), the harsher your feelings (humiliation, disgust, despair). One of the ways to be more accepting is to stop making moral judgments of your experience and to describe them objectively instead.

Self-acceptance is enlightening. With self-acceptance, you don't blame yourself morally or judge yourself. Your evaluations of your experiences are simply descriptive of current reality. You are free to say what you like and don't like, but you don't engage in contempt or moral judgments.

Self-Acceptance Is Right Now

When you're not resisting what happened six days, six months, or six years ago, you're up to date. Self-acceptance allows you to enjoy the present.

Pat and Gary have a favorite drinking glass made out of thin blue glass. They have had it for over eighteen years, and it has become one of their favorite possessions. They use it regularly, even though they run the risk of breaking it. Independently, they have discovered that they both have accepted its eventual loss. To them, it's already broken; this frees them to use and enjoy it. Similarly, accepting the eventual loss of your life allows you to enjoy it.

Being up to date (not worrying about the past or the future) feels inherently good. To experience the eternal present moment, accept the now—including who you are—as it is: complete and total.

Self-Acceptance Is Feeling Good

When you talk about being "up" or "down," you're really talking about being in or out of acceptance. When you're in a state of self-acceptance, you feel up; when you're out of it, you feel down.

When you reject any part of the universe (yourself included), you reject all of it. All emotional distress has this feeling of separation, of being cut off and isolated. Acceptance allows you to reconnect and feel part of the universe again.

Paradoxically, by being responsible for yourself, you feel closer to others ("I can be myself because I don't have to worry about the person hurting me. I don't have to put any walls up"). When you accept the responses you make and acknowledge the choice of responses you have, you accept yourself:

"I accept the fact that I responded to the party by overeating and overdrinking. I acknowledge that I have new choices today. I can eat only when I'm hungry and only what I want."

"I accept the responses I made to my boss when I was upset. I acknowledge the new choices I have today and that I can create the good relationship I want with him."

Your good moods will let you know whether you're moving toward or away from self-acceptance, because you feel good when you accept yourself.

Self-Acceptance Transcends Toxic Beliefs

When you accept yourself, you are able to rise above the beliefs that keep you from getting what you want. You adopted many of your beliefs when you were a child and had trouble thinking logically. That's why many beliefs contain logical errors—they have a Catch 22 that puts you in a no-win situation. You may, for example, have trouble finishing jobs.

These examples are related to housecleaning, but the thinking patterns apply to most other tasks, like writing important reports at the office or finishing academic assignments:

"I can't do the housework because I have too much housework to do."

"I can't clean the house because I might find I can't do it."

"I can't clean the house because I am worthless and I'm worthless because the house is dirty."

"I can't clean the house because I didn't clean the house earlier."

"I can't clean the house because I don't like myself and I dislike myself because I don't clean the house."

"I can't clean the house because then it will get dirty again."

"I can't clean the house because I can't do it the way I want to do it."

"I can't clean the house because then I would feel stupid for not having done it before."

"I can't clean the house because I'm depressed, and you know why I'm depressed."

"I can't clean the house because I might like doing it, and then I will want to do it again."

"I can't clean the house because a dirty house makes me feel disorganized."

"I can't clean the house because I can't work in a dirty place."

Accepting yourself frees you to do what needs to be done to get you what you want ("I accept the reality that the house is dirty and that I don't want to clean it, but I have vision of a clean house and I will take steps to achieve that vision"). Because you don't spend energy on fighting who you are, you have more energy to create what you want.

Positive beliefs can also block acceptance ("I'm smarter than others"; "I'm always nice"; "I never make big mistakes"; "I'm always good to those I care about"; "I'm always honest"). You may, for example, reject the unnoble thoughts, unpleasant feelings, and unbrilliant actions that go against your ideal image. Because your positive images clash with what you are really doing, you don't tell yourself the truth. When you accept yourself, including your imperfections, you see who you *truly* are and can be honest with yourself.

Self-Acceptance Is Being Accountable

You are free from excuses. You own your choices and their consequences. When you are accountable, you don't need excuses ("I have a bad back"; "I didn't get any support"; "I don't have enough money").

The unproductive, unrewarding change system is the excuse system. You place the cause of your experiences outside of you. No matter what goes wrong in your life, you always have an outside hook to hang it on ("The alarm didn't go off"; "I had blisters"; "No one told me").

In the choice system, the causes of your experiences are within you. You know that at any moment you can create the experience you want by using the ACT Formula:

1. *Accept* current reality.
2. *Choose* and envision the experience you want to have.
3. *Take action* to get it.

Self-Acceptance Is Freedom

It detaches you from what you've been resisting and therefore frees you from it.

Have you ever worn eyeglasses? The first few days you see the outline of the rims and feel the weight on your nose. At some point, you accept the glasses and stop thinking about them. The same process happens in all acceptance: After putting what you have been resisting to rest, you stop thinking about it. You are free from it.

III. ADVANCED STRATEGIES AND PRINCIPLES

11. Separate the Choice World from the Change World

I f you want to understand the differences between choice and change, you need to know that you live in your own unique psychological world and that you share a common physical world with everyone else. Each world has its own separate principles and characteristics. For example, choice is derived from your psychological world, and change from the physical world.

You can get rapid relief from emotional distress when you divide the physical from the psychological ("The deal went sour but I don't have to *feel* sour"). The two worlds are different and not directly related, and yet they do coexist and do influence each other.

EXERCISE

Notice how you feel right now. Write a description in your notebook. Now sit back and tense your whole body. Tense every muscle in your body; hold this tension for six seconds and then quickly relax. Do this six times. Then compare your feeling to what you felt before the exercise. Do you see a difference?

This exercise, which is a good first-aid strategy for all forms of distress, offers an excellent example of how the psychological realm (your choice to do this exercise) influences the physical world (your tense muscles) and how the physical world (your relaxed muscles) influences your psychological world (your experience of relaxation and sense of well-being).

Your Two Different Worlds— the Physical and the Psychological

The physical world is a world of things that occupy space—your body, your house, your neighbors. The psychological world is beyond space and time and consists of your being, feelings, and experiences. The physical world is finite and has limits and boundaries. The psychological world is limitless and has no boundaries. One client, for example, said, "I don't have enough love for my kids and my girlfriend, too." He was confusing an infinite psychological experience (love) with a limited physical resource (time, energy, money).

EXERCISE

Think about an experience you had today. It need not be a painful one and can be as simple as brushing your teeth or cooking breakfast. In your notebook, write down what in the experience was physical and what was psychological ("*Physical:* putting toothpaste on toothbrush, brushing teeth, rinsing mouth. *Psychological:* deciding to brush for at least two minutes, deciding to use dental floss, enjoying the fresh smell of the toothpaste").

The purpose of this exercise is to teach you to recognize the difference between the physical world and the psychological world. When you are able to recognize this difference, you can separate the two worlds more easily ("The toothpaste fell off my toothbrush into the sink [physical world], but I don't *have* to get angry" [psychological world]).

The psychological world exists separately from the physical world. If someone hits you, you feel physical pain: cause and effect. When someone says something unpleasant to you, however, you may or may not feel psychological pain. If your husband or wife says, "You're really thoughtless," for example, it hurts you psychologically only if you resist it (need to change it). You cause yourself emotional pain by mixing the two worlds—by attempting to change or resist something that can't be changed.

Therapists would become obsolete and about 90 percent of mankind's psychological pain would be eliminated if we all learned one simple formula that warns against mixing the two worlds: "Sticks and stones may break my bones but words will never hurt me."

You are the one who adds emotional coloring to your world. Each person in a group often experiences the same event differently. A Republican and Democrat can hear the same speech and each come away more positive than ever that his or her point of view is right. What you tell yourself about an event is what determines your psychological experiences. You can't see the psychological world; you can only experience it. You can attempt to understand another's psychological world through empathy, but you can't ever be sure that what you experience is what others experience.

Your senses often fool you. Your sense of sight, for example, tells you that objects have color even though scientists have proven that objects are colorless. Your eyes have tiny cones in the retinas that color objects. People who are color blind (their retinas don't have these cones) see objects closer to their true nature.

Similarly, you color events emotionally ("That speech was terrible"; "That show was wonderful") and then see the coloring you have added as if it were part of the event and caused your feelings ("He made me mad"; "The show made me happy").

We have an extensive and concrete language to describe the physical world but a limited vocabulary for the psychological world. We usually use physical metaphors to describe the psychological world ("I feel like a million bucks"). These metaphors often cause problems: "I feel worthless. Dirt is worthless. Therefore I'm dirt"; "Physically you can hurt me. I feel hurt. Therefore you hurt me."

Physical principles—change, work, time, pressure, control, avoidance— cause problems when you try to use them in your psychological world. Pain in your physical world is helpful to avoid harm (you learn to keep your hands out of the fire). Your coexisting psychological world gives you the awareness and choice to avoid physical pain ("I know that if I stick my hand in the fire I'll get burned, so I'll choose not to"). You want to avoid physical pain. But if you avoid psychological pain, you often create serious problems for yourself. For example, if you avoid the anxiety of driving after you've had an automobile accident, you'll create a phobia.

As we've remarked previously, the principles of the two worlds often are opposites: When you give away something physical (possessions, money, land) you have less. When you give away something psychological (love, anger, freedom, resentment) you create more within yourself. And you can give away something physical (donate money to a worthy cause) and psychologically feel expanded. Many people operate from the physical world and can only see that when they give away something, they have less. They dislike sharing because they have not learned the psychological experience of feeling good by giving something away. The more you know about the psychological universe, the faster you can create emotional relief.

Five Important Facts
About Your Psychological World

1. *You* run your psychological world.
2. Knowledge and awareness expand your psychological world.
3. You expand your psychological world by being open to others and to the physical world.
4. Your psychological world can conjure up images of everything that exists or could exist in the physical world.
5. When you identify your psychological self with the physical world or with others' psychological world, you become vulnerable to emotional distress.

1. You Run Your Psychological World

Others and events can influence you psychologically, but they can never psychologically dominate you unless you let them. *You are always in charge because you are 100 percent responsible for your psychological world—your thoughts, feelings, and actions.*

Frank, one of Gary's clients, suffered from anxiety and despair. He attributed this to working under a manipulative boss. He had worked for this boss for three years. He was too frightened to quit his job because his sons had college expenses coming up and because of his high mortgage payments. As a result of his extreme anxiety, Frank had become passive-aggressive at home, expecting to be babied by his wife and children. When he wasn't waited on hand and foot, he sulked, threw tantrums, or stalked out of the house.

"I feel trapped," Frank told Gary. "My boss gives me mixed messages. I never know for sure what he wants. Then he rants and raves if I screw up." Frank was convinced that his boss had caused his anxiety and depression. It was not until his third therapy session that Frank suddenly understood that *he* could run his psychological world.

"What you were saying suddenly hit me," Frank said. "The last time my boss was putting me down I began thinking that while he might be the boss of the company, *I* am the boss of my psychological world. Just like that I felt better. He can yell at me, make unreasonable demands upon my time, pile my desk with work, and even fire me, but he can't make me depressed and he can't make me afraid. Only *I* can do that. I felt like laughing out loud right in the middle of one of his sentences. I felt like I was getting out of jail. I might have to keep this job for the rest of my life, but I don't have to be depressed or scared."

Once Frank learned that he ran his psychological universe, he no longer felt as if he had no choices. At home he stopped using his anger and withdrawal to manipulate his wife and sons. They, in turn, were more attentive, because he was more fun to be around. At work he still had his reality (a manipulative boss), but because he felt psychologically free, he stopped distressing himself over his boss's unreasonable actions and felt more energized to act to improve his job situation.

2. You Expand Your Psychological World Through Knowledge and Awareness

In the choice system you see your current reality as a source of information rather than as something you must change and control. For example, if someone tells you, "I don't like the way you look," you regard it simply as information or feedback. You waste energy if you try to change what the other person said. Whether or not you alter how you look is your choice.

Frank eliminated much of his distress when he simply viewed his job situation as a source of information. "I used to try to manipulate my boss whenever I felt he was manipulating me. I wasted a lot of energy thinking of what I could do to get even. Now I know that I don't want to work there.

I looked objectively at how I spend eight hours of my day, and I decided I don't want to do it anymore."

Not only did Frank decide to create a new job, he went all out looking for information. He found out about college tuition at various schools for his sons, talked with them about working their way through school, talked with his wife about the possibility of selling the house to accrue cash and perhaps reduce expenses, and went for job counseling at the local university, where he was given an interest test. "I was a little surprised to find out I had interest in teaching," said Frank. "In college I did a lot of volunteer children's work for my fraternity, but I never considered employment in that area."

The job placement counselor at the university recommended three night courses Frank could take to get his teaching credentials. "At times it was hard to work all day, go to school at night, study during lunch and on the weekends, and still maintain a relationship with my wife and sons. But I kept the vision of a new satisfying job, and that helped me do what I had to do."

A year after he first came to Gary for therapy, Frank got a job teaching. His salary was less than his previous one, but he and his wife were able to keep the house; their sons got jobs after school and on weekends to save for college. By using psychological principles Frank learned how to relieve his distress (in his psychological world) and how better to create what he wanted in the physical world.

More Gain, Less Effort Psychological principles are "senior" to physical principles—they are more effective in creating what you want in both worlds. Those areas in life where you are most successful are the ones where you're using psychological principles.

Whether you're building shopping malls, writing books, or discovering cures for cancer, you'll be more successful if you use the psychological principles of choice, vision, and awareness rather than the physical principles of effort, force, change, and control.

3. You Expand Your Psychological Universe by Focusing on Others and on the Physical World

You obtain knowledge—the fuel of your psychological world—by focusing on others and on the physical world. When you focus solely on yourself, you shrink. This is why the best way to overcome depression (a state of destructive self-absorption) is to get interested in the world.

We humans have evolved and survived because of our ability to master the physical world—build shelters, grow food, conquer disease. Nature has biologically wired us to feel good when we master the physical world and to feel bad when we acquiesce to the forces of the physical world. You master the physical world by directly confronting it at times and by yielding to it at others.

One of the easiest ways to feel better when you're feeling down is to master a piece of the physical world—wash your car, get a haircut, clear out a closet, write a letter. To master the physical world, you need to focus on it and connect with it by taking action. Once you do this with one or two small tasks, you usually begin to feel connected to the world and others. You feel that you are in the flow and ready for bigger tasks.

As we've said earlier, *To create the physical world you want, you need to connect and cooperate with others. You influence others and you allow them to influence you.*

You can't stand still. You are either expanding and influencing more of the physical world, or you're being constricted and pushed around by the physical forces.

The more of the physical world you can influence and shape, the more you will be reinforced by society. Doctors, plumbers, bakers, painters get paid for changing the physical world.

You usually like the physical world (your house, job, neighborhood) when you feel like a winner. And you usually dislike the physical world when you feel like a loser ("I hate this farm . . . dirty house . . . overwhelming job"). We are biologically set up to win by being internally rewarded for creating what we want.

The ultimate aim is to create the psychological and physical worlds that you want. The trick is to use psychological principles (choice, acceptance, self-accountability, awareness of current reality, creating your visions) with both worlds.

After Frank talked with his wife and sons, he discovered that they wanted to help the financial situation, not just rely on him. He learned that his wife would be willing to sell the house and his sons would be willing to work. Once he stopped blaming his family for his having to work at a job he hated, he was free to connect with them. He found that through the use of cooperation a wealth of choices appeared.

4. Your Psychological World Can Conjure Up Images of Everything That Exists or Could Exist in the Physical World

Psychological imagery has its advantages and disadvantages. You can imagine disturbing scenarios ("What if I'm attacked?") that frighten, depress, and enrage you. You can then react to the images as if they were real, become upset, and forget all about creating your vision. It is as if the physical world has a fifth column that can defeat you through propaganda—"Why even try? Look at all the things that could happen to you."

The advantage of your imagery is that you can create visions of what you want to happen even before you know how to make it happen. You create what you want *in your imagination* even though you don't yet know *how* to create what you want *in reality*. Your imagery helps to provide you with the *how*. It gives you a blueprint. Your imagery also provides you with an impetus to move toward the vision, as if the images were a magnet pulling you. Frank, for example, was able to create a new job by imagining teaching in a high school and the financial freedom to make the move.

5. Identifying Your Psychological Self with the Physical World or Others' Psychological Worlds Makes You Vulnerable to Emotional Distress

Your psychological self is pure experience or being. The most accurate definition of your psychological self is "I am." The psychological world is about being, the physical about having. When you start to add traits from the physical world to your self-identity, you develop problems ("I am my car, my job, my house, my body, my family, my bank account"). If something happens to the physical reality—you get fired, get sick, lose your money—you take it as an assault on your psychological self.

Often people confuse events with self-identity—for example, seeing your identity as a failure or a loser instead of accepting the reality that you *had* one failure or that you lost something in *one* specific situation. In the physical and the psychological world, no two events are exactly the same, so to identify with one is always a mistake. One of Gary's clients, Martha, had been left by her husband after nineteen years of marriage. She said, "Acceptance won't help me. I don't want to accept that I'm unlovable." Gary asked her to separate what happened to her in the physical world (her husband left her) from her feelings in the psychological world (self-identify). Martha paused a moment, then lit up. "You mean, I can accept the fact that my husband left me, but that doesn't mean I accept that I'm unlovable, even if my husband told me I was."

To create the life you want you have to let go of errors, traumas, setbacks, bad patches, and misadventures. You stop identifying with them and move on.

The Most Useful Set of Principles

Because your psychological universe and physical universe coexist, many situations use both physical principles (change, work, time, force, effort, control) and psychological principles (choice, awareness, acceptance). For example, learning Russian is both psychological and physiological. You use some biochemical means to store and control the language, yet you would also have to use psychological means (choosing to study grammar, choosing to memorize vocabulary words) to learn the language.

In the same way, emotional distress is both physical and psychological. However, except in rare cases (manic-depressive psychosis, schizophrenia) where drugs are helpful, psychological principles are the best way to eliminate emotional distress.

Psychological principles are quicker and more effective in creating the experiences you want. If you think only from the perspective of the physical world, you believe that to create a different experience you have to put time and effort into changing ("I've got to change how I feel").

If you want to change something in the physical world, you must generally look for three items: tools, time, and energy. For example, if you decide to change the desk at which you are writing into a chair (physical principles), you will need an array of tools such as a saw, hammer, square, glue, screws, drills, sandpaper, and so forth. You would need some time (especially if you are not much of a carpenter) and you would spend a lot of energy before the job was completed. Actually, as you look around, you probably can see several hundred places in the room where you could sit, so perhaps you will choose to use one of those for the time being. The choice you make is based on a psychological principle that will save you many problems and much time in the physical world.

No matter how bad you feel, you can get relief with choice. Even if your current reality remains the same, *you can make a snap decision to enjoy yourself or choose to snap out of a funk in a moment.* Nothing in your physical world may change, but you can create a different experience. Rather than try to change your experience, you make a choice to create a different experience.

We know that when clients come to see us, we can help them get rapid relief. The reason is that we are using psychological principles in the psychological world. If we had to help people change their other circumstances, it would be a different story. In the physical world, things are often cemented together and change takes time. In the psychological world everything is liquid, fluid, and flexible. No matter how distressed patients are feeling when they come to see us, we know that they can leave the office feeling good.

Change equals *waiting.* To get rapid relief, you need to stop thinking of change. The work and time that change requires can psychologically defeat you. Change amounts to slow relief from emotional distress. It is not a response (thought, feeling, action) *you* can make. When you want to change something, you have to wait because change is accomplished over time with an expense of energy. When you choose something ("I choose to get along with my mother"), you give your brain instructions for something it can do immediately.

EXERCISE

Look back in your notebook at your list of three disappointments. Recall how much time you spent waiting for others, events, or yourself to change. How did you finally resolve the problem? At some point, did you simply make a choice that created a desired experience? ("I decided to quit holding a grudge and called my brother to talk about the problem"; "I decided the marriage was over.")

You may have to take a leap of faith to use the psychological principles. One client said, "I know I don't really understand all the principles of the change and choice worlds, but this stuff works for me, and I don't want to spend a lot of time on figuring out how it works. I act as if I understand everything you've told me, that when I feel bad I'm trying to do a physical thing [change] to a psychological situation. I accept the fact that I cannot *change* the psychological world, so when I feel bad I say, 'Okay, this means I'm trying to change something, so I better start making choices instead.' I'm not sure if the premise is true or not, but it works."

EXERCISE

Think of something you have been trying to change: weight, smoking, shyness, procrastination, public speaking anxiety. How long have you been trying to change it? (Probably for a long time.)

Trying to change something helps maintain the *status quo*. Change sabotages you in many ways ("I'm going to change tomorrow and never eat junk food again, so I better eat as much as I can tonight"). You are trying to use a physical concept to create a psychological experience ("If I make myself feel guilty enough, I'll change and stop putting off my studies").

EXERCISE

Take a problem where you have been trying to bring about change and see yourself using the psychological principles to create what you want. Take a leap of faith here. For example, instead of saying, "I have to make myself stop smoking," say, "I accept the fact that I want to smoke. However, I choose to be healthy. I will take action by throwing away the cigarettes I have, by not buying any tomorrow, and by doing something I enjoy when I feel the urge to smoke."

How You Become Trapped
In the Change System

The change system's thinking is caused by confusing the physical world with the psychological world, a confusion that is a legacy from childhood.

You underuse psychological principles mainly because you lack awareness of how they operate and how effective they are. In elementary school, you learned about the physical world. Later you learned abstract facts about the physical world (history, economics) and more sophisticated knowledge of the physical world (physics, chemistry). But there is no specific curriculum that teaches the principles of the psychological world.

You first learned about the physical world—that it can be changed and controlled—as a child. You learned how to control your bladder, tie your shoes, coordinate a knife and fork, and use a pencil. Your early success in life depends on mastering such physical world principles. Until you became eleven or twelve years of age, you were developmentally unable to separate the psychological world from the physical world or to use most of the psychological principles. You used tears and smiles to get your way, and each time you succeeded you reinforced the basic premise that others are responsible for your experiences and you are responsible for others.

Developmentally, you needed to think this way when you were a child. You were dependent on others to take care of you, and you needed a way to manipulate them so that they would. In psychological terminology, this self-centered thinking is called *parataxic thinking*. You tend to believe you're the center of the world and the cause of whatever is going on. In your primary learning years (ages two through eleven) you were a parataxic thinker.

In childhood blame felt right. Parataxic thinking is why, as a child, you blamed yourself when something went wrong, such as your parents' fighting, drinking, divorcing, or dying. You used a frame of reference that confused the physical world with the psychological. As a result you saw life mainly from a blame perspective ("I got mad at Dad and thought something bad about him; that's why he died"). You thought your feelings (psychological world) were connected to events (physical world), so you blamed yourself or others when events went wrong.

You were developmentally unable to see emotional trauma any other way. You couldn't uncouple bad events from bad feelings ("I broke my toy so I have to feel bad"). Small children often can distinguish between what they cause and what is caused by outside forces. However, when something traumatic happens, they have trouble being accountable for their actions and want to blame someone else.

A four-year-old can understand he is "blaming" when he is alone, trips, falls down, and says his mother caused it. He can correct this error and see his mother was not present when he fell. However, he needs a higher level of development to have his mother scold him just before he happens to fall and still be able to say his mother was not to blame. And if somehow his mother did trip him, it would be nearly impossible for him to see how he was responsible for his psychological feelings about the situation and not blame his mother for his hurt feelings.

As an adult, you have the mental hardware to separate what happens to you physically from how you experience it psychologically. You may, however, be heavily conditioned by your early parataxic thinking processes, and this thinking often determines the way you feel.

Early in the development of rapid therapy, Jim saw a young hospital patient who was almost always upset. Jim had worked with her for several months and had given her numerous interpretations of why she acted the way she did. They helped very little. One day, at his wits' end as to how to help her, he asked how come she always seemed to be so upset. She thought for a moment and said, "If you're not upset, how will people know you care?" Her comment, more than anything else, helped Jim realize that the way you think determines the way you show your symptoms. Her comment about the relationship between caring and being upset was more revealing than the dynamic formulations he had attempted to put together.

EXERCISE

Read over your notebook account of your three disappointments. Ask yourself what painful emotions you had in each one of the situations. For each experience, write down what belonged to the physical world and what belonged to the psychological world. (*"Physical:* divorce proceeding, property division, custody decision, angry spouse. *Psychological:* depression, anger, fights, resentment."

Be aware that what you have written under "physical world" cannot cause what you have written under "psychological world." The physical world cannot cause anything psychological.

In childhood tying X to Y felt right. In early learning you glued events and feelings together. For all practical purposes, you saw the event and feeling as inseparable. When you said, "My friend made me mad," you believed that to be completely true. You perceived X (an event) and experienced Y (a feeling), and therefore you concluded that X caused Y. This was how your brain processed information during your early years. As you grew up, you recorded and linked numerous event-and-feeling episodes in your mind, and most of them have probably stayed with you.

Why Change Seems So Right

Here are some common questions about change.

"Doesn't the Need to Change Motivate Me?"

When you confuse the physical and psychological worlds, you believe you need a strong physical incentive (pain) to get what you want. Jill, a premed student, said, "I used to motivate myself to study by picturing the negative consequences if I didn't—like flunking out of school or not getting into medical school. After I got myself anxious, I would start to work to reduce the anxiety. It was like Chinese water torture. Each bad thought of what would happen to me if I didn't study was like a drop of water on my forehead. Eventually the drops became so painful I would open my books.

"Since I started thinking of choice instead of change, I do the opposite. I imagine getting into medical school and becoming a doctor. Rather than manipulate myself with anxiety, I magnetize the vision of what I want and let that image pull me. Weird as it seems, I often jump out of bed these days to get my studying done."

"If I Change, Won't I Permanently Solve My Problem?"

You may desire change because change implies permanence. You want assurances that you'll never have the problem again, but your struggle to change things only compounds your problem. While some choices ("I'll stop smoking") can last for years, the original choice or option does not disappear ("I'll have just one cigarette"). Choice doesn't create permanence, but choice is permanently yours to use.

"Why Does Change Often Feel Right?"

Change frequently seems right because it is often an escape fantasy. It seems to take you away from your painful current reality. You want everything to change and be wonderful, so you dream it and struggle for it. You may believe you can change into a different person ("If I get a job . . . if I move . . . if I finish school . . . if I get married . . . if I get a divorce . . . if I retire . . ."), but you set yourself up for failure because you are labeling something physical (for example, losing weight) as the cause of something psychological (feeling good).

After some initial success with change strategies ("I've lost weight"; "I've saved some money"), you become disappointed when you realize that you are still the same person. Then you give up on your vision and think, "It must be something else that will make me happy," and you struggle after that, continuing to assign the power to make you happy outside of yourself.

"What About Changing Others for Their Own Good?"

Do you have relatives or friends who are their own worst enemies—a son who drinks too much, a daughter attracted to abusive men, a husband killing himself by smoking two packs a day, a friend pushing others away while suffering from isolation and loneliness? The futility of change is obvious when you look at your efforts to change others.

EXERCISE

List the names of three people you have tried to change. Rate (from 0 to 10) how much effort you put into trying to change each person. Then, rate (0 to 10) how much you were actually able to change the person. What does this exercise tell you about trying to change others?

Change, whether you're trying to change yourself or others, is lack of acceptance. Change naturally creates resistance. Choice, on the other hand, implies acceptance. You will get much more cooperation if you ask people to make different choices instead of asking them to change.

The more you believe you can change others, the more you feel like a failure. You do, however, indirectly influence others. For example, you can influence others to use a seat belt by using one yourself. One of the best ways to influence people is to do what you want them to do. Being an influence is far different from trying to change someone. We can help increase others' awareness, but we can't change them. If someone decides to be happy, you can't make them unhappy. If someone decides to be unhappy, you can't make them happy.

"Shouldn't I Change What Makes Me Unhappy?"

All of our clients in some way have failed to divide the two worlds: "Rain makes me overeat"; "Rain depresses me"; "I was really mad that it had to rain on our vacation"; "Thunder and lightning make me panic."

You can easily spot this in others, but it's usually difficult to see in yourself. For example, Gary's son Zach had a bad morning recently. He had trouble uncoupling the physical world from the psychological. First, he was upset because he couldn't find his Superman T-shirt. Then he was upset with his father because Gary wouldn't immediately stop what he was doing to help him find it. Gary was fairly good at separating the two worlds. He was able to keep his sense of well-being uncoupled from Zach's tantrum.

You Have a Powerful Means
for Feeling Better

Once you get the hang of dividing your psychological experiences from physical outside events and from other experiences, you possess a powerful means to feel better. Instead of trying to change things, you can create the experiences you want.

• You no longer need to operate from the assumption that more of the physical (money, status, or approval) will make you happy ("I can create happiness no matter how much money I have").

• You no longer have to operate from the assumption that less of the physical (less weight, fewer hassles, or a simpler life) will make you happy ("I can create peace of mind no matter what the demands of life").

• You no longer have to wait to change apartments, to graduate, or to go on vacation to be happy. One client said, "I went shopping and the place was packed. There was only one register open in the women's department, and the clerk was overwhelmed. Everyone in the line was moaning and groaning. I was tired and irritable. So I remembered what you said about separating the physical from the psychological. I decided to make a good time out of the awful physical situation. I joked with people in line and got into conversations. I started to encourage the clerk, who was having trouble figuring out how to work the register. I'd been mentally blaming her, thinking she must be retarded or something. It turned out that I had a great time."

  • You don't have to undo the past ("Why did it happen?") or wait for the future ("Only ten more years until I retire") before you can enjoy the present ("I'll love what I'm doing right now").

  • You don't have to demand perfection to feel contented ("If I can fly, I'll soar; if I have to crawl, I'll crawl, but I refuse to be unhappy").

Allison, a client, saved good books for the perfect reading time so that she could enjoy them at her leisure. Consequently, she never read at all. She thought that by waiting for a perfect time for reading she could avoid the anger she experienced when she was interrupted by her children or by a phone call. In fact, her avoidance only created resentment toward others. She said, "It dawned on me last Saturday night. I finally got it. I wanted to read, so I read. I was interrupted three times, but I just accepted that. That was part of the physical world. I finally understood that the interruptions had nothing to do with my psychological world. They don't have to make me angry, and they don't have to keep me from enjoying a good book. My reading time may be far from perfect, but I can just accept that. I've even started a bookmark collection."

  • You can create separate psychological and physical visions instead of believing that one causes the other. One client replaced his sense of dread about making an upcoming speech by switching from "I have to do it" to "I'll create an interesting talk that I'll feel proud of."

  • You're better able to create what you want. One woman was able to use the division of the two worlds to lose thirty pounds and keep them off. She was able to learn to separate what her physical body wanted from what she wanted psychologically. She learned to listen to her body and to eat only when she was physically hungry. She asked herself, "What do I really want to eat?" and then was true to herself by eating what she wanted. She learned she had been confusing her psychological desire to feel better with her genuine physical hunger, and she was able to say, "When I'm hungry for food, I'll eat. When I'm hungry for love or attention, I'll create that for myself."

  • You can separate what you are responsible for (your psychological world) and what you are not responsible for (the physical world and others' psychological worlds). If people in your physical presence are having bad moods or not enjoying themselves, you don't have to take personal responsibility for them ("It's a hundred degrees outside and he's in a rotten mood, but I'm choosing to have a good time").

  • You can be more congruent (together). You know that these two worlds coexist, so you can cause them to move in the same direction. When you decide to do something, rather than go physically yet resist psychologically ("I'll go to the movie with him, but I'll hate every minute of it"), you

can decide to be fully there. You get your thoughts, feelings, and actions going in the same direction.
• You don't have to be devastated by physical traumas once you separate the two worlds ("Okay, I've been diagnosed as having cancer. This is a fact, but how I respond to the diagnosis psychologically is up to me").

Dividing

Choice creates experiences. Mike, one of the first clients Gary counseled using the methods of rapid therapy, was a scientist who had just been appointed to university position. He had gotten great satisfaction in working hard to put himself through graduate school. However, once he had his degree and accepted the position, he grew increasingly angry at his sister, a cocaine addict who was constantly in trouble, and his mother, who often called Mike for advice and invariably ignored every suggestion he offered.

Mike was angry at his sister for taking money from their mother, and he was angry at his mother for allowing herself to be manipulated. He resented the intrusion of these constant crises on his time, and he resented his mother for being more involved in his sister's problems than in his successes. The joy and pride he felt in his achievements were quickly buried under his resentment. He obsessed over how unfair it all was.

"I can understand how my choices to work and study hard created my experiences of graduating at the top of my class and feeling good about my accomplishments, but my sister and my mother are making me angry. It's not me. I'm not making any choices for them. If they weren't so self-destructive, I'd feel just fine. They are making me responsible for their irresponsibility."

Mike didn't see that by making different choices he could get what he wanted in the psychological world and often create what he wanted in the physical world. As a scientist, he clearly understood cause and effect on a physical level. He failed to understand, however, that in the psychological world *he* was the cause of his feelings (effect). After Mike learned that he could design his own life, he put the ACT Formula into practice.

"I figured it out one night when I was packing my books for the big move," Mike said. "My mom called and complained for two hours about my sister. I told her the same old stuff I've said for months. She just ignored what I said, and I got really angry. When I hung up, I threw the phone at the wall and broke it. Then I realized that if the situation never changes, I could spend lots of money on new phones. That's when I got it. I could be unhappy the rest of my life if I make my happiness contingent on my mother and sister. They might never change. I decided I wanted to be happy anyway." Once Mike saw that his own choices were creating his experiences, he decided to design the life he wanted and he put the ACT Formula into practice.

1. He decided to *accept* the current reality of what was happening be-tween his mother and his sister.
2. He *chose* to imagine a positive feeling toward both his sister and his mother.
3. He then *took action* by telling both of them he thought what they were doing was self-destructive but that it was their business. He also said he would like to help them if they wanted it, but he wasn't going to force them to change.

Mike was amazed to find that his anger and resentment disappeared immediately. Instead of wasting his psychological energy (focus) trying to change his family, he used it to create the life he wanted. He enjoyed his new appointment and started making friends at the university. At last report, Mike's sister is still on drugs, and his mother continues to lend her money. Mike remains loving toward both of them, but he refuses to lend money to either one and uses an answering machine when necessary to forestall the long, futile calls from his mother. Mike called Gary recently to say he was up for tenure at the university and was dating a woman he liked.

You Can Start Winning

When you learn to divide the two worlds, you have already won. You know that nothing in the physical world can cause you to feel emotional pain. What you *choose* to believe will have consequences, and you can create the consequences you want by choosing what to believe. How you choose to see an event is up to you. You can see it in one way ("It's awful!") or another ("It's great!"), but what you choose creates your experiences. You can choose to believe in honesty or dishonesty, in love or hate, in goodwill or ill will, in your worth or worthlessness, in manipula-tion or cooperation.

Even with the death of a loved one, you can get relief from emotional pain by what you choose to believe. One of Gary's clients, Jessie, was able to get relief after two years of depression, which began after the death of her husband and daughter in a car accident. She just accepted the physical loss of her husband and daughter by using many of the acceptance strat-egies described in Chapters 2 and 3. The "flooding" strategy was most helpful to her. Next she accepted the psychological feelings that sur-rounded the death (grief, depression, anger, loneliness), using many of the same strategies.

Jessie realized that she could not immediately affect her feelings just by deciding to be happy, but *she could choose to believe that she could be happy again and that her belief would have consequences.* Her former belief ("I'll never recover from their deaths") had left her so seriously depressed that she wanted to die as well, but she felt she had to live for her other two children. "That belief doesn't work. I don't like the consequences," she said. "And I understand now that, although I can't choose to change what happened to my husband and daughter, I can choose how I am going to respond from now on—how I am going to live." She used the psychological principles of acceptance, choice, and vision to help her create what she wanted in life (to be happy again and to go forward with her life).

The ACT Formula was helpful to Jessie as she learned to separate her physical world (the deaths of her husband and daughter) from her psychological world (the responses she could make to be happy again).

1. "*I accept* the feelings I have now (anger, depression, grief, loneliness)."
2. "*I choose* to envision myself being happy again."
3. "*I will take action* to reach my vision by being more physically active around the house, by getting involved in my children's school again, by joining a support group, by looking into ways I can develop and utilize my interests (handicrafts, knitting, quilting)."

Jessie used awareness a great deal in her action strategies. Whenever an activity gave her pleasure, she tried to be aware of that pleasure and then chose to do that activity again. In this way she found that doing handicrafts with other women (in classes, in the PTA) gave her a great deal of pleasure. She pursued this pleasurable activity.

When Jessie last spoke with Gary on the phone, she reported that she was happy again. She continued to use the psychological principles whenever she felt grief or depression and reported that those painful emotional episodes were becoming increasingly rare. "It's amazing to me that I am happy," she said. "My husband and my daughter would have wanted that. When I was in the midst of my depression, I would never have believed that I could feel good again and that it was *my* choice, not death's choice."

The power of psychological principles was demonstrated in what happened between the United States and China in 1972. Almost overnight twenty-five years of entrenched, at times violent, animosity between the two countries was eliminated. The leaders accomplished this instant transformation by making one choice: They made up their minds to have good relations despite their policy disagreements. In essence, they used the ACT Formula.

1. *They accepted* their differences.
2. *They chose* to have good relations.
3. *They took action* to work out the details.

The current reality—that there are differences between the United States and China—did not change. Yet this one decision had far-reaching ramifications—from the price of tea in China to whom Americans cheered for in the 1984 Olympics.

If the United States and China had tried to use physical principles (change, control, force) to solve their problems, hostility between the two countries would still exist. This use of the ACT Formula is not an isolated one. Anwar Sadat's decision to visit Israel in 1979 created a similar rapid shift in international relations. Because psychological principles can so easily and effortlessly create a completely different experience, the results can seem almost miraculous.

Choices create your life. This is cause and effect—karma. What you choose is what you sow. When you die, your life will be the sum of all of your choices. *You are always your own worst enemy or your own best friend.*

12. Responsibility and Self-Accountability

The meaning used for *responsibility* in the change system is the glue that inaccurately cements the physical world to your psychological world. The physical world (your parents are fighting again) can make you feel down only if you glue the two worlds together ("I'm responsible for my parents' fights, and their fights are responsible for my feelings"). The meaning you give the word *responsibility* is often a physical world meaning that has little or nothing to do with your current reality.

When dealing with physical events, we can often say that we have caused them. If you run over someone with your car, you are physically responsible for hurting the person. If you shoot off a gun in your neighborhood and hit an innocent person, you are responsible for the damage, even though the actual damage was done by the bullet released from the gun. In the physical world there is often a causal relationship between sequential events (events that follow each other)—the bullet would not have caused the damage if you had not done something to cause the gun to fire.

In the psychological world, however, the relation between sequential events ("You criticized me and I feel bad") is seldom if ever directly causal. When you try to tie the two worlds together you can create guilt, shame, and low self-esteem. The psychological concept of responsibility (as the ability to respond), instead of binding the two worlds together, allows you to separate the physical from the psychological.

Old-fashioned responsibility keeps you helpless. For many people, *responsibility* means being blamed and getting into trouble. This old-fashioned "responsibility" is a burden, something you try to escape ("Who's responsible here?" "Not me!"). Furthermore, it's confusing. The teenaged son says, "My parents don't give me any responsibility," and his parents say, "He's irresponsible." Thinking of responsibility this way keeps you stuck ("My wife wants a baby, but I don't want the responsibility"; "I'd like to expand my business, but I don't want the responsibility"; "I'd like to let my ex-wife go, but I still feel responsible for her"; "I can't accept the death of my son because I feel responsible"). You often end up feeling helpless and hopeless ("There's nothing I can do; I'm not responsible for what happens to me").

Ten Principles of Choice Responsibility

When you operate from the choice system, "responsibility" is like a magic wand. You create choices, seemingly almost out of thin air. To teach yourself to think this new way about responsibility, do the following ten exercises. Each is geared to help you learn about the ten principles of "choice" responsibility.

1. Anyone Who Has the Ability to Respond in the Here-and-Now Has Responsibility

One of Jim's clients, Carol, came to the office for her second visit. After she sat down, Jim asked her, "Who is responsible for the coffee cup sitting on the table in front of you?"

EXERCISE

Stop and think about this question. If you were in Carol's place, what would you say?

Carol said, "Whoever put it there." Jim then asked her to think about the question again, using the definition for *responsibility* as "the ability to respond." She said, "Well, I guess you are."

Rather than response ability, Carol's answers reflected blame or assigning accountability to others for what she could do. Both Carol and Jim *had the ability* to move the cup, so both were responsible for whether it stayed on the table or not. Carol's first answer ("Whoever put it there") is a good example of making responsibility mean blame. Her second answer ("Well, I guess you") is a common attempt to avoid blame.

Often people will insist that anyone or anything else has the responsibility for the cup being on the table ("gravity . . . the janitor . . . whoever was here last . . . whoever owns it"). They are related sequentially in that they happened before, but that is all. None of these answers has anything directly to do with responsibility: the ability to respond in the here-and-now. Carol and Jim could both respond in the here-and-now, so they were both responsible.

When you equate responsibility with blame, you overlook what you can do to get what you want. Remember that the psychological world is the world of the present. Practice responding in the here-and-now. A number of here-and-now responses you might make are given below:

• If you want to hear from someone and it's their turn to call, make use of your ability to call them.
• If you're seeking permission to do something, use your ability to do it yourself, without permission.

• If you're bothered by trash in your neighborhood, pick it up yourself. Gary often suggests to depressed clients that they pick up litter in order to get active and to become constructively connected with the physical world. Many report that it is a liberating and powerful experience. Options that were hidden, because the clients didn't think it was their responsibility ("Someone else littered") appear like magic ("I can choose to keep my street clean").

• Carry out activities you don't want to do but would like to have done (make a phone call, check the oil).

• Deliberately do a job you believe is someone else's task. Make the coffee for your secretary, for example, or take the car in to be serviced.

• For a certain period of time (a week, a month) do everything you catch yourself wishing were done. For example, if you wish that the dishes were done, do them; if you wish the car were washed, do it. Wishing something were done usually leads to blaming others for not getting it done.

Remember your intent: to become aware of your ability to respond in the here-and-now. You may be thinking that "ability to respond" means that other people will take advantage of you—you'll always end up doing the dishes, fixing the coffee, or checking the oil. But as you will learn later in this chapter *"able to do" does not mean "have-to-do."* Being aware of your ability to respond liberates rather than restricts you. It liberates you in two ways:

1. *You eliminate the painful emotions that accompany blaming* ("I get so mad when he doesn't do his share").
2. *You see that you can create what you want* ("If I want a clean house, I can have it by cleaning it myself, by hiring someone to clean it, by rearranging the division of housekeeping chores with my spouse, by being honest with my spouse about how much I want to create a clean house, by trading with a neighbor something I can give for housekeeping").

Others may be upset when you do tasks they believe are their responsibility. You may need to explain to them that you are doing it because you want the end result, not to take something away from them.

2. Responsibility Is Separate from Blame, Intent, or Right-or-Wrong

You ask your partner for directions and those that she gives you are wrong. As a result, you get lost. Who is responsible for getting lost?

A. You ☐
B. Both of you ☐
C. Your wife ☐

Your wife is responsible for giving you the wrong information but not for your getting lost. You were already lost or you wouldn't have needed directions. You're responsible for accepting the directions and for remaining lost. In situations like this your tendency is to hold your wife "responsible" (blame her), and you may want to victimize her (get even).

Blame takes you away from the problem at hand. You believe that if you fix the blame, you fix the problem. You become more interested in finding out who spilled the milk (blamestorming) than in cleaning it up. Rather than trying to change the fact that the milk spilled, you can choose to clean it up.

Switch onto the result track from the blame track as quickly as possible:

• When something is lost, don't jump to conclusions ("Someone stole it"; "She lost it"). Focus on the result you want—finding it.
• When something goes wrong (the car breaks down), don't go on a witch hunt ("American cars are worthless"; "The mechanic did a lousy job"; "Why didn't my wife check the oil?"). Focus on what you want—a smooth-running car—and take steps to create that. You can buy a new car, find a new mechanic, or buy a do-it-yourself manual.
• When you blame someone for something that went wrong, choose to be self-reliant. Blaming is a form of dependency. If you blame your wife because you don't have a clean shirt, you are dependent on her for your clean clothes. Self-reliance means that you can have clean clothes whenever you want. You simply get into the habit of washing your own clothes.
• When you find yourself blaming an event of the past (a traumatic childhood, the loss of a limb, your parents' divorce) for your present unhappiness, focus on what you want in the future. Let a future vision pull you forward rather than allow a past tragedy to pull you down.
• If you blame yourself for being too stupid or too ugly or too fat to get what you really want, focus instead on what you can do. Focus on your abilities, not your disabilities. You don't have the choice to win a beauty contest if you weigh too much. That is the judge's choice (even if you are the perfect weight). You do, however, have the ability to learn about exercise and healthful eating, to buy fashionable clothes, to experiment with makeup, to find a new hairstyle.

3. Responsibility Is Part of a Given Situation and Is Inseparable from It

EXERCISE

Your sister moves in with you. You tell her that she can stay, rent-free, as long as she cleans up the place while you are at work. You come home from work the first day and find that she has dumped her clothes everywhere, filled the sink with dirty dishes, and left a note saying she went to a movie with a friend. Who is responsible for cleaning up the mess?

A. Both you and your sister ☐
B. You ☐
C. Your sister ☐

Because your sister is gone, she can't clean up the mess. If she walks in while you are cleaning, she then has the ability to respond and you both become responsible for cleaning up the mess.

People out of the picture at the moment aren't responsible. To be able to respond, a person must be present. *And if you're in the picture and you can do it, then you're responsible.*

Remember, "can do it" does not mean "have-to-do it." Because you are responsible (you can respond to the mess in the living room), you can choose what you want to do about it. You can leave it or you can clean it. Don't get into the martyr complex and believe that you have to do it because no one else will do it. Let the job go undone for a while, and you will usually find that others will start doing what they want done.

4. Each Person Is Responsible for His or Her Own Feelings

EXERCISE

John says that he will meet you for lunch and, as he has done before, he stands you up. When you see him, you tell him off in front of his friends. He feels hurt. Who is responsible for John's hurt feelings?

A. Both you and John ☐
B. You ☐
C. John ☐

You are responsible for your anger, your verbal attack, and its timing and circumstances, but John is responsible for his hurt feelings.

Others will typically assign the accountability for their unhappiness. Similarly, you want to blame something outside of you for your bad feelings. Feeling bad, however, is each individual's own response; therefore each person is responsible for his or her own feelings. Even if your parents brainwashed you into believing you're a loser, you are still responsible for your personal experience of feeling like a loser.

5. Responsibility Is Affected by Inner and Outer Influences

Inner influences on your responsibility include how you physically feel, how smart you are, and how much you pay attention. Your responsibility is affected by anything that alters your mental state—drugs, alcohol, fatigue, illness.

Externally, your responsibility is influenced by location, strength, access to resources, support from others, and physical restraints (anything from a locked door to paralysis). A handicapped mother may have less responsibility for the care of her baby than a nonhandicapped mother. You can move from a position of almost total responsibility for the care of your baby to one of little responsibility when you leave the baby with a babysitter—you can't respond to the baby when you're gone. You are *responsible,* however, for who you get to babysit and whether or not you leave instructions for your baby's care. You can be just as accountable or answerable when you are with the baby as when you are away from the baby.

EXERCISE

Three people watch two youths rob a man. A fifty-year-old man sees the crime from several feet away. An athletic police officer sees the crime accidentally through binoculars from several blocks away. A ninety-year-old woman sees it from an apartment across the street. Who is most responsible for doing something to help the victim?
A. The fifty-year-old man   ☐
B. The police officer   ☐
C. The ninety-year-old woman   ☐

You don't have enough information to answer the question because you don't know all the influences bearing upon the three witnesses. The police officer could be on foot or could be beside a squad car; the fifty-year-old man could be a karate expert or could be in a wheelchair; the ninety-year-old woman could be deaf or could have keen hearing and be within reach of a telephone.

All three have the responsibility to help the victim in some way, but their abilities to act are obviously different. The ninety-year-old woman, assuming that she can hear reasonably well and has a phone to call the police, might have the most effective responsibility of the three.

This exercise can help you understand that outer and inner influences affect the boundaries of your response ability. If you are tired, for example, you may not be able to study effectively for an exam even though you want to do well on it (just as the athletic police officer in the exercise, if he was on foot, didn't have the response ability to help the man being robbed). You may want to learn the material for the exam, but you can't because you are overtired (outer influence). You *can* choose to get a good night's sleep, but there are some influences you cannot affect. If you are permanently paralyzed, your response ability is defined within the boundaries of your paralysis. If you think you can't be happy until you can walk again (*not* within your area of response ability), you will not be happy. If, however, you realize that a response you can make is to be happy *despite* your paralysis, you can choose to be happy and take actions that will get you there.

6. Responsibility Is Limited or Expanded by Awareness

Awareness plus ability equals responsibility (range of responses). Suppose you took an individual out of the jungle, showed him his first electric light, and then asked him to turn it off. He would have the ability to turn it off but would lack the awareness of how to carry out your request because he had never learned how an electric switch works.

You cannot transfer responsibility to another person. You can, however, provide knowledge that allows the person to use innate ability. You could show the person from the jungle, for example, how to use the light switch. He then would have the ability and the awareness to turn off the light and thus his responsibility would be expanded.

In the choice system, you increase your abilities to create what you want in your life by expanding your awareness of available choices or responses.

EXERCISE

A husband arrives home after a terrible day at work. He finds a sinkful of dirty dishes. Who is responsible for washing the dishes?
    A. His wife   ☐
    B. He   ☐
    C. Both of them   ☐

As soon as the husband becomes aware that the dishes are dirty, he is responsible (he has the awareness and the ability to clean up the mess). He shares the responsibility with others who know that the dishes are dirty and are capable of washing them.

Lack of awareness limits your ability to respond. Unless you know that the electric wires behind your walls are bare, you are unable to respond by tearing the wall out and rewiring; unless you know that need equals pain, you may not think of acceptance as the antidote; unless you know about the choice system, you're unlikely to use it.

Lack of awareness may limit your responsibility but not necessarily your *accountability* (what you are answerable for). When you park your car, you may overlook a No Parking sign, but the policeman will nevertheless hold you accountable and give you a ticket. The parking ticket is on the concrete level (it simply is) and has nothing to do with blame. You're assessed a cost for not following the rules. You are, of course, free to waste

your energy and blame anyone from Henry Ford for inventing auto-
mobiles to the mayor for establishing the No Parking zone.

7. Responsibility Is Not Obligation or Duty

Several members of your family see the newspaper on the floor when they
return home. Two of them, whose job it was to tidy up the living room that
day, become angry when you confront them. They both say that they didn't
see it. Who is responsible for the paper remaining on the floor?
  A. The person who dropped it   ☐
  B. Whoever's job it is to clean the floor   ☐
  C. Anyone who sees the paper   ☐

Whoever sees the paper has the ability to pick it up. Responsibility is
often confused with obligation or duty. Responsibility involves choice, not
obligation. Because you come home and find the bed unmade doesn't
mean *you* must make it. Responsibility means that you are capable of
making the bed, not that you have to.

It's a common assumption that because you can do something, you
should ("You're off work today, so you should be responsible for waiting
for the delivery"). Harried housewives and overworked executives believe
they are duty-bound to do something because they "can do." *But "can do"
does not mean "have-to-do." During a day you have many potential
responses (can do's) that you may choose not to make.*

"Have-to-do" is usually said as one word. You use the phrase to prod
yourself and others along ("*have-to-do* the taxes"; "*have-to-do* the
dishes"). It's a way to show that you are a responsible person ("I have-to-
do something about my son's eating habits"). You can use the phrase to get
sympathy ("There's so much work around here I have-to-do"). Because
most people hate the phrase, you also can use it to bug others ("I made the
phone calls, so you have-to-do the letter writing").

In the unproductive change system, you conjure up the worst case
("We'll live in a pigsty"; "We'll be broke and living on the street"; "We
won't have any clothes to wear") and then use the "have-to-do" to manipulate yourself ("I have-to clean the house"; "I have-to go to work"; "I
have-to-do the laundry"). By the end of the day you're drained from
reacting to the negative demands you have created.

In the choice system, you separate the words. The activity is an option
or choice that you have ("I have the option to do the laundry and the
option not to do it"). Beyond the *have to do* is usually something you want
to have happen. By focusing on what you want, you free yourself from the
bondage of the *have-to-do.*

In the choice system, you acknowledge current reality, then visualize
the best case ("I imagine living in a clean house"; "I have money in the

bank"; "I have my clothes and drawers full of clean clothes"). The positive image generates good feelings and energy. You then look at getting what you want as an act of creation ("I'll create a clean house"; "I'll create some cash"; "I'll create some fresh clothes").

Practice switching from self-coercion to self-creation whenever you catch yourself in the have-to-do mentality.

"I'll create some money" versus "I have to go to work."

"I'll create a great visit" rather than "I have to see my mother this weekend."

"I'll create some groceries" rather than "I have to go to the store."

"I'll create a clean desk" versus "I have to pay bills and answer letters."

"I'll create some free time" versus "I have to do my homework before I can do anything else."

"I'll create a thin body" rather than "I have to go on a diet."

"I'll create good health" rather than "I have to go to the doctor for a checkup."

8. Responsibility Is Not Control

EXERCISE

You are called on the carpet by your boss for something you didn't do. Afterward, you sit at your desk and find that you are crying uncontrollably. Who is responsible for your feelings?

A. Your boss ☐
B. You ☐
C. Both of you ☐

You are responsible for your feelings. You are responsible for staying healthy, but you may be unable to control whether you get sick. In a similar way *you are responsible for your feelings even though you may be unable to control them.* You are still the person with the ability to do something about how you feel.

Trying to control your feelings often causes you to feel out of control. Your emotions are usually kept in control by an elaborate physiological method. Trying to use the physical principle of control adds to the problem.

Because you cannot directly control your emotions, you tend to blame them on outside events ("I don't want to feel bad, so something outside of me must be doing it to me"). For example, in any phobia (such as an airplane phobia) you believe the outside event (flying) is causing your fear. In fact, all you have to do is expect that you will have anxiety and this in itself will be enough to create the anxiety. You will scan the environment until you find a hook to hang your anger, anxiety, and depression on—you can always find something or someone to blame ("It was your fault I was angry").

You can see what triggers your feelings but not how you actually make them. Generally, the triggers are other people, so you're inclined to blame them for your bad feelings. Whenever you find yourself blaming someone or something for your feelings, remind yourself that you are responsible even if you are not in control of them.

9. Taking Too Much or Too Little Responsibility Leads to the Problem

EXERCISE

Joan takes great pride in taking care (cleaning, counseling, cookies) of her children, even though they are now adults. As a result, her children have not learned to take care of themselves. Who is responsible for the deficits of Joan's children?

    A. Joan   ☐
    B. Her children   ☐
    C. Both   ☐

Joan has had a large influence on her children's lack of development; however, her children are directly responsible for their own actions.

One of the best steps you can take in behalf of others is to stop doing so much for them. This includes such activities as making excuses to family, friends, and employers, driving the person to work, bailing the person out of trouble, and doing his or her everyday housekeeping chores.

Teaching children to increase their responsibility often starts with getting them to do the simple, everyday tasks—make their beds, take out the trash, do their homework.

The parent may use rewards or costs to help the child learn to master the job. The parent can also introduce and encourage the idea of choices. This way the child not only has the ability to do the task but a sense of self-determination as well. If the child does not learn how to master the ability, he or she will have difficulty later in life. And if the child doesn't learn about choices, he or she will develop a slave mentality and not feel free or competent to create desired experiences.

10. Responsibility Doesn't Mean Capacity

EXERCISE

John wanted to impress his boss, so when his boss asked if he could write a difficult computer program—which John didn't even understand—John said he could. In this instance John was:

    A. Being responsible   ☐
    B. Being irresponsible   ☐
    C. Being stupid   ☐

John was fired from several jobs for pretending he could do something that he was in fact unable to do at the moment. Privately he admitted he didn't believe he was very smart.

He pretended that he knew more than he did in order to keep up the image of a responsible person. This got him in a great deal of trouble. He had the capacity to learn the skills, but he did not have the ability at the moment. His concern with his image often prevented him from accepting the current reality of his ability and creating new skills and capabilities.

In the choice system, you accept and admit the current level of your ability ("I can't write that particular computer program because I don't know how") and choose to create new skills: "I would like to learn that type of programming. Can you suggest a good workshop or extension course?"

How to Put Responsibility into Practice

Use the following methods to practice the principles of responsibility.

• Tune into times when you use the change system meaning of responsibility to glue the psychological and physical worlds together:

"He hooked me in."
"She pushed my button."
"I fell for it."
"She set me up."

Then mentally divide the two worlds:

"He made alluring promises about the deal. I made the choice to buy into the deal."
"She teased me with my failures. I made the choice to get angry."
"They told me lies about the club. I chose not to check out the facts and to ignore the discrepancies."
"She told the others I would do something. I chose to do what she said."

• Divide the word *responsibility* into two words when you hear it. Ask yourself, "Do I have the ability to respond in this situation?"
• Divide where you are from what you want. If where you are (facing a sink of dirty dishes) is not where you want to be (watching TV with the dishes done), tell yourself that you have the ability to respond to the first to create the second ("I accept the fact that the dishes are dirty. I choose to have clean dishes, and I'll do the dishes"). When you combine the two ("The dishes are dirty, and they should be clean so I can relax") you end up in blame ("Why didn't I do them this morning? Why didn't he do them?").
• Whenever you use the word *responsibility,* silently add the phrase *equals awareness plus ability.* Then ask yourself if you have the awareness and

the ability to do something about a situation. If you do, you are responsible.

• Purposely look for situations where you often blame ("I do the bills, he should vaccum"). Rephrase the situation in your head ("I can choose to do the bills or not; I can choose to vaccum or not").

• Whenever the phrase *have-to-do* comes into your head, change it to *have the option to do.*

• Look around you and ask yourself if you are responsible for objects in your physical environment. Do this as an exercise, to practice the new meaning of *responsibility.* For example, ask yourself, "Am I responsible for the couch being in that corner?" "Am I responsible for the TV being dusty?" "Am I responsible for the pile of papers on my desk?" Think through whether or not you have the ability to respond to each situation.

• Whenever you feel an uncomfortable emotion, tell yourself, "I have the ability to respond in any way I want. I can create my own feeling." Although your feelings may not subside immediately, you will eventually come to understand that just because your brother-in-law put you down again, you don't have to become upset.

• Whenever you notice people around you expressing uncomfortable emotions, say silently, "I have not created that emotion for that person. I can only create my own emotions."

Self-Accountability— How to Create Your Own Life

Self-accountability (the ability to hold yourself accountable) includes what you are directly responsible for and what you can indirectly influence (see Figure 3). When you create your life through choice, your circle of responses and influences expands.

If you have understood the ten principles of responsibility, you have already expanded your circle of response. You've given yourself more choices because you've increased your awareness. Learning how to hold yourself accountable also increases your choices. *When you hold yourself answerable or accountable for all of your experiences (what has happened in the past and what you can do in the present and future), your potential is unlimited.*

Five aspects of self-accountability help you expand your ability to create your own life.

1. Self-Accountability Grounds You in Current Reality and Helps You to Accept It

Lightning strikes your house and burns it to the ground. Who is accountable for this?

    A. No one, since it was an accident   ☐

    B. Fate or God   ☐

    C. Yourself   ☐

FIGURE 3

AREA OF SELF-ACCOUNTABILITY

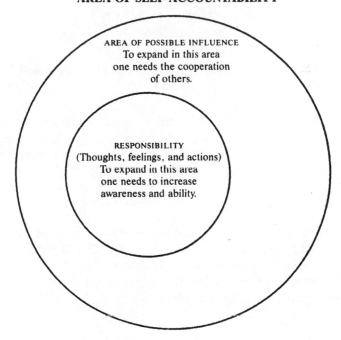

You chose to move into the house, so you had an indirect role in living in a house hit by lightning. You can take responsibility for rebuilding it or for finding a new place to live.

When you hold yourself 100 percent accountable, you move out of the victim role ("Why did this have to happen to me?") and into the creating role ("Okay, this happened. What are my options to create what I want in the future?"). At times you may have to stretch to see how you had some influence in an adversity. However, the more you can hold yourself accountable, the easier you will find it to accept the problem.

Self-accountability helps you accept reality because it is objective, concrete, and descriptive of what you did or what you can do. You're able to see the relationship between what you do and what happens in your life.

Because you are looking at something concrete—actions and experiences—you can choose new actions to produce new experiences. You may be unable to prevent lightning from striking your house again (that is outside your area of responsibility), but you can take steps to increase your area of influence (buy fire insurance, keep valuables in fireproof containers, make copies of favorite photos for a safe-deposit box, get professional help in grounding the house).

When you try to change your current reality, you blame yourself or others or the weather or fate. But the reality is that you can't see, feel, or touch blame. Blame and change don't give you specific guidelines for what to do in the present. *Once you hold yourself accountable for what happens to you, you can start getting directions on what needs to be done.*

2. Self-Accountability Allows You to Collect Wisdom and Let Go of Blame

Blaming Yourself Self-blame is often a misguided attempt to feel better. The good you (the real you) puts down the bad you (the unreal you) in order to feel better. You try to feel better rather than get better. Agree with a self-critical person ("Yeah, you are a jerk"), and you'll see that he or she usually isn't sincere ("What do you mean I'm a jerk?").

When you're self-accountable, you collect wisdom from all your experiences and let the blame go. You become a wise observer: "This is what happened . . . This is where I could have had influence or impact . . . This is how I could have influence in the future." The unproductive, blame observation says, "That was bad and I was stupid to have done it." Blame, like many subjective abstractions, is often in error. What you call bad today often turns out to be good tomorrow.

Blaming Others Just as you hold yourself accountable for your actions, you hold others accountable for their actions (you do not hold them accountable for your thoughts, feelings, and actions). If you are in a position of authority, you don't have to blame people; you merely hold them accountable. If you have an employee whom you hold accountable for doing a job, you simply provide consequences (such as a probation period) if he or she doesn't follow through on a task. You don't have to become angry or blame anyone.

When you are self-accountable, you allow yourself to be influenced by others and you are willing to influence others. You, however, do not take responsibility for others or make them responsible for you.

FIGURE 4

SUMMARY OF SELF-ACCOUNTABILITY VERSUS BLAME

SELF-ACOUNTABILITY (CHOICE SYSTEM)	*BLAME—ASSIGNED ACCOUNTABILITY* (CHANGE SYSTEM)
"What I can do something about; my direct ability to respond." (CIRCLE OF RESPONSI-BILITY)	"What others should do something about. What I should do about others."
"What I can do indirectly to influence the outcome." (CIRCLE OF INFLUENCE)	"I assign to others accountability for my thoughts, feelings and actions."

Characteristics	*Characteristics*
• *Choice* "I choose to stay and face them."	• *Choice is absent* "I don't have any choice. I'm to blame or he's to blame."
• *Constantly changing* "I am here, I can start the salad."	• *Frequently fixed* "It's her job to fix the meals. She's to blame if it's not done."
• *Not transferable* I am accountable for all my experiences."	• *Transferable* "I blame whoever seems to trigger my bad feelings."
• *Concrete here-and-now* "I can do something now to get what I want."	• *Abstract negative judgment* "God's given me a life of suffering."
• *Internally influenced* by intelligence by attention by ability to process	• *Internally influenced by need to change self and others*
• *Externally influenced* by time by distance (proximity) by strength	• *Independent of external influences* time distance (proximity) strength

3. Self-Accountability Allows You to Transcend Tragedy and Trauma

EXERCISE

Your child is run over and killed by a drunk driver. Who is accountable?
A. You   ☐ ☐
B. The drunk driver   ☐ ☐
C. Both A and B   ☐ ☐

You and the courts hold the driver (who is physically responsible) accountable. You can hold yourself accountable as well.

Random, unexplained traumatic events happen. When you need to change current reality, your emotional distress can be overwhelming. Because you want so desperately to change what happened ("I can't stand it; I won't accept it") you are unable to emerge from your grief and despair. The most helpful approach in this kind of situation, difficult as you may find it to do so, is to hold yourself accountable. You are accountable because you decided to have a child and because with having a child comes the possibility of losing the child. You also take personal responsibility for psychologically handling the loss of the child and for what you can do to prevent similar tragedies.

For example, we all can hold ourselves self-accountable for drunk drivers and do something to correct the problem:

• Join groups to lobby for tougher laws.
• Stop giving alcoholic drinks to someone who is going to drive.
• Organize against the excessive numbers of bars and liquor stores in your neighborhood.
• Volunteer to drive people who have had too many drinks home after parties.
• Refuse to bail someone out of jail for drunken driving.

Parents who have lost children to congenital illnesses, cancer, cystic fibrosis, and other terminal diseases have formed support groups, established foundations for research, and written books in order to share their experiences. They have held themselves accountable and done what they could do. Death, especially the death of a child, is one of the hardest realities to accept. Self-accountability helps you to accept it and to move toward healing. One of Gary's clients used the following sentences to help her get relief from grief over the loss of her baby son to heart disease.

"I am self-accountable because I chose to have a child, and with having a child came the possibility of disease and death."

"I am self-accountable for how I psychologically handle his death."

"I am self-accountable for how I act to prevent similar deaths in the future."

These three steps very closely parallel the ACT Formula:

1. "*I accept* that having a child means the possibility of death."
2. "*I choose* to envision myself psychologically able to handle the death."
3. "*I will take action* to create my vision by joining a support group, being a support resource to parents whose children have heart disease, working to raise money for congenital heart disease, volunteering in the pediatric ward, opening my home to grieving brothers and sisters of dying children when their parents must be at the hospital."

4. Self-Accountability Is a Success Force

Self-accountability leads to success because of its unlimited expansiveness. Candy Lightner, a mother whose daughter was killed by a drunken driver, held herself accountable and formed Mothers Against Drunk Driving. In just the few years since its founding, M.A.D.D. has affected legislation against drunk driving in many states. History is filled with examples of people who have indirectly affected the course of nations because of their attitudes and acts.

When you choose what you want instead of resisting current reality, you are free to focus on what you can directly and indirectly accomplish. Success often follows. You never know what you can influence until you push the limits. Because you hold yourself accountable, your options (what you can do and influence) expand. You're able to create more success.

To release your success force:

• Focus energy on your responsibility by separating and verbalizing "can do's" from "can't do's" ("I can't make my husband happy, but I can have a good time").
• Remain alert so that you can see what responses you do have ("I don't like what happened here, but let me see what options I have to get what I want").
• Recognize that your individuality (self-accountability) is compatible with the universal human bond ("Being for myself means I can be for you, too").
• Operate from a level of abstraction that is compatible with the issues being dealt with ("I don't have to develop a theory for who caused the accident before I can help fix it"). If action is called for, don't get lost in thought; on the other hand, if reflection is needed, don't impulsively jump in.
• Accept the truth that current reality doesn't create your feelings ("Although it feels like her criticism hurt me, I know I'm doing it to myself").
• Consider long- as well as short-term consequences ("The big choice is to save money for a car; the little choice is to say no to buying this jacket").

• Acknowledge current reality and hold your vision in mind ("I'm unhappy right now, but I'm choosing to feel good in the long run").
• Expand your self-accountability by expanding your ability to see and master current reality and to create your visions.

5. Self-Accountability Influences All Areas of Your Life

No area of your life is unaffected by your degree of self-accountability. *Psychology Today* magazine conducted a health survey of 25,000 people. The healthiest group consisted of the "health vigilantes." People in this category were self-accountable for their own health. When they felt sick, they were the most likely to say that it was because they did not take care of themselves. Those in the most unhealthy group believed that health came from outside of themselves. When stricken with a minor illness, they were most likely to believe that it was caused by outside stress.

The vigilantes, or self-accountable people, in the study were the least likely to have a chronic illness. They had the fewest physical and psychological symptoms and took the fewest sick days.

The researchers of the study concluded, "Perhaps the vigilantes, for all their unrealistic confidence in their own powers, have found the psychologically healthiest approach to health."

The physical world usually holds you answerable even if you don't psychologically hold yourself accountable. You may not hold yourself accountable for smoking ("My nerves make me do it"), but the physical world of your body will levy a cost. Furthermore, the physical world often has no sense of fair play. It has no sense at all—it just is. Even if you admit your error ("I know I shouldn't smoke"), the physical world may exact a price (lung problems).

You can greatly influence your health when you hold youself accountable. What you eat, whether or not you exercise, how you relax, whether or not you drink, take drugs, or smoke—all these are within your circle of responsibility and will have a direct or indirect influence on your health.

When you become self-accountable for your health, make sure that you don't take personal responsibility for your body or body functions. Your body is part of the physical world. You can influence it, but you are not responsible for it so you cannot control or change it. If you have developed problems because you have made yourself responsible for your body (as opposed to influencing it), you can get relief by learning to let go.

• If you have insomnia, let go of the responsibility for your body sleeping. Let sleep come on naturally.
• If you hyperventilate, let go of the responsibility for breathing. Stop trying to control it. Put your attention on something else and let your body do it.

• If you have a cancer phobia, let go of the responsibility for your immune system and have more faith in your body.
• If you develop fears of not swallowing, let go of the responsibility and let your body be responsible for swallowing.

In the last two chapters we have described why choice works and change doesn't. Because they are more theoretical than the first chapters, you may find it helpful to review Chapters 1 through 6 with your new understanding of responsibility and accountability and the importance of dividing the psychological world from the physical world.

13. Staying in the Choice System: Relief for Life

Let's say you play tough tackle football every Saturday afternoon. You hurt. All week long you hurt. Week after week you're in pain. You finally decide to do something to stop the pain. You have three options.

1. Hang in there but get upset at yourself for being unable to avoid getting hurt so often.
2. Hang in there while you get upset at everyone else for playing so rough.
3. Get out of the game entirely and spend your Saturdays at the beach.

When you believe you need to change reality, you use double-barreled blame—you blame others and you blame yourself. You are both a victim and an aggressor ("They did it to me, so I'm going to do it back to them").

Needing to change the world is like the football game. You have the same three options:

1. Try to change yourself.
2. Try to change others.
3. Quit trying to change the world and use choice to create what you want.

If you've spent your life in the change system, you will find the choice system a whole new universe. The more you get to know it, the more familiar it will become.

Learning to use choice is like learning a new language. First you learn the grammar or rules of choice ("I'm responsible for my choices, others are responsible for theirs"). You may feel self-conscious and artificial when you begin to use the techniques. But after you have practiced the choice system for a while, you forget about the basic rules or grammar because choice comes naturally.

With practice you will become fluent in using choice. Under stress you may regress back to trying to change things, just as an immigrant who has learned a new language may regress back to the mother tongue.

If you live and work with people who assign accountability for their lives to you and to others, you may find yourself going back to your old change ways. However, you can quickly bring yourself back to the choice system with the methods given below.

Mary, one of Gary's clients, was able to put the principles of choice and acceptance into practice very quickly. She refused to let her coworkers, friends, or husband draw her into the change system. Yet when she visited with or talked to her family, it was a different story. She regressed back to change almost automatically. Her mother pressured her ("You should dress better and settle down"). Her father gave her disapproving looks, and her sister began telling her all of her problems. Before she knew it, Mary was back to trying to change everybody. Her desire not to change her family was completely forgotten.

Mary was able to overcome regression by practicing the methods listed below. As the result of her practicing, in subsequent visits, Mary has been able to stay in the choice system.

To help yourself let go of change and stay with choice, use the following methods:

Stop rescuing others. Helping and serving others is one of the secrets of leading a happy life. However, helping people who don't want to help themselves serves nobody. Social scientists now believe that this kind of help enables the problem to continue. Experts in fields such as obesity, smoking, alcoholism, delinquency, drug abuse, and emotional disorders believe that your attempts to help people with these problems allow them to continue the problem.

The most common pattern is for one person (usually a woman) to take on excessive responsibility for another person (usually a man) who takes on little responsibility for himself. She may take on many jobs for the person, such as waking him in the morning and getting him to work. She may take on his emotions for him (feel bad when he messes up). The more she does for him, the less he does for himself. He sleeps late, for example, won't work, and blames his bad feelings on her.

If you take on overresponsibility, you are just as unhealthy as the one you are rescuing. You are the mirror opposites of one another—your degrees of immaturity are parallel. If the other person does almost nothing for himself or herself and you do almost everything for him or her, then you are just as psychologically impaired as he or she is.

Many people say, "I can't just let the other person go down the drain." This plumbing metaphor is correct—you *are* caught in a trap. The more you try to pull the other person out of the drain, the more determined the other person is to go down. *You do have to let go.* That's the only way out of the trap. You must focus on yourself and save yourself. If you don't, ultimately both of you will go down the drain.

If you let go, the other person may indeed go down the drain; you have no guarantee that the other person will ever hit rock bottom and start climbing back. But unless you let go there is little chance that the person will ever accept reality and start making new choices.

Claudia Bepko and JoAnn Krestan, experts on alcoholism, talk about this in their book *The Responsibility Trap: A Blueprint for Treating the Alcoholic Family.* They suggest that the "co-alcoholic" (the family member trying to help the alcoholic) accept the reality that he or she cannot change the alcoholic. The authors believe that once the people around the alcoholic have "hit bottom" and stopped trying to rescue the alcoholic, the alcoholic is likely to "hit bottom," too. They describe hitting bottom for the would-be helper as "a process of acceptance that the attempt to change another person is doomed to failure. . . ."

Letting go of the need to change others is the hard/easy approach. You may have to tolerate some uncomfortble feelings in the beginning as you stay true to yourself in the face of others' manipulation. Letting go of the need to change others is not hating the other person but detaching for the good of both of you. You can be responsive *to* other people without being responsible *for* them. You can, for example, help others out of a sense of choice, as opposed to helping them because you feel responsible for them.

Regard each new encounter with other people as a new experience. Recognize your past patterns so that you become aware of whether or not your distress is simply a repeat (from habit) of past experiences. If in the past you responded to manipulation with guilt, you may fall right into it again when you encounter the person who manipulated you. Now that you know about the choice system, choose to discard your old patterns. Make each experience you have a fresh chance to create your life.

Beware of vibes. In a sense, each one of us has a degree of telepathy. We can sense others' emotional states without having rational reasons for doing so. You sense that the other person is angry at you or that you are in a hostile, unfriendly place. Often the vibes you sense can be a result of your own projection, but often they are true.

Even though you can pick up bad vibes, you may misread them. For example, you visit someone and you sense unfriendly vibes; you speculate that he or she is angry with you when the truth is that the person has been arguing with his or her spouse.

Don't take responsibility for others' bad vibes, even if they are blaming you. By using the ACT Formula (*accepting* vibes, *choosing* to have a higher level, and *acting* as if the vibes are good) you often can raise the emotional tone of the situation and influence other people positively.

Bad vibes can be contagious. If you are entering a "bad vibe" situation, inoculate yourself beforehand ("They are usually into blaming me and others, so I'll stay alert to the choice system while I'm there").

Be aware of manipulation. Many people in authority like to keep you in the change system because it's a way to control you. Some religious groups, governments, judges, police officers, children, and parents can be skillful at manipulating you into believing that you are responsible for making them happy, comfortable, and satisfied.

Often you are unaware of manipulation. For example, one couple who saw Gary for marriage counseling was unaware of their manipulations. The husband was sensitive to rejection. During the therapy session, when he made a self-blame remark ("I know I made her unhappy"), she would bend close to him. When he made a self-accountable statement ("I know I'm only responsible for my own experience"), she would bend backward and away from him. Once they both became aware of her body language responses and his reaction to them, they made rapid progress toward creating the type of relationship they both wanted.

Don't let others' facial expressions throw you into the change system. Facial expression is the most common form of manipulation. A face has fifteen pairs of skilled muscles that can be used to show feelings. Facial expressions can be read universally. The more you feel responsible for others' experiences, the more sensitive you will be to facial cues.

When you're being manipulated, the elegant solution is to hold your ground and endure others' displeasure. This may mean holding your tongue when the other person is trying to bait you into a fight and to speak up when the person expects you to acquiesce. You also have available to you an inelegant but still useful solution: to leave the situation or to avoid the situation until you have the courage to be true to yourself.

Model the choice system. Pointing out to others that they are trying to manipulate you often backfires. This heats up the discussion, and before you know it, you're trying to change the other person. Note what happens, for example, in this exchange between a wife and husband:

WIFE (*complaining*): "Your mother makes me so mad."
HUSBAND (*angrily*): "It really makes me mad that you let my mother upset you like that. When are you going to stop letting outside events control your feelings?"

Now see how they could have handled the same situation more satisfyingly by using the choice system:

WIFE (*complaining*): "Your mother makes me so mad."
HUSBAND: "I find when I'm self-accountable around my mother, I feel good even if she nags us about our children. I could choose never to see her again, so I hold myself accountable for choosing to visit her despite her nagging."

Model what you want: "I find when I'm self-accountable I usually feel good" versus "If you would be responsible for your own life, I wouldn't feel so bad").

Be your own authority. Parents are the first people you feel you need to change. They seem to have all the power and you have none. (Small children's love affairs with guns and superheroes have to do with this sense of powerlessness.) In your early experience you deduce that some people seem to be superior and others seem to be inferior. Your observation is reinforced by cultural distortions (poor people are inferior to rich people; slow kids are inferior to bright kids; athletes are superior to nonathletes; old people are inferior to young people).

People usually feel more responsible for those above them than below them, which is why when you met a rich, successful person you're more likely to be nervous—you're taking responsibility for them liking you.

Develop a sense of democracy. Actively argue with your tendencies to put people below you or above you. As you do, you will find that you regard yourself as the equal of all people—and therefore your own authority.

Choose to be socially free. Whenever you find yourself uncomfortable around other people, ask yourself if you're trying to live up to a social role you believe you should be playing ("I'm the boss/father/lawyer/friend" or "I'm the life of the party/the one who always listens and sympathizes/the follower/the leader"). Make the conscious choice to be free and to be yourself. Say and do what feels natural to you at the moment.

Be true to yourself. You would give your life away if you tried to do everything everyone expected of you. Your boss, your parents, your children, your husband or your wife, your friends, and neighbors all expect you, at times, to do what you don't want to do and not to do what you want to do. To be true to your visions and to create your own life, you have to go against others' expectations. Be willing to pay the price by knowing that what others think or say about you is their business, not yours.

Be willing to let go of the temporary securities and benefits of the change system. Part of your mind wants to hang on to the belief that you need to change yourself, others, and the world. To keep this belief alive, your mind will tell you that if you let go of trying to change or blame, you will lose something important.

The benefits of holding others accountable for your experiences may seem so valuable and necessary that you are afraid to let go of them. Blaming others for your problems lets you off the hook. At one therapy session, Gary told a client her test score indicated that she was moderately depressed. She came in even more depressed for her next session and said, "You made me depressed at the last session." Gary asked how. She said, "You made me depressed by telling me I was depressed."

Blaming others for your feelings seems to offer an apparent advantage in that you can manipulate others, but the benefits are short-term. People may initially do what you want, but eventually they resent you.

When you become accountable for your life, some people may turn away from you, particularly those who like being able to manipulate you. In the long run, however, you'll attract more people to you.

Keep your energy high. You're most likely to go into the change trance when your energy is low. Then you use more energy trying to change current reality and the problem becomes self-perpetuating.

After a good night's sleep or a few days' rest away from a dilemma, you come back ready to solve it. When your energy is low, your best move is to seek isolation and build up your energy level. Focusing on what you don't want drains energy. Focusing on *what you do want* creates energy.

Eating and sleeping right and avoiding excesses can help you keep your energy level up. If you have trouble letting go of your distress, you may be overloading yourself. You may need some balance (more or less work), some time out, or help with your situation, such as hiring a cleaning person.

Care for others in a healthy way. You can care about and help others without taking responsibility for their well-being. Treating others well is usually beneficial to you. If you treat people well, most of the time they will move toward you, and if you're wise, you'll make choices that bring you the types of experiences you want to have. This usually includes the enjoyment of others and their goodwill.

Keep it simple. When you're distressed, you often feel overwhelmed. You think your problems are too complex and too big for any simple solution.

No matter how complex a situation may be, you can always make it more complex or more simple. Accept the reality that you are overwhelmed, then look for simple choices that will appear in your current reality.

Keep your feelings in perspective. You may be thrown because your feelings will validate the change system. The choice system, at first try, may not seem to be working for you. Rather than intellectualizing your feelings away or ignoring them, accept them and start moving toward what you want to happen. A byproduct of moving toward what you want is good feelings. If you continue to operate from the choice system, your feelings will begin to validate it.

Predict, prepare, and let go. You will probably try to change something in some situations more than in others. You will find it useful to predict how you would handle the situation if you were in the change system and how you would handle it with choice and creation. Write each potential approach in your notebook. This use of contrasts allows you to preempt the change situation. For example, suppose you were going to talk to your boss about upgrading your job:

Change System

1. "I'll wait and hope he brings it up."
2. "I'll try to change him and feel like a failure if I can't convince him."
3. "I'll get my feelings hurt if he disagrees with me."
4. "I'm afraid I'll hurt his feelings by asking for this."

5. "I'll resent him for putting me in this position."
6. "I'll feel helpless—as if he's an adult and I'm a child."
7. "If he refuses, I'll feel hopeless about ever getting to do what I want."
8. "I'll be devastated if he disagrees with me or criticizes me on any point."
9. "I won't want to tell him what is really on my mind because I don't want to make him mad."
10. "I'll end up feeling more isolated and alone."

Choice System

1. "I'll talk to him the first chance I get."
2. "I'll see cooperation, not control or power."
3. "I'll refuse to feel bad, no matter what happens."
4. "I'll totally accept myself and the situation."
5. "I'll choose to be confident and true to myself."
6. "If we have a difference, I'll acknowledge it and still go for what I want."
7. "If he refuses to go along with what I want, I'll see what other options I have."
8. "I'll hold myself accountable for the whole situation."
9. "I'll learn something from it, no matter what happens."
10. "I'll keep my eye on the ultimate vision of doing what I want to do and feel free, connected to others—and hopeful."

Once you have written out your two possible approaches and their outcomes, you are in a better position to create what you want. You can preempt (let go of) the change plan and choose the choice plan.

Relief for Life

As you have seen, creating your life from choice is something that is always available to you. At first the choice system may seem artificial, but in time it can become second nature. The practical suggestions in Part I of the book (Strategies for Rapid Relief) and the specific applications to anxiety, anger, loneliness, and depression in Part II (How to Apply the Choice System) give you many ways to *practice* choice. Remember: You don't have to wait to practice *until* you feel better. As you practice, you will find that you *already* feel better.

Practice, however, is what makes the choice system seem natural. It is the way in which you lay claim to choice for life. Chapters 11 and 12 (Advanced Strategies) explain the basis of the choice system on a more theoretical level. If you use these two chapters in conjunction with the other chapters, you will find that the practical enhances the theoretical and vice-versa.

This chapter has been about *staying* in the choice system. When you get rapid relief from emotional distress by stepping into the choice system, you may find yourself wishing that you could always use the choice system, always have that kind of *miracle* available. You can!

Living in the choice system gives you relief for life. You always have choices, no matter what situation you are in. When you accept your current reality and choose what you want in life, the choices you need to get there will appear. A whole life is open to you—your life—and you can make it the life you want. When you step from the change system to the choice system, the relief is not only rapid, it is yours to create for life.

Appendix

Strategies You Can Use to Get Immediate Relief in Tough Situations

Here are simple five-minute strategies you can use for:

- Confusion
- Disappointment
- Envy
- Facial tics
- Frustration
- Guilt
- Feelings of helplessness

You can have relief immediately or shortly after you use a specific strategy. At times using a strategy only once will give you relief. At other times you may have to repeat the strategy several times until your distress is eliminated. The key to rapid relief is to *use the strategy immediately and catch your distress as quickly as possible. Don't let your distress simmer,* or you may have to apply the strategy more frequently.

After we describe each distress, you'll find four simple steps you can use to let go of it and begin to create the experience you want. We also provide tips to use if your distress is more complicated. To help you practice using the ACT Formula in these difficult situations, each section also shows you how to apply the formula to the specific problem.

The strategies work. You don't need to take our word for that—try them out and you'll see how effective they are. To get the most out of them, act and think *as if* they work—this will increase their effectiveness. With practice, you will get better at catching your distress and using the strategies to eliminate it. You also will find yourself feeling less distress and actually becoming free of it in areas that were once troublesome.

Confusion

Cause: You experience a feeling of confusion when you're unwilling to make a necessary decision. Confusion is a smoke screen you employ to hide from yourself what needs to be done. When you look at the decision that you're facing, you become anxious. You then use your confusion as a way to back away from the anxiety. But the pressure to make the decision does not go away, and so the anxiety and confusion remain.

Solution: To eliminate your confusion and create clarity, take the following steps:

1. Tell yourself the truth about what decision you are trying to avoid. Writing down a description of the decision can be helpful in seeing the truth.
2. Consciously decide whether you are going to make the decision now or if you are going to put it off until later. If you decide to wait you have to be honest about what the consequences of that will be and be willing to accept them. Again, writing your choice down, as well as its consequences, will help you to establish reality.
3. If you decide to face the issue now, you need to make a decision. You usually know what the right decision is for you; the reason you have been avoiding it is that you don't like the consequences.

You rarely have to make the perfect decision. What actually happens is that you make a number of decisions that you correct along the way.

And remember: *What you do after you make your decision is crucial.* The specific decision is secondary to this.

Complication: Your mental and physical state may add to your confusion. When you're sick or have low energy, you often experience even more confusion about a tough decision. For example, when you are too hungry you even have trouble deciding what to eat.

In this case you may need to take care of your physical needs before you can face the psychological side.

ACT Formula:

1. "*I accept* the fact that I'm feeling confused and that I'm avoiding making a decision."
2. "*I choose* to envision myself feeling clear and good about the decision I make."
3. "*I will take action* by writing out a one-sentence description of the decision."

Disappointment

Cause: You feel disappointed when you have expectations that are unmet. Your emotional response is caused by a mismatch between what you thought should have happened and what actually did happen. You are caught in a reactive mode where you are counting on something outside of you to create what you want. But the crucial issue is how you are labeling the setback. How you label the situation will determine what you do. If, for example, you label the situation as a failure, it will be.

Solution: To eliminate disappointment and create enthusiasm, take the following steps.

1. Create a label that will help you bring about what you want. Some examples are:

   "This is just a missed appointment, not a disappointment."
   "This isn't the right means to get what I want."
   "This is the removal of an obstacle to a higher vision. I'll get something better."
   "The shortest point between two lines isn't a straight line, but the path of least resistance." (To get the job you want, you may have to go on a number of different interviews. Rarely do you go straight from *A* to *B.)*

2. Rechoose the vision of what you want to happen.
3. Let go of expectations and let the *how* develop naturally.
4. Do something physical to take your focus and energy off your distress, such as cleaning out a closet or playing handball.

Complication: You may be so devastated by your feelings of disappointment and discouragement that you have trouble thinking of anything else. You have a problem in accepting current reality. Use the acceptance strategies in Chapters 3 and 4 to get past this. Keep in mind that you can accept the disappointment and that your feelings will change ("I'm feeling hopeless, but I know I'll feel different in a day or so").

ACT Formula:

1. "*I accept* the reality that I have had what looks like a setback."
2. "*I choose* to label the situation in a way that helps me create my vision."
3. "*I will take action* in the physical world to create energy by focusing on something I can master ("I'll do a crossword puzzle"; "I'll redo my address book")."

Envy

Cause: You feel envy when you believe that others' successes take away from your own. You feel only envy for those who are in a similar position to yourself. The yacht owner envies the person with a bigger yacht.

Envy is a symptom of low self-esteem. When you fully accept yourself, you don't make comparisons. When you're envious of someone else, you usually also have contempt for the other person. You discount their success and the way they achieved it. You often wish them misfortune and hope that they lose the next round. And then, because envy is an ignoble emotion, you dislike yourself for having it.

Solution: To eliminate envy and create goodwill in yourself toward others, take the following steps.

1. Acknowledge (tell yourself the truth about) being envious and about being the one who is creating the envy.
2. Visualize having what you envy; if this is what you want, then choose to have it.
3. Choose to have goodwill toward the person you envy. Do this for practical reasons. If you put people down for having something, you greatly diminish your ability to acquire it for yourself.
4. Act *as if* you're happy for the other person. Wish him or her well and tell others that you believe the other person has earned all of the good fortune he or she has created.

Complication: You may be experiencing jealousy along with your envy. They are similar feelings, but jealousy is potentially more self-destructive. Jealousy has the added component of fear. You are afraid that someone will take something away from you. Unfortunately, jealousy often brings about what you are afraid of. If you act on this fear, you can drive others off by being overly possessive and overly intrusive in their lives. You need to learn to accept and tolerate your feelings of jealousy and to act as if you are not jealous, even though you have these strong feelings. As you practice this, these strong feelings will diminish.

ACT Formula:

1. "*I accept* the fact that it is because I have low self-esteem that I am feeling envious."
2. "*I choose* to have an image of myself as a person who is able to get what I want in life and who rejoices in others' good fortune."
3. "*I will take action* by speaking well of others and wishing them luck."

Facial Tics

Cause: Facial tics may have a physical basis. If you have a tic, you should check with your physician to find out whether it is of organic origin. Frequently, however, a facial tic is a symptom of anxiety and stress. It is automatic and involuntary. The tic could be an eye blink, a darting tongue, or a twist in any of your facial muscles and tends to occur when you are tense and feeling under pressure. You may feel shame and embarrassment about the tic, and your anticipation of the shame and anxiety helps to keep the problem going.

Solution: To eliminate the facial tic and create social comfort, take the following steps:

1. Often you want to avoid thinking about the tic because it is unpleasant, but it is important that you become aware of the kinds of situations in which you have the tic. With practice your awareness will increase.
2. Ask others close to you to help you become aware of it.
3. Hold the appropriate part of your body with your hand for one minute,

to prevent the tic from occurring. If you have an eye-blink tic, put your hand on your eye and don't let the eye blink for one minute. If you have a tongue tic, hold your tongue for one minute. When you hold the tic, you will feel the muscles moving. Holding the tic sends the message back to the brain to stop the movement.
4. When the tic returns, which may be right away, repeat Step 3. If you repeat this each time you experience a tic of emotional origin, the tic will go away.

Complication: Your tic may be the result of severe anxiety. To lower your anxiety, use the methods outlined in Chapter 7. If you have multiple or severe tics, that may be an indication that you have a neurological problem that requires medical care.
ACT Formula:

1. "*I accept* the fact that I have the tic and that I feel embarrassed about it."
2. "*I choose* to accept myself and all my idiosyncrasies totally and to be free of the tic."
3. "*I will take action* by holding the muscles for one minute when I become aware of the tic."

Frustration

Cause: You feel frustrated when you believe others or events are responsible for your feelings. Feelings of frustration do not come from others or from events, however, but from yourself. When you're feeling frustrated, you feel blocked because you can't change what you think you can change. The choices you believe you need are unavailable to you at the moment. Your focus becomes stuck behind the obstacles and you're unable to see any way around them.
Solution: To eliminate frustration and create movement, take the following steps:

1. Tense your entire body—your feet, legs, stomach, chest, shoulders, arms, hands, neck, and face—for ten seconds. Then quickly let go. Repeat this six times.
2. Let go of the unavailable choices. Tell yourself, "I choose to accept the reality that I don't have the choice available to me right now."
3. Refocus on the vision you want to have and choose to have that.
4. Take some action in the physical world (get up, move around, talk to someone, take a different approach to what you are working on).

Complication: When you feel frustration, you will have a strong inclination to want to manipulate others to solve the problem for you. You may get angry and try to bully others into doing what you want. A common ploy includes telling others that they are morally, emotionally, or intellectually defective for not doing what you want them to do. Or, you may take the opposite approach and use withdrawal. The way out is first to see if you create what you want on your own; if you want others' help, ask in a clear and straightforward way.

ACT Formula:

1. *"I accept* the fact that I'm making myself frustrated over unavailable choices."
2. *"I choose* to create my vision anyway."
3. *I will take action* by releasing tension in my body and putting my focus on choices that are actually available to me."

Guilt

Cause: Guilt represents fear of the consequences of your actions—you feel guilty when you're unwilling to pay the price of your choices. If, for example, you feel guilty about having an affair, you don't want to pay the price of having your spouse find out. Similarly, you feel guilty about not going home for Christmas because you don't want to endure (pay the price of) the anger or silent treatment you may get from your family. Most often the price you don't want to pay is the loss of your own approval or self-image ("I couldn't live with myself if I did that"). Guilt is not a moral issue but an economic one—are you willing to pay the price or not?

Solution: To eliminate guilt and create self-accountability, take the following steps.

1. Stop and think of what the likely consequences (price) of your actions are. List them in your notebook to create reality.
2. Decide whether you're willing to pay the price for your action. To determine if you're willing to pay the price, you have to decide what matters most to you. If, for example, your marriage matters most to you, then having an affair may cost too much. On the other hand, if your marriage doesn't mean that much to you, the chance of ending it may be worth the price. To be true to yourself, you often need to let go of past self-images ("I'll *ask* for what I want even though I have an image of always being self-reliant").
3. Act on your choice if you're willing to pay the price.
4. Let go of the choice if you're unwilling to pay the price.

Complications: You may feel guilty about something you have already done. You can accept the consequences of what you've done (pay the price), or you can make some amends for your behavior. For example, you might return something you have stolen. However, making amends can become a game in which you placate others to avoid paying the price. The alcoholic who gets drunk and abusive and then apologizes profusely the next day is an example of someone who tries to reduce guilt by reducing the consequences. Over time, others become tired of this pattern and avoid you. When you consider the cost of your behavior, *figure in long-term as well as short-term costs.*

ACT Formula:

1. "*I accept* the fact that my actions could have real negative consequences."
2. "*I will choose* to pay the price of the action to be true to the vision of what I want for myself."
3. "*I will take action* by doing what I believe is in my best interest."

Helplessness

Cause: You set yourself up to be helpless by making yourself responsible for others and others responsible for you. You feel helpless when you believe you need to change others and you can see that you're unable to change them.

Solution: To eliminate helplessness and create resourcefulness, take the following steps:

1. Draw two circles like those below.

FIGURE 5

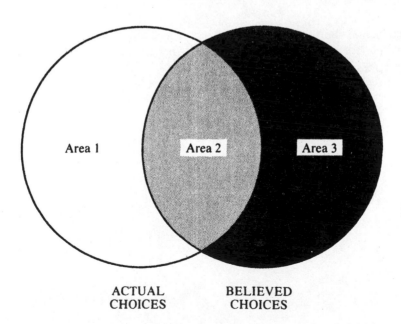

Area 1   Area 2   Area 3

ACTUAL   BELIEVED
CHOICES   CHOICES

Circle A indicates your actual choices, circle B represents your believed choices. Your success occurs where actual choices and believed choices overlap (area 2). Area 1 is all of the choices that you do have and are not seeing. Area 3 is believed but unavailable choices: This is the area that causes you to feel helpless.

2. Write down those choices that you have believed were yours but are not available (area 3).

3. Increase area 2 by listing at least 10 responses or choices you can make. They do not have to be related to the problem: You might, for example, have the choice of taking a walk, calling a friend, or cleaning out a desk drawer. Or you can do something about the problem.

4. Do one of the activities on the area 2 list. This will give you a sense of mastery and put you in the effector mode and out of the helpless mode. After you are in the effector mode, other solutions for creating what you want in the situation will start to emerge.

Complications: You may have a life-style based on being a victim or being powerless. In the past, because you could not see how your choices created your experiences, you learned helplessness and developed corresponding attitudes. As a result you may have developed many dependent relationships that keep you in the victim role. *Even if you believe you are helpless, you must act as if you can take care of yourself.* Create a different reality, and you'll create a different belief. Do as much for yourself as you can. You will find that you can do much more than you realize and will observe yourself switching from helplessness to resourcefulness.

ACT Formula:

1. "*I accept* the fact that I'm confusing real choices with believed choices."
2. "*I choose* to hold onto the vision of what I really want and refuse to be helpless."
3. "*I will take action* in the present to put me in the effector mode."

Recommended Reading and Tapes

Barksdale, L. S. *Essays on Self-Esteem*. Idyllwild, Calif.: Barksdale Press, 1970. Available from Barksdale Foundation, 53625 Doubleview Drive, Box 187, Idyllwild, CA; 714-659-3858.

Beck, A. T., and Emery, Gary. *Anxiety Disorders and Phobias: A Cognitive Perspective*. New York: Basic Books, 1985.*

Beecher, Willard, and Beecher, Marguerite. *Beyond Success and Failure*. New York: Pocket Books, 1981.

Berman, Steve. *The Six Demons of Love*. New York: McGraw-Hill, 1984.

Carrington, Patricia. *Releasing: Tapes I and II*. Available from Pace Educational Systems, P.O. Box 113, Kendall Park, NJ 08824; 201-297-9101.

Durst, G. M. *Napkin Notes: On the Art of Living*. 1982. Available from The Center for the Art of Living, P.O. Box 788, Evanston, IL 60204.

Easwaran, Eknath. *Dialogue with Death*. Petaluma, Calif.: Nilgiri Press, 1981. Available from Nilgiri Press, Box 477, Petaluma, CA 94953.

Ellis, Albert, and Harper, Robert. *A New Guide to Rational Living*. New York: Prentice-Hall, 1975.

Emery, Gary. *Becoming More Self-Reliant* (Audio tape). Psychology Today Tape Series, 1985.

———. *Controlling Your Depression Through Cognitive Therapy* (Audio tape series and workbook). BMA Audio Cassettes, 1982.

———. *Emery News* (Newsletter).

———. *A New Beginning*. New York: Touchstone, 1984.

———. *Overcome Anxiety* (Audio tape series and workbook). BMA Audio Cassettes, 1987.

———. *Own Your Own Life*. New York: Signet, 1984.

———. *Stress Free Home Study Course* (Audio tapes and workbook). 1986.

———. *Stress Free Tape Club* (Audio tapes, subscription information and available tapes from address below).

Ferrucci, Piero. *What We May Be*. Los Angeles, Calif.: Tarcher, 1982.

Fritz, Robert. *The Path of Least Resistance*. Salem, Mass.: DMA, 1984. Available (along with information on DMA courses) from DMA, Inc., 9 Pickering Way, Salem, MA 01984; 617-741-0780.

James, Jennifer. *Success Is the Quality of your Journey*. Available from Inner Cosmos, 3903 E. James, Seattle, WA 98122.

Koller, Alice. *An Unknown Woman*. New York: Bantam Books, 1983.

Reynolds, David. *Playing Ball on Running Water*. New York: Morrow, 1984.

Rogers, David. *Constructive Living*. Honolulu, Hawaii: University of Hawaii Press, 1984.

————. *Fighting to Win.* New York: Doubleday, 1984.
Siegel, Eli. *Self and the World.* Definition Press, 1981. Available from Aesthetic Realism, 141 Greene Street, New York, NY 10012.

Books and audio tapes by Gary Emery are available from the L.A. Center for Cognitive Therapy, 630 South Wilton Place, Los Angeles, CA 90005, 213-387-4737.

Audio and video tapes by James Campbell are available from the Institute for Cognitive Therapy, 4747 West Country Gables Drive, Glendale, AZ 85306; 602-978-4272.

Index

Dreams, use of, to accept losses and set-
backs, 55
Drug use, dealing with, 32, 207–208
Dunne, Dan, 157

E

Eastwood, Clint, 142
Easwaran, Eknath, 69
Emery, Gary, xiv
Emotional crisis management, 18
Emotional distress
causes of, xi
possibility of getting rapid relief from,
3–4
steps toward immediate relief from, 5–
14
use of, psychological principles to
treat, 175–177
vulnerability to, 175
Emotional overflow, 17
Emotional pain, 5–6
Emotions. *See* Feelings
Empathy, in dealing with anger, 130
Energy, as aspect of choice system, 6
Enjoyment, 80
Enright, John, 156
Envy, strategy for handling, 219–220
Ethnomethodology, 56
Euphemisms, 152
Events, reviewing, 38–39
Exaggeration
of negatives, 50–51
of positives, 51
Expectations, letting go of, 63, 125–126
Experiences
learning from past, 37
learning to laugh at painful, 46–47
and thoughts, 49
Explosive words, 135
Expressed emotionality, 125

F

Facial expressions, as form of manipulation, 209
Facial tics, strategy for handling, 220–
221
Fact gathering, 37–38

Failure, sense of, as change symptom, 5
Faith, 105
Family relationships
acceptance in, 32
manipulation in, 121–122
and teaching responsibility, 196
Farsighted creativity, 75–76
Fast talk, 137
Fear
accepting responsibility for, 20–21, 41,
78
and anger, 118
in change system, 146
modeling as means of overcoming, 113
Feedback, getting in communication,
141
Feelings
accepting chains of, 44
effects of, 18–19
experiencing, 40–41
expressing, 41–42
functioning of, 16–17
loving, 46
making yourself responsible for, 20–
21, 191, 195–196
and self-manipulation, 17–18
welcoming, 41
Feeling strategies, 21, 40–48
Feynman, Dr. Richard, 35
Fight or flight response, 115
Fitzgerald, F. Scott, 62
Flexibility, need for, 57–58
Flooding strategies, 45, 184
Focus/Focusing, 173–174
and dealing with anxiety, 106–107
direction of, 79–80
getting to know, 77
managing, 77
training of, 78
and visioning, 106–107
Focused listening, 78–79, 143
Fonda, Jane, 142
Forgiveness, and acceptance, 53
Fox, Matthew, 91
Fritz, Robert, 34, 74
Frustration
and anger, 119
as change symptom, 5, 145
strategy for handling, 221–222
Future, as cause of present, 65–66

About the Authors

Gary Emery, Ph.D., received his doctorate from the University of Pennsylvania, where he worked with Aaron T. Beck, M.D., in helping to develop cognitive therapy. He is the author of five previous books on the subject, including *A New Beginning*, 1981; and *Own Your Own Life*, 1982, and coauthor with Dr. Beck of *Cognitive Theory of Depression*, 1981, and *Anxiety Disorders and Phobias* (1985). He received his master's degree in counseling psychology from Creighton University and bachelor's and master's degrees in sociology from California State University at Long Beach. He lives in Los Angeles, where he is director of the Los Angeles Center for Cognitive Therapy and assistant professor in the department of psychiatry at UCLA.

James Campbell, M.D., received his medical degree from the St. Louis Medical School in 1965. He began to work with Dr. Emery while serving as a resident in child psychiatry at UCLA. Currently he is in private practice in Glendale, Arizona.